Scenic
Driving
INDIANA

Douglas Wissing

D1468835

FALCON®

AFALCONGUIDE®

Falcon® Publishing is continually expanding its list of recreational guidebooks. All books include detailed descriptions, accurate maps, and all information necessary for enjoyable trips. You can order extra copies of this book and get information and prices for other Falcon® books by writing Falcon, P.O. Box 1718, Helena, MT 59624, or by calling toll-free 1-800-582-2665. Also, please ask for a copy of our current catalog. Visit our website at www.FalconOutdoors.com or contact us by e-mail at falcon@falcon.com.

Cover photo by Connie Ricca.
Back cover photo by Richard Cummins/The Vesti Collection.
All black-and-white photos by the author unless otherwise noted.

Cataloging-in-Publication Data is on file at the Library of Congress.

CAUTION

Outdoor recreational activities are by their very nature potentially hazardous. All participants in such activities must assume responsibility for their own actions and safety. The information contained in this guidebook cannot replace sound judgment and good decision-making skills, which help reduce exposure, nor does the scope of this book allow for the disclosure of all the potential hazards and risks involved in such activities.

Learn as much as possible about the outdoor recreational activities in which you participate, prepare for the unexpected, and be cautious. The reward will be a safer and more enjoyable experience.

 Text pages printed on recycled paper.

Contents

Map Legend

Scenic Drive - paved

Scenic Drive - gravel

Scenic Side Trip - paved

Scenic Side Trip - gravel

Interstate

Other Roads (paved)

Other Roads (gravel)

Bridge

Building

Point of Interest

Campground

Hiking Trail

River/Creek

Lakes

Interstate 00

U. S. Highway 00

State and County Roads 00

Forest Service Roads 000

Wilderness Area National/State Park

National Forest Boundary

State Boundary I L

Map Orientation N

Scenic Drive Location

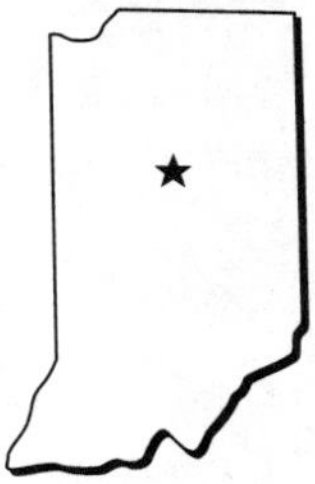

Locator Map

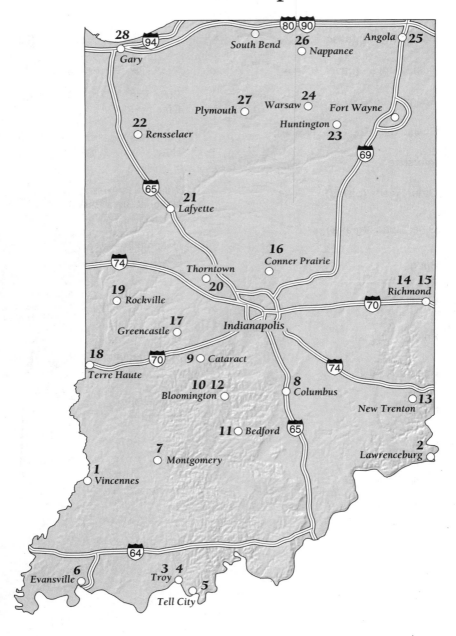

28 Gary
94
80 90
South Bend
26 Nappanee
Angola
25

27 Plymouth
24 Warsaw
Fort Wayne
Huntington
23

22 Rensselaer

69

65
21 Lafyette

16 Conner Prairie

74
Thorntown
20
14 15 Richmond
70

19 Rockville

17 Greencastle
Indianapolis

18 Terre Haute
70
9 Cataract
74
8 Columbus
13 New Trenton

10 12 Bloomington

11 Bedford
65

7 Montgomery
2 Lawrenceburg

1 Vincennes

64

6 Evansville
3 4 Troy
5 Tell City

Introduction

What is the song of Indiana? Perhaps it's a Cole Porter or Hoagy Carmichael tune, a song by John Mellencamp, or "Moonlight on the Wabash." Maybe it's a Gregorian chant from the St. Meinrad monks or a Tibetan chant from Bloomington or a Bean Blossom bluegrass lament or a Shipshewana Amish hymn. Or maybe it's the jingle of the reins as the draft horses pull through the fields or the murmur of a brook or the shush of Lake Michigan waves, the pushy cry of a red-winged blackbird, the heart-rend of a whippoorwill, or the chuff of a train; the silence of a Quaker service or the scream of an Indy racer. Or maybe it's all these things.

I've driven from one end of this great state to the other, zigzagging across the dimples and folds and flatlands of Indiana, winding down countless country lanes. And I can testify there is a lot of Indiana to experience. The glint of the dawn on the Ohio, the sugar powder hills of the dunes, canal boats, vintage cars and old-time trains, fireflies dotting a summer field into a pointillist canvas, forests ablaze with autumn color stretching to the horizon. The smell of new hay, old wine, and campfires flickering on a cool evening.

Ah, Indiana. Here's to your rivers and roads and endless prairies. To your expansive forests and deep lakes. To your layers of history and the energy of your many cultures. And especially to your people, who twang out their greetings and take the time to tell you how to get there.

Indiana is a long state, stretching from the pine forest lands near Lake Michigan down to the cypress bogs of the Wabash and the lower Ohio. Across its 36,000 square miles, an almost unimaginable diversity thrives: hardwood forests and fecund wetlands, glades, barrens, savannas, and immense prairies.

There are several distinct natural regions in the state. The southern hill country is a rumpled swath of limestone hills and ravined forest. Caves, rushing streams, and dense forests are part of the ecology and culture of the region. With sprawling floodplains and unique aquatic life, the watersheds of the major southern Indiana rivers—the lower Ohio, the Wabash, and the White—are themselves a distinct natural region. The southern lowlands in the southwestern section of the state are bottomlands where rich agricultural land coexists with teeming wetlands and the state's best oil and coal deposits. It is the hottest part of the state, and the one closest to America's Deep South in both climate and culture.

The central flatlands display quite graphically the impact of glaciation, in some places laying flat as a poker table on the landscape, in others, rolling in swell and swales like a kindly sea. The Kankakee Swamp that stretched for 5,300 square miles across northwestern Indiana is just a memory, but a collection of state wildlife preserves along the Kankakee River give a hint as to the wonder of the wetlands. Lakeland in Indiana's northern belt is pocked with hundreds of kettle lakes, liquid memories of the ice-blocks left by the retreating glaciers. The Calumet Region's dunes at the Lake Michigan lakeshore are among the most diverse environments in the world, where the tenets of ecology were parsed out by pioneering biologists two generations ago. Diversity—there's diversity here in Indiana.

Prehistoric man found Indiana a nice place to make a home. The state is blanketed with evidence of their exuberant lives—mounds and mussel banks, millions of potsherds, arrowheads for a hundred thousand hunters. And their descendants roamed the state from one end to the other—the Miami, Delaware, Potowatomi, and Iroquois, to name a few. When the Europeans found the land, they came in the droves that have never ended. First the French hunters and trappers, then the British "long knife hunters," followed by the settlers of northern Europe, and then the great waves from eastern and southern Europe that peopled the burgeoning industrial cities. In one way or another, they're all still here, and they make Indiana what it is.

The first European settlements were along the rivers of southern Indiana—the Ohio, Wabash, and Whitewater—and accordingly the towns with the longest history and finest vintage architecture are found there. The canal boom of the 1830s left a string of port towns along its path that are intact memories of a short-lived boom, when the commerce of the world floated to their docks. The first great national road ran straight as a die across the belly of the state, and towns like Centerville still tell the story. The coming of the silver railroad tracks changed the face of Indiana, withering the river and canal towns and accelerating the development of hundreds of others. Dozens of small Hoosier towns still radiate out from their time-worn stations—sometimes poignantly empty, more often converted to shops and visitor centers.

When the Automobile Age arrived, Indiana took to it with a passion. Hoosiers pioneered the infant industry, creating many of the nation's early models, along with legendary ones like Cord, Auburn, Stutz, and Duesenberg. The mythic brick racetrack in Speedway, Indiana, and the near-ubiquitous car museums across the state live to tell the tale. That and the small-town root beer stands, the post–World War II motor hotels now used as transient housing, the swooping '50s-style signs that hang on the fronts of buildings that are a hundred years older. They tell the story of an Indiana on wheels, too.

Driving is easy here. With a few exceptions, the routes in this book are on paved roads, mainly highways. I've aimed down the two-lanes for the most part, leaving the big highways for those in a hurry. Campgrounds and services abound in this well-settled state. You'll seldom be far from our modern world, though sometimes it may seem as though you are a long way from anywhere.

Most of the drives in this book are day trips, though any of them lend themselves to overnight jaunts or saunters that can last a week. There are plenty of delights for those who take the time to explore a bit.

The weather in Indiana is classified as temperate-continental, but any native will tell you that is only part of the story. "Hang around awhile if you don't like the weather," they say, "it'll change soon." And they are right. The mid-latitude westerly wind belt that passes over Indiana, and the jet stream and hemispheric storm track associated with it, guarantee lots of different things happening weatherwise, often in a short period. In general, there is about a ten-degree shift in annual average temperatures from the north (48 degrees) to the southwest (57 degrees).

What the north and south have in common is humidity. The great waves of moisture that boil up from the Gulf of Mexico ensure this is a well-watered place, essential for our dense forests and rich agricultural lands, though somewhat wilting for humans at times. Indiana gets almost 40 inches of rain a year, with the south getting most of its precipitation in the winter, the central and north in the early spring. For all, the driest month is October.

While there are ample reasons to visit the state throughout the year, spring and fall are particularly inviting. In the spring, the blooming redbuds and dogwood turn the forests into ethereal landscapes. Fall foliage is almost iconic, with hundreds of thousands of acres on fire with reds, oranges, purples, and yellows—exotic biotic changes happening for our viewing pleasure. Indian Summer in Indiana is a special time after the first frost. Days are warm and sunny with low humidity, the nights cool and crisp—another ideal time for touring.

Recommended Reading

The Natural Heritage of Indiana, edited by Marion T. Jackson (Indiana University Press, Bloomington, Indiana, 1998), is a beautiful exploration of Indiana's extraordinary natural diversity.

Indiana's Wildlife Viewing Guide, by Phil T. Seng (Falcon Publishing, Helena, Montana, 1996), showcases 89 of the best wildlife viewing spots in the state.

The Indiana Way, by James H. Madison (Indiana University Press, Bloomington, Indiana, 1986), is an overview of Indiana history written by one of the state's most respected historians.

Indiana: A New Historical Guide, edited by Robert M. Taylor, Jr., Errol Wayne Steven, Mary Ann Ponder, and Paul Brockman (Indiana Historical Society, Indianapolis, 1989), a guide to the compendium of the state's history.

Southern Indiana

1

River to River
Vincennes to the Falls Cities

General description: The 112-mile drive follows the path of Indiana's first highway, the old Buffalo Trace blazed by the vast buffalo herds as they migrated from the prairies of Illinois to the salt licks of Kentucky. The trip commences in the early French fur-trading town of Vincennes and concludes in the Falls Cities of New Albany, Jeffersonville, and Clarksville across from Louisville, Kentucky.

Special attractions: In Vincennes: George Rogers Clark National Historical Park; Old Cathedral Complex; The French House; Grouseland; Indiana Territory Capitol building; Fort Knox II. In Orange County: West Baden Springs Hotel; Paoli Courthouse; canoeing at Fredericksburg. In the Falls Cities: Falls of the Ohio State Park; historic homes.

Location: Southern Indiana.

Drive route numbers and names: U.S Hig.hways 50/150 and 150.

Travel season: The route is drivable in all but the worst of snow seasons. Spring and fall are particularly beautiful.

Camping: Oubache Trails Park in Vincennes and KOA Kampground in Clarksville.

Services: Gas, food, and lodging in Vincennes, Washington, Loogootee, French Lick, Paoli, and the Falls Cities.

Nearby attractions: Louisville, is just across the Ohio from the Falls Cities.

 The drive

The oldest town in Indiana, Vincennes was founded in 1732 as a French fur-trading outpost. The town is located at a strategic ford in the Wabash, which connected the Great Lakes and the St. Lawrence with the Mississippi. For many decades the village was a remote part of the far-flung French North American empire. Each spring, hardy voyageurs canoed down from Quebec to exchange trade goods for the beaver pelts that fired so much conquest and exploration in the New World.

French culture remained intact in Vincennes well into the twentieth century. Today there are still remnants of the old French days. When the French parishioners began building the Old Cathedral in 1826, it was the third in the little town, the first to be constructed of logs. It remains a spiritual lodestone of the community. The basement crypt, accessible by stairs to the right of the altar, is the final resting place for the pioneer bishops. The adjoining French and Indian cemetery is the final resting place of many of the original families with gravestones dating back to 1800. The Brute Library is the state's earliest library with volumes dating back to the twelfth century.

The George Rogers Clark Historical Park celebrates the great Revolutionary War victory of the Americans and the French that won the Northwest Territory for the young republic. The Old French House at 509 N. First Street is a fine example of an early fur trader home. Michel Brouillet constructed his log home in 1806. Each May the French Commons resounds to the sounds of a Revolutionary War battle and the fifes and fiddles of eighteenth-century musicians at the annual Spirit of Vincennes Rendezvous.

Grouseland at Park and Scott Streets is the anchor of a group of historic structures that represent Vincennes heyday as a great inland frontier political capital in the post–Revolutionary War period. Grouseland, a Federal-style house built from 1802 to 1804, was the home of William Henry Harrison, the first governor of the Indiana Territory. From this structure he negotiated five treaties with the Native Americans that opened the Middle West to European settlement. On the lawn the fabled Shawnee chief, Tecumseh, met with Harrison. Harrison later was elected the ninth president of the United States. There is a visitor center in the log cabin behind the house.

The Territorial Capitol on Park Street served as Indiana's capitol from 1800 to1813. The Western Sun print shop next door was Elihu Stout's frontier newspaper and printing company, which began in 1804. Across the street, the tiny white house is the birthplace of famous turn-of-the-century author, James Maurice Thompson, best known for *Alice of Old Vincennes*. The Vincennes University (VU) campus to the east is the home of the first institution west of the Alleghenies and north of the Ohio, founded in 1801.

Fort Knox II is a 44-acre park that is the site of Fort Knox, one of several military forts built near Vincennes. Follow the river road on the west edge of the VU campus 0.4 mile to Portland Avenue. Turn left and proceed two blocks to Oliphant Drive and turn north 1 mile to Fort Knox Road, and drive 1.9 miles to the Fort site. Oubache Trails Park adjoins the site.

The River to River Scenic Drive follows Indiana Highway 150, the historic path formed by the buffalo herds' migrations across Indiana from the Illinois prairie to the Falls of the Ohio at today's Falls Cities, where they

Drive 1: River to River
Vincennes to the Falls Cities

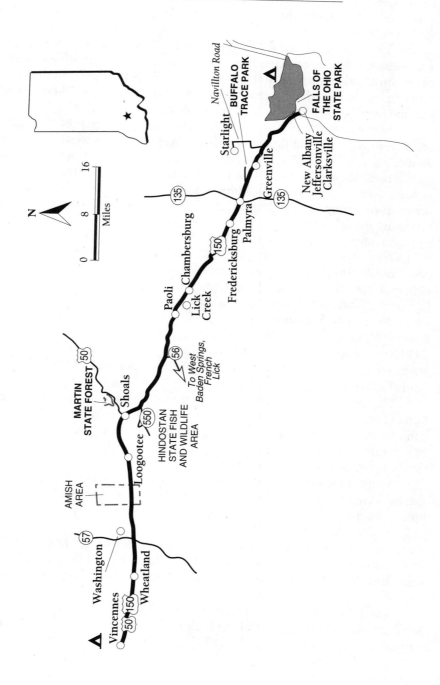

crossed in low water to the Kentucky salt licks. It was the first natural highway in the region, beaten six feet deep into the earth in some places, used by Indians, frontiersmen, invading armies, and militia. Take Sixth Street north to the edge of town and the intersection of US 50/150. Drive east 10.5 miles to Wheatland.

Wheatland, founded in 1806, was the home of James "Blue Jeans" Williams, the fourteenth governor of Indiana. In 1876, when he defeated Benjamin Harrison, son of William Henry, it was considered the first election of a common man over the blue bloods of the early state. There is a 30-foot memorial to Williams at Walnut Grove cemetery south of Wheatland.

The road continues through rich agricultural land, part of the Southern Bottomland Natural Region. In 1817, Daviess County was termed "the garden spot of Indiana" and it remains fourth in the state in agricultural production. Maysville, 4 miles east of Wheatland, is part of the Vincennes Donation Lands, granted by Congress to the heads of French families in hopes of resolving the tangled claims arising from French land grants and communally held property.

Washington, 1.2 miles east, flourished with the arrival of the railroad in 1857. By 1889, the town was a major refurbishing depot for the Baltimore and Ohio Railroad, employing more than 1,000 workers, though little remains of the previous bustle. On Hefron Street, a block from the Daviess County Courthouse square, the Helphenstine House is a fine example of Greek Revival architecture, built at the height of the fashion in 1847. The Robert Graham House on Maple, owned by an Indiana car manufacturer, is a 1912 example of Frank Lloyd Wright's Prairie School of Architecture, with marble fireplaces, crystal-glass French windows, parquet floors, and a billiards room.

The Daviess County Historical Society Museum is a 15-room collection of Daviess County and Indiana history, including a vintage schoolhouse, bank, church sanctuary, parlor, and embalming room, as well as an Amish folk exhibit. The museum is 2.1 miles south of Main Street on IN 57. Turn east 0.3 mile to Donaldson Road.

Return to Washington and continue east on US 50/150. The drive continues through a region of Amish farms. More than 500 Amish families live in the eastern half of Daviess County. This area is covered more completely in Drive 7, "Southern Indiana Amish."

Loogootee, 14.1 miles east of Washington, is part of Martin County, where lowland region begins to give way to the dramatic topography of the Crawford Upland, a region of cliffs, deep valleys, dense forests, and towering ridges.

Shoals, 8.1 miles east, is the county seat. Just before the city limits, the Jug Rock is on the north side of the highway, a natural formation that is the wonder of the county. It is the only free-standing "stand rock" west of the

The Culbertson Mansion in New Albany is a fine example of Steamboat Gothic architecture.
Photo courtesy of Clark/Floyd Co. Convention Visitors Bureau (CVB).

Mississippi. The 1877 county courthouse and jail four blocks south of the highway on Capitol Street is the site of a famous lynching. The Archer boys, accused of torturing and killing a local farmer, were hung from the trees in front of the jail in 1886.

Shoals greatest claim to fame was its near-monopoly of mother of pearl buttons in the years around World War I. The buttons were made from the mussels harvested from the rich White River beds. There were seven button factories in the Shoals area at one time. Today the town depends on the deep gypsum mines discovered in the mid-twentieth century for employment. Two major producers employ more than 400 workers. The National Gypsum mine 2 miles east of Shoals is the nation's deepest at 515 feet.

Take IN 150 south 2 miles to IN 550. Hindostan Falls, the site of a once-flourishing village, is 0.5 mile down the road. Hindostan State Fish and Wildlife Area resides where the community once did. Cholera devastated the town a decade after settlement and it never recovered. During periods of high water the falls are not visible. Return to IN 150 and continue east 10.9 miles, then turn south 0.9 mile on IN 56 to West Baden Springs and French Lick. Springs Valley, as the two towns are collectively known, is the home of renowned turn-of-the-century mineral springs spas. The French Lick Springs Resort still operates as a large golf and tennis resort, and the West Baden Springs Hotel, after years of neglect, has gone through a remarkable restoration to restore its grandeur. It is open for tours.

Continuing 22 miles east on IN 150, Paoli is an old Quaker town with a historic Greek Revival courthouse, built between 1848 and 1850. Quakers were instrumental in the operation of the Underground Railroad that transported runaway slaves from the South to freedom in Canada in the years before the Civil War. One branch of the road ran through Paoli.

The road continues south through the Hoosier National forest, past a couple of nineteenth-century villages, Rego and Hardinsburg then onto Fredericksburg founded in 1805 as a toll road on the New Albany–Vincennes plank road. Tolls were collected according to the number of wheels and horses. Persons going to church, funerals, muster, or elections were exempt. The town also sat astride the Blue River that empties into the Ohio, affording flatboat transport in high-water springs. Today canoes are available for rental in the old mill, which also serves as a ginseng-buying depot.

Palmyra, 4.9 miles to the east, dates to 1810. The town is at the junction of two of Indiana's earliest roads: the Mauckport Road (IN 135) and the Buffalo Trace (now IN 150) that crossed Indiana from Vincennes to New Albany. Buffalo Trace Park, 0.7 mile east of Palmyra, celebrates the historic trail. The 146-acre park includes recreational facilities and primitive camping.

Greenville, 6 miles east, was first settled in 1807 and was a manufacturing center for barrels, wine kegs, and wooden clocks, due to the fine white oak forests that surrounded the town. It also was a toll stop on the old pike, which operated from the 1820s to the 1880s in spite of the emergence of the railroads.

To the east 2.9 miles, Galena, originally called Germantown, was another toll stop on the road. The old mill, built in 1857, was a steam-powered flour mill. Because of the many nearby streams, the area abounded with Native American villages and burial grounds.

The scenic drive passes through the Knobstone Escarpment, Indiana's most prominent phsysiographic feature, which rises nearly 600 feet from the Ohio River valley below. The knobs above New Albany are a long-time truck farming area for the Louisville market. For many generations, the mostly German farm families hauled berries, melons, and tobacco to the Louisville wholesale market. The Starlight area is known for agri-tourism. The Huber Orchard and Winery, established in 1843, is at 19816 Huber Road. Take Navilleton Road off IN 150. Nearby Stumler's also has a restaurant, party barn, petting zoo, and farm market. The Joe Huber Family Farm, 2421 Scottsville Road, has more than 50 varieties of fruits and vegetables for sale, and a farm restaurant rated four-star by the Louisville *Courier-Journal*.

North of New Albany 2 miles on IN 150, The Mary Anderson Center is a nationally renowned artists' retreat focused on providing a haven for creative work.

The Falls Cities—New Albany, Jeffersonville, Clarksville, and neighboring Louisville, Kentucky—got their name from the Falls of the Ohio. In Ohio's 981 miles from the Allegheny mountains to the Mississippi, the Falls of the Ohio were the only obstacle, where the river dropped 24 feet in 2 turbulent miles. The Ohio raced over the Falls in a series of rapids and chutes and waterfalls for thousands of years until canalization and damming in the nineteenth- and twentieth-centuries subdued it. This immense natural barrier has created a node of ecology, history, and commerce over the last 12,000 years. The Falls of the Ohio neatly divided the river into the Upper and Lower Ohio. East to Pittsburgh was the Upper; from the Falls west to Cairo, Illinois at the junction with the Mississippi, was the Lower.

New Albany was the first town below the falls, located in a lowland east of the Knobstone escarpment. Three Scribner brothers arrived from New York in 1813, bought the platted town and named it after the capital of their home state. The Scribner house at 106 W. Main, owned by the Daughters of the American Revolution, was built by brother Joel in 1814.

Steamboat building was the primary industry in New Albany until the Civil War, with four to seven shipyards working constantly. Town Clock Church at 300 E. Main Street is a remnant of river days. It was built with a tall steeple in the mid-nineteenth century, a landmark for river pilots since. New Albany's Mansion Row Historic District was named to the National

Register in 1983. It includes Main bounded by State and Fifteenth, and Market Street between Seventh and Eleventh. The stately homes range in style from Federal to Italianate to French Second Empire.

The Floyd County Museum, 201 E. Spring Street, offers paintings from regional artists, both historic and contemporary, as well as the Yenawine Diorama, an animated hand-carved expression of early Indiana life.

Next-door Jeffersonville was designed by Thomas Jefferson in 1802 with an alternating checkerboard of green spaces and buildings to protect the town from yellow fever and other pestilences that plagued the early settlers.

The nineteenth-century Old Jeffersonville Historic District was listed on the National Historic Register in 1983. The district is bounded by Court and Graham Streets, the Ohio, and IN 65. Within the district, the quirky 1837 Grisamore House at 111–113 W. Chestnut, and the 1832 Henry French House at 217 E. High are on the National Registry. Schimpff's Confectionery at 347 Spring Street has been serving candy since 1891, and you can enjoy soda fountains under their old pressed-tin ceiling.

The Howard Steamboat Museum in Jeffersonville is a trove of steamboat memorabilia.
Photo courtesy of Howard Steamboat Museum.

The business of government has always been a major part of Jeffersonville. It was the early county seat and home of Indiana's second land office. The 1874 U.S. Quartermaster Depot at 10th and Meigs was the major dispensary for the armed forces from the Civil War to the Korean War. The depot warehoused everything from mule saddles to army shirts—71,000 different items in all. Since the depot closed in 1957, it has become the census processing center for the nation.

The Howard Shipyards dominated Jeffersonville from 1848 until well into the twentieth century. On the 52-acre site along the historically deepest section of the Ohio, the Howard yards produced more than a thousand boats. At 1101 E. Market, the Howard Steamboat Museum brings this world to life with a collection of steamboat memorabilia relating to the Golden Age of river travel, a wide array of bells and whistles, ships wheels and models, tools, photographs, and documents. The museum is housed in the Howard family mansion dating from the 1890s. Many of the rooms are decorated in high-style Victorian furnishings and elaborate trappings brought from Chicago's World Colombian Exposition.

Across the street, the giant Jeffboat complex continues Jeffersonville's maritime tradition. Through World War II, the shipyards produced many of the landing craft used in the invasions on both fronts, with 13,000 workers laboring in the yards by 1944. Today, Jeffboat encompasses the old Howard shipyards, producing the tugs and barges that are ubiquitous on the river. In 1979, it launched a $20-million floating palace, the *Mississippi Queen*, the only steam-powered stern paddlewheeler built in this century. Jeffboat is America's largest inland shipbuilder.

Take Riverview Drive 0.7 mile west to Clarksville, the oldest American town in the Northwest Territory. It was chartered in 1783 by George Rogers Clark, revolutionary war hero and brother to William Clark, who joined Meriwether Lewis on his journey of exploration to the Pacific. There is a marker at the location of George Rogers Clark's home west of the corner of South Clark and Harrison Avenue. The Clarksville Museum in the Town Hall at 230 E. Montgomery has a collection of memorabilia relating to Clark.

Clarksville was also the site of one of the first instances of government privatization. The old Indiana Reformatory for Men was the First State Prison for Men, built in 1821. It was built with publicly subscribed funds and then leased to private individuals who incarcerated the prisoners on a per capita basis. The first prison operator, Captain Seymour Westover, was killed with Davy Crockett at the Alamo. The red-brick Romanesque complex was sold in 1923 and remodeled into a Colgate-Palmolive-Peet Company soap factory, which operates today at South Clark Boulevard and Woerner Avenue, one of the area's largest employers. The Colgate Clock on the building is the second largest timepiece in the world.

The most unique aspect of Clarksville, however, is the Falls of the Ohio State Park, 201 W. Riverside Drive. In 1981, the United States Congress declared the Falls of the Ohio the country's first National Wildlife Conservation Area, a 1,404-acre site that is a favorite of birders. The conservation area protects the habitat of migrating birds who visit the falls to feed in the wetlands and potholes of the limestone reef. Over 265 species of birds throng the falls area. In the river below the falls, 125 species of fish swim, including the endangered paddlefish.

Congress also protected the immense fossil beds that constituted the limestone reef, the largest exposed Devonian Age fossil beds in the world. The Indiana state park opened in 1990 on 68 acres, overlooking the fossil beds and offering a dramatic view of the Louisville skyline. A few feet down from the park's interpretation center, visitors can hike the 220 acres of fossil beds through a landscape of natural arches and tiny canyons, fossilized coral, and clusters of miniature crinoids and trilobites. Adventurous souls can cross the McAlpine Dam spillway to explore the outer fossil beds.

The 16,000-square-foot interpretation center encapsulates much of the history of the Falls of the Ohio area. A multi-screen video explains the epochal geologic story of the falls. There are exhibits on everything from coral reefs and the fossil beds to mastodons and early humans, steamboats, George Rogers Clark, the legendary Welshmen, and the ecology of today's falls. Three aquariums show the varied life of coral reefs and the Ohio River.

2

Greek Revival Indiana
A drive along the Ohio River

General description: A 68-mile drive along the Ohio River shore through a series of nineteenth-century towns that are a national treasury of architectural styles and small town life. The route follows the nationally celebrated Ohio River Scenic Route.

Special attractions: Madison's 133-block National Register of Historic Places district, Lawrenceburg, Aurora, Rising Sun, Vevay, riverboat casinos at Lawrenceburg and Rising Sun, cruise boats on the Ohio.

Location: The extreme southeastern corner of Indiana.

Drive route numbers and names: Indiana Highways 56, 156, and 62.

Travel season: The route is drivable in all but the worst of snow seasons. Spring and fall are particularly beautiful. Traffic is heavier during the Madison Regatta.

Camping: There is camping at Lake in the Pines in Sunman, north of Lawrenceburg, and Clifty Falls State Park, west of Madison.

Services: There are services in Lawrenceburg, Aurora, Rising Sun, Vevay, and Madison, as well as numerous spots along the route.

Nearby attractions: The urban charms of Cincinnati are 25 miles east of Lawrenceburg.

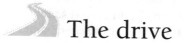 The drive

The drive begins in the old riverport town of Lawrenceburg and neighboring Greendale. The scent of fermenting mash has hung over this part of the valley since the towns' early days, as the area is known for whiskey production. By 1809 the region's abundant grain and clear, cold well water stimulated whiskey production as the pioneers discovered the ease of transport and profitability of the distilled elixir versus raw grain. As late as 1941, there were still three major distilleries in town. Considered the largest distillery in the world, the Joseph E. Seagram and Sons, Inc. is the last remaining.

In Greendale, turn 0.5 mile north on Nowlin Street to the Greendale Cemetery. The cemetery was founded in 1867 on land given to Colonel Zebulon Pike in 1803 for service in the Revolutionary War. His son, Brigadier General Zebulon Montgomery Pike, was the famed one-armed explorer of much of the West and the Grand Canyon.

Lawrenceburg, founded in 1802, is the fourth oldest city in Indiana. In the heyday of the steamboat era, Lawrenceburg was a favorite port of call.

The architecture of Lawrenceburg is still a remarkable example of a nineteenth-century mercantile center. In 1984, the entire downtown district, bounded by Charlotte, Tate, William, and Elm Streets and the railroad tracks, was added to the National Register of Historic Places.

There are at least 30 significant historic buildings in the downtown area. In 1997 a three-block section of downtown Lawrenceburg was added to Historic Landmarks Foundation of Indiana's list of eleven most endangered historic sites. Among many historic structures in Lawrenceburg, the Dearborn County Courthouse on High Street is an exceptional example of Greek Revival architecture. The small county museum inside has walking tour maps. At 508 W. High Street, the 1818 Vance-Tously House, was considered the finest house between Cincinnati and Louisville, a Federal-style structure built with plans brought from England. The 1818 Jesse Hunt three-story brick building at Walnut and High was Indiana's first "skyscraper," an awe-inspiring sight to the pioneers. An important group of Federal row houses are located at 124–136 E. High Street. The commercial Italianate building at 316–318 Walnut was jacked up one story in the nineteenth century, a common occurrence. Indeed, Chicago's entire inventory of buildings in the Loop were raised ten feet in the same period, while business went on as usual.

At 229 Short Street, the 1882 Queen Anne–style Presbyterian Church was the first congregation ministered by famous abolitionist Henry Ward Beecher, the brother of Harriet Beecher Stowe, author of *Uncle Tom's Cabin*. Beecher was ordained here in 1837 and served as its minister until 1839.

The American Legion at the corner of Second and Short Streets has the Flying Red Horse "Peggy" in a glass case outside the club. She is a customized Model T Ford, built by two World War I vets who wanted a parade vehicle. Peggy's giant wings flapped as she reared on her hind wheels and spun at American Legion parades all over America from 1936 to 1972. She was put out to her glass pasture in 1994.

East of the town on U. S. Highway 56, there are signs for the Argosy Casino on Argosy Parkway. The immense Las Vegas–style complex boasts one of the world's largest floating casinos. Nearly four million people crossed the gangplank to gamble in 1997.

Two miles west, the town of Aurora was founded in 1804 on a picturesque bluff above the river bend. In its heyday, steamboats constantly pulled to the public dock to unload passengers and load the manufactured goods of the town: foundry work, whiskey, furniture, and caskets.

Drive 2: Greek Revival Indiana

A drive along the Ohio River

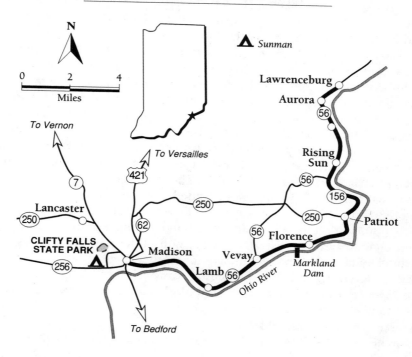

The downtown area, bounded by Importing, Water, Market, Fifth, and Exporting Streets, is a National Historic District. There are several exceptional examples of Gothic Revival structures in Aurora, commingling with other nineteenth-century styles. They include the 1878 St. John's Lutheran Church at 214 Mechanic Street, the mid-1870s First Evangelical Church at 113 Fifth Street, and houses at 318 Fourth Street and 403 Judiciary, the latter a Queen Anne–hybrid built between 1870 and 1890.

The crown jewel of Aurora is the grand Hillforest house at the end of Main Street. It's as though an enormous steamboat ran aground high on the hillside. "We say it is Italian Renaissance meets Steamboat Gothic," Hillforest Director Sue Small said. The circular porches wrapping the semi-circular front, the rooftop cupola resembling a steamboat pilot house, the slender columns and arched windows, all contribute to the steamboat effect.

Even higher on the hillside, the landmark 1810 Veraestau displays nearly two hundred years of Greek Revival enthusiasm. The house has been owned by two families since its original construction, who maintained the original style through two major renovations. Take Market Street at the west edge of town 0.7 mile to Glenmary Lane.

At the west edge of town, look for Riverview Cemetery. Laughery Creek is at the southern end of the cemetery, where Mohawk leader Joseph Brant and one hundred warriors attacked and soundly defeated Colonel Archibald Lockry and 107 Pennsylvania volunteers in August 1781. The troops were en route to join George Rogers Clark. Lockry and approximately half of his troops were killed, and the survivors taken prisoner. There is a memorial to the Lockry Massacre in the cemetery, and another at the south end of the new Laughery Creek Bridge (the creek name was misspelled when it was recorded and was never corrected).

The old Laughery Creek Bridge is the only structure in Ohio County on the National Register of Historic Places. Built in 1878, it is an extremely rare iron triple-intersection Pratt through-truss span.

Rising Sun is 6.5 miles west. Platted in 1814, Rising Sun boomed in the 1830s and '40s with as many as 2,500 people thriving in the town. Each spring 300 to 400 flatboats left Rising Sun daily, headed downriver. There were eight factories, two steam-powered mills, three potteries, a newspaper, a clutch of churches, and a seminary for teachers.

Today, the population is about the same. The sprawling Grand Victoria Casino & Resort by Hyatt sits a few blocks east of downtown, connected by a newly constructed Riverwalk. The casino is decorated like a vintage gambling palace, with gilded corbels and wooden turnings. It has a 200-room hotel, and a 1,000-seat show room for acts like Tom Jones and Wayne Newton. Unlike the Argosy casino boat, the Grand Victoria boat actually cruises down the river for about a mile and a half before returning.

The Ohio County Historical Society Museum at 212 S. Walnut is a good starting point for a walking tour of the town. It has a collection of quilts and farm implements, diverse and sundry music machines, and the town pride: the famous 1920s "Hoosier Boy" speedboat. Be sure the tour guides tell you about Smith Riggs, a local blacksmith who invented the first modern electric chair.

The Ohio County Courthouse, an 1845 Greek Revival structure on Main Street, had no inside stairs until a 1980s restoration. An 1840s Federal/Greek Revival–style house is at 316 Fourth Street and an 1860 Gothic Revival house at 510 Main Street.

Take Indiana Highway 156 south out of Rising Sun. The road runs through the flood plain along the Ohio with cabin cruisers and coal barges coursing down the river almost at the level of your car. Sand and gravel quarries dot the roadside.

The Switzerland County line is 4 miles west. A land of steep and rolling hills, the county sits at an elbow of the Ohio. Switzerland County was separated from Dearborn and Jefferson counties in 1814, at the behest of Swiss-French settlers who migrated to Indiana to pioneer wine production in America. The Vevay vineyard prospered, becoming the first commercially successful vineyard in the country. By the mid-nineteenth century, more than 30,000 acres of grapes were in production along Indiana's Ohio river shore, from the eastern border over to the Falls of the Ohio at Louisville, which became known as "The Rhineland of America." By 1880, Indiana was a top–ten grape producer in the nation, but black rot, phylloxera, and the inevitable death knell of Prohibition devastated Indiana production. The industry was moribund until passage of the Indiana Small Winery Act in 1971, which permitted wineries to sell directly to the public. Currently, there are 19 wineries scattered throughout the state, with fully a third of the state's wineries clustered along the Ohio from Cincinnati to Louisville.

Ohio River traffic declined through the nineteenth century, and the railroads and major highways passed Switzerland and Ohio Counties by. People migrated to more economically vibrant areas as the soil showed signs of depletion and the river markets dried up. The lack of modern transport deterred large industries and preserved the historic air of the region. When architects surveyed Vevay, the county seat, in 1980, they discovered that 86 percent of the structures in the town were more than fifty years old, and nearly two-thirds were built before 1883.

On the right side of the highway, 1.2 miles from the county line, the Federal-style brick Merit-Tandy-Tillotson House sports a balustraded widow's walk on its roof, a somewhat incongruous folly for a one-story cottage. It sits in a stretch of countryside known as Mexico Bottoms that commemorates the Mexican-American War veterans who cleared the bottom of the giant trees.

Patriot, 2.8 miles west, looks worse for wear, as befits a town that has suffered from numerous catastrophes. At one point, Patriot had several mills and distilleries and substantial river traffic. A fire in 1924 destroyed most of the commercial district. The disastrous 1937 flood swept away the wharf, bank, boats, mills, and distilleries, and the town never recovered. There are still a number of structures scattered through the village from Patriot's boom years, including several Queen Anne buildings. There are also a couple of vernacular buildings worth noting: the tiny whitewashed old stone jail at 106 First Street, and a nineteenth-century tavern on Fifth and Front Streets.

At the junction of IN 156 and 250, there is a marker to Patriot native Dr. Elwood Mead, "the engineer who made the desert bloom." He built the Hoover Dam and Lake Mead was named for him. Traveling south on IN 156, the lowland is called Egypt Bottoms because the fertility of the soil yielded corn crops of biblical proportions. It is an area of upright I-houses (named because they are most often found in states that start with

I—Indiana, Illinois, and Iowa), hand-hewn rock walls, and clapboard Country Gothic churches.

Florence, founded in 1817, is 11 miles south of Patriot. At one time it was the home of the Anti-Swearing Society which fined its 75 members for profanities. South of Florence, the brick, green-shuttered Armstrong House was built in 1880. The road is through a bit of vintage Burma Shave and Mailbox Tobacco Americana.

The Markland Locks and Dam and Generating Station is 4.5 miles south. Constructed in 1956 and 1963 near the village of Markland, the dam is 1,416 feet long, with two parallel locks on the Kentucky side of the river that are 110 feet wide. Across the bridge in Kentucky, an observation tower overlooks the locks. An information signboard presents a history of the Army Corps of Engineers projects that dammed the Ohio.

Markland is 600 river miles below Pittsburgh and is 455 feet above sea level. By the time the river reaches Louisville it is at 420 feet and is down to 358 feet at the Newburgh dam. In 1930, the river carried 20 million tons of freight. By the mid-1980s 160 million tons of material moved down the Ohio, more than either the Panama or Suez canals.

Vevay (pronounced vee' vee), a tidy town with well-kept nineteenth-century buildings, is another river town that deserves a stroll. The Knox House at 302 W. Main has New Orleans–style iron grillwork, as does the Grisard-Sieglitz home at 306 E. Main. The Switzerland County Historical Museum is in a hundred-year-old Presbyterian Church at Main and Market.

At 209 W. Market Street, the Ulysses P. Schenck House was built with the best elevations facing the river, the important avenue of the day. Schenck was called the "Hay King" from his success in dealing timothy hay from the Switzerland County fields downriver on flatboats. The Dufour Cottage to the east is one of several houses in Vevay built by Jean François Dufour. The unusual fish scale–shingled Vevay Christian Church on Market was built as a Unitarian Church in 1863. The 1817 Morerod homestead on Arch Street still has a 500-gallon wine cask in the cellar to vint the grapes from builder Jean Daniel Morerod's extensive vineyards. The clapboard Armstrong Tavern at 201 W. Market was built in 1816. Slaves were ferried over daily from Kentucky to work in the tavern in the early days. The Edward Eggleston and George Cary House at 306 W. Main is on the National Register of Historic Places, as is the Old Indiana Theater at the corner of Ferry and Cheapside.

The magnificent 1870s Benjamin Schenck House sits on a hill overlooking the town. It boasts the finest furnishings of the day, including walnut tin- and copper-lined bathtubs. Down at the end of Market Street, The Rosemont Inn Bed and Breakfast is another restored merchant prince home, lavishly furnished with period antiques.

Madison is the Williamsburg of the Midwest.   Photo courtesy of Jefferson Country CVB.

But Vevay's most unique entry in the Historic American Buildings Survey is the Switzerland County Courthouse privy, a hexagonal brick outhouse, built in 1864 with a louvered cupola. The courthouse is very nice, too, a Greek Revival structure. The basement has a deep cellar that served as a waystop on the Underground Railroad.

At the west end of town, the contemporary Ogle Haus Hotel is a good place to sit on the terrace and watch the river traffic. The tall stacks of the Markland Generating Plant and the endless lines of passing river barges are a reminder that the Ohio is sometimes known as "America's Ruhr." It is the most heavily trafficked river in the world.

Lamb, 16.5 miles west on IN 56 is the site of Indiana's oldest existing brick house, the George Ash House, built at the turn of the eighteenth century. Turn left at the town sign and proceed .25 mile to the dead end, then go left 0.3 mile along the river. The upright little house is on the north side of the road.

Cedar Cliffs parallel the highway a few miles west of Lamb, offering a 12-mile view down the river for those energetic enough to make the climb.

Four miles farther west, look for an old rusting red crane on the north side of the highway. The roofless, two-story fieldstone house on the hill behind the crane is the home of Chapman Harris. The Underground Railroad came through here, as it did many places along the river, sheltering the refugees following the North Star. Chapman Harris was an ex-slave who worked as a minister and blacksmith. During the day, he preached of the evils of slavery and the joys of heaven for the righteous. Come nightfall, Chapman Harris went to his anvil on the river shore. As his hammer rang out across the wide, black waters, the fugitives on the far bank knew it was safe to cross to the other side, and the skiffs set out on the voyage to the promised land of Canada.

Madison, 0.5 mile west, is known as "The Williamsburg of the West." The town was founded in 1810 in a bend where the Ohio curled the farthest to the north. The 133 blocks of the National Historic District are an extraordinary ensemble of Greek Revival, Federal, Italianate, Queen Anne, Bungalow, and vernacular architecture, most well-maintained and in everyday use. While much of vintage Madison is in private hands, there are several outstanding historic buildings open for tours, including the 1844 James F. D. Lanier mansion, considered the finest house on the Ohio. By 1839, the pioneering Madison-Indianapolis Railroad, the first railroad in Indiana, conquered the high bluffs that surround the old town and reached the town of

The Switzerland County Grape Stomp in Vevay celebrates the oldest wine region in the country. Photo courtesy of Switzerland County CVB.

Vernon. The 311-foot climb over 1.3 miles was the steepest standard-gauge track in the world. The incline can be seen at the corner of Main and McIntire. The matrix of river, rail, and road funneled the region's raw goods into Madison for manufacture and processing and trans-shipment out into the larger markets.

In a brief period, the town became a bustling industrial city with brick smoke stacks belching and dozens of products being produced. There are wagon, tack and spoke factories, shipyards, six wharves, castor- and lin-seed-oil factories, distilleries, and breweries. Madison was a major pork-packing center, rivaling Cincinnati. By 1850, Madison led the state in manufacturing capital and total number of products shipped. Banks, mansions, stores, and stately churches rose where only wilderness existed a few decades before.

The brick commercial architecture of the downtown area was constructed during Madison's heyday from 1830 to 1850. After that, new railroads linking Louisville, Indianapolis, and Cincinnati de-emphasized river traffic, sending Madison into a slump. A burst of economic activity in the 1870s "modernized" Main Street with cast-iron fronts that added Italianate touches like elaborate cornice brackets. Today, even the bars and cafes are historic: The Historic Broadway Hotel and Tavern at 313 Broadway is Indiana's oldest family tavern, serving customers since 1859. The beautifully restored JWI Confectionery at 207 W. Main serves candy and ice cream made with the same equipment that was used when Valentino and Elvis were the big stars. The town is rich with bed-and-breakfasts in lovely old homes.

The Madison Area Convention and Visitors Bureau, 301 E. Main Street, has a wealth of information about the town. The 1818 Jeremiah Sullivan house at 304 W. Second is considered one of the finest examples of Federal architecture in the old Northwest Territory. It is open to the public, as is the Schofield house at 217 W. Second Street. The 1820 Talbott-Hyatt house has extensive restored gardens and outbuildings.

At Poplar and First Streets, the Shrewsbury house radiates the austere grace of classical antiquity. Magnificently proportioned, the Shrewsbury house has a spectacular spiral staircase that rises through the house's three stories, unsupported except by its own thrust.

At 511 W. First Street, the grand 1844 James F. D. Lanier home overlooks the broad Ohio. It was considered the finest house on the Ohio in its day. Neo-Corinthian columns soar 30 feet to the 50-foot-long portico. Behind the Lanier house, the charming John Eckert cottage at 510 W. Second Street was built by a local tinsmith in 1872. The octagonal building at 615 W. First Street was Madison's railroad terminal and now houses a museum. The Holstein-Whisett house at 718 Main Street is a Greek Revival structure built in 1840 and reminiscent of the townhouses of Salem and Portsmouth.

Main Street has a fine collection of mid- and late-nineteenth-century commercial buildings, many with Italianate facades. Mulberry Street has a remarkable collection of unaltered 1830s commercial buildings.

Seven miles north of Madison, the Eleutherian College sits proudly on a ridge. Founded by New England Baptist abolitionists in the 1830s, the three-story fieldstone structure was the first college in the United States where African-American and white students of both genders could study together. To reach the college, travel north on IN 7 for 6 miles. Turn west on IN 250 and drive 1 mile to the village of Lancaster. The college building is on the south side of the road.

At the west edge of Madison on IN 62, Clifty Falls State Park has a rugged terrain of deeply cut canyons, waterfalls, and scenic walking trails. The nearby Clifty Creek Generating Plant was opened in 1955, the largest steam-powered generating plant in the world.

3

The Haunts of Young Abe Lincoln
Southern Indiana hills, valleys, and forests

General description: The 47-mile drive winds through the hills of southern Indiana where Abraham Lincoln spent his formative years and where his beloved mother and sister are buried.

Special attractions: Troy, where Lincoln first arrived in Indiana and later argued the law; Grandview, where he worked and played; Gentryville, featuring Lincoln State Park and Lincoln Boyhood National Memorial; Holiday World and Splashin' Safari in Santa Claus; and Lincoln Pioneer Village, at Rockport, where Lincoln commenced his flatboat trip south to the slave states.

Location: Southern Indiana.

Drive route numbers and names: Indiana Highways 66, 245, and 162; U.S. Highway 231.

Travel season: Summers can be blistering in Spencer County, but the entertainment complex at Santa Claus can offer respite with its water park. Except for inclement winter weather, the roads are negotiable in all seasons.

Camping: There is camping at Lincoln State Park in Gentryville and Lake Rudolph Resort in Santa Claus.

Services: There are services in Troy, Grandview, Santa Claus, and Rockport.

Nearby attractions: Benedictine monasteries at St. Meinrad and Ferdinand; Huntingburg for antiquing and league baseball; Jasper for German culture and food (see Drive 4).

 The drive

Abraham Lincoln arrived in Indiana with his family in 1816 as a seven-year-old boy and trundled down the old buffalo trail by oxen cart to Illinois in 1830 as a robust raw-boned man. "I grew up in Indiana," he said, pioneering on a farm on Little Pigeon Creek, surrounded by the cabins of Kentucky yeomen like his father, earning his keep by farming the land and clearing the woods.

The scenic drive begins in Troy, where Lincoln landed with his family in 1816. The Lincolns crossed the Ohio at Troy on Thompson's Ferry and followed a wagon trail that was cut from Troy to Hurricane, the township where Thomas Lincoln had staked his claim. The wilderness road passed within 4 miles of the Lincoln homestead, and Thomas felled trees the rest of the way to make a path for the wagon. Abraham Lincoln later said he "never passed through a harder experience than he did going from Thompson's Ferry" to their home site.

At the age of 17, Abe was back working in Troy, helping out on a ferry boat and picking up extra money selling wood for 50 cents a cord to the steamboats. He also hauled passengers out to midstream to catch the passing steamboats in a small skiff he built. A Kentucky ferryman lodged a complaint and hauled Abe into court for operating a ferry without a license. Lincoln, 17 at the time, studied the law and pled his own case before Justice of the Peace Samuel Pate across the river in Kentucky. Lincoln argued that since he only traveled to midstream and never crossed the river, the law didn't apply. He won the case, and his success cemented his interest in the law and learning.

The old trail to Hurricane that the Lincoln family traveled when they arrived in frontier Indiana is no more, so this route will take a more circuitous but ultimately far easier way. Proceed west on Indiana Highway 66 along the Ohio River 9.4 miles to Grandview. There is a large barge-loading operation about 5 miles down the road, primarily handling the area's abundant soft coal.

Grandview sits at a wide bend in the river, affording a fine view. The town has a gas station, a bar, and a good bed-and-breakfast. The tiny town dates back to settlement in the early 1800s, and the Lincoln family lived nearby.

Drive 16 miles north on IN 245 to Santa Claus, Indiana, famous for Christmas mail. Being the only town in the country named Santa Claus, the post office prepares for an annual onslaught of half a million pieces of Christmas mail needing the special postmark.

Beginning in 1914, local postmaster Jim Martin began responding to the "Dear Santa" letters that made their way to Santa Claus. Today, the entire town is involved in the yearly task, responding to up to 10,000 letters from around the world. "Everyone around here is so aware these letters have to be sent out," Pat Koch said, queen mother of the Holiday World and leader of Santa's Elves, the organization that coordinates the letter-writing.

Santa Claus Land, the original name of Holiday World, began in 1946, the first themed amusement park in the world, predating even Knott's Berry Farm by a bit. The Kochs' theme park was renamed Holiday World in 1980 and boasts the wooden Raven roller coaster, ranked one of the three best roller coasters in the country. State-of-the-art amusement rides share the park with charming vintage rides that are lovingly preserved. The park also has a collection of Lincoln memorabilia. The Splashin' Safari water park features a wave pool, water slides, and an action river.

Drive 6.2 miles west on IN 162 to Lincoln State Park and Lincoln

Drive 3: The Haunts of Young Abe Lincoln
Southern Indiana hills, valleys, and forests

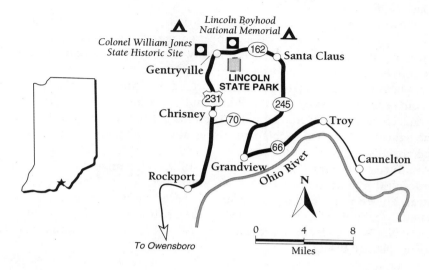

Boyhood National Memorial and Living Historical Farm. The 196-acre complex encompasses the 100-acre farm that Thomas Lincoln sold when the family moved to Illinois in 1830. The Memorial Building houses a museum dedicated to the life and times of Lincoln, a visitor center, and auditoriums, designed with the esthetics and culture of the Lincolns in mind. The nearby gravesite of Nancy Hanks Lincoln, Abraham's mother, is the focus of the park.

The National Park Service developed the Living Historical Farm in 1967, one of only two in the park system. The farm is a well-interpreted working pioneer farm, portraying life on the Indiana frontier. Self-sufficiency was the rule, with nearly everything consumed on the farm needing to be grown or made.

Across the road, Lincoln State Park is an extensive 1,700-acre recreation area with an 85-acre swimming and boating lake, 200 campsites, cabins, hiking trails, and a nature center. Many of the park's original structures and trails were constructed as part of the Depression-era Civilian Conservation Corps (CCC) program.

From June through September every Tuesday through Sunday, the 1,514-seat Lincoln Amphitheater presents theatrical performances such as *Young Abe Lincoln* and Broadway musicals. Nearby, a historical reproduction of the log-constructed Little Pigeon Primitive Baptist Church is erected on the site of the church that served the Lincolns as a spiritual haven. The gravestone of Sarah Lincoln Grigsby, Abe's beloved older sister, is in the church cemetery. Sarah died in 1828 during childbirth. She and her still-born child are buried together.

Proceed 1.4 miles west on IN 162 to a marker for the site of the James Gentry homestead. Gentry was a pioneer entrepreneur, the founder of Gentryville and a friend of the Lincoln family. The crossroads hamlet of Gentryville is 0.1 mile farther west. For several decades, Gentryville has been most famous for the creative antique clutter of the Antique Shak, housed in an old general store and other buildings at the junction of IN 231. But it was at this crossroads that Abe Lincoln began his political education, absorbing the banter and bluster of the days' issues at Gentry's Store as the Whigs of the area debated the Democrats.

Turn south on IN 231 to the next road west, County Road 1575N, and proceed 0.7 mile to the Colonel William Jones house, Lincoln's political tutor. The 1834 Federal-style brick home reflects Jones' economic position when his neighbors were housed in log cabins. In 1990 the Jones home was named an Indiana State Historic Site. It is also listed on the National Register of Historic Places.

Return to the intersection of IN 231 and turn south. IN 231 follows for a large part the old Yellow Banks Trail that ran from Rockport to the Delaware Indian town at the forks of the White River. Travel 11.7 miles south of Gentryville to Rockport. South of Crisney, the mammoth AK Steel Plant looms, which is having a dramatic economic impact on the area. The twin 1,040-foot towers and boiling vapors in the distance are part of the AEP (American Electric Power) generating plant.

The early nineteenth-century settlers of Rockport clustered at the bottom of the bluff on which Rockport now sits. The riverside bluff is also where Abraham Lincoln cast off on his fateful flatboat journey to New Orleans. A marker at the end of Bluff Road commemorates his trip to the South. In 1828, James Gentry decided to send trade goods down the river to New Orleans, and he contracted 19-year-old Abraham Lincoln to help man the 65-foot-long flatboat. During the three-month journey, Lincoln saw slavery first-hand, first along the plantations on the Mississippi where they stopped to trade, and later in the New Orleans slave markets. To return to Indiana, Lincoln and his crew churned back up the rivers on one of the steamboats, making their way through the West. If their trip was like most, it probably took about nine days.

The current Spencer County courthouse in Rockport features a large interior stained-glass dome. Built in 1921, it is the county's fifth. A marker at Second and Main Streets denotes the site of the Rockport Tavern where Lincoln spent the night in 1844 when he was stumping for Whig candidates. Just south of Ninth and Main, the Lincoln Pioneer Village is located in the city park. The 4-acre plot has an inn, church, school, law office, store, and homes. A museum was added in 1950 that includes one of Thomas Lincoln's cherry-inlaid corner cupboards, his specialty as a frontier craftsman. The Pioneer Village was listed on the Indiana Register of Historic Places in 1998, the first step toward national designation, and recently was awarded rehabilitation grants.

The 1867 Mathias Sharp House at 319 S. Second is listed on the National Register of Historic Places. The interesting, octagonal 1859 Crooks-Anderson house is located at 419 Walnut Street. The Federal-style Rockport Inn at 130 S. Third was built as a private residence in 1857. South of Rockport on IN 231 and several eras away, the nostalgic Holiday Drive-In Movie Theater screens the latest in Hollywood films on five huge screens every night in the summer and on the weekends in the fall.

4

Land of the Indiana Germans
Exploring the heartland of Indiana's German colonies

General description: A 48-mile drive through the heart of Indiana's Old Country, where small towns and farmland still retain the flavor of the Fatherland. The region has maintained its traditional appeal due to the strong, family-oriented German culture and the importance of the Catholic Church in the area.

Special attractions: The Ohio River at Troy, St. Meinrad Archabbey and Monastery, Monastery Immaculate Conception, Jasper's Germantown culture and Schnitzelbank Restaurant, Huntingburg's Victorian delights.

Location: Southern Indiana.

Drive route numbers and names: Indiana Highways 545, 62, and 162; U.S. Highway 231.

Travel season: The route is along all-weather roads. Fall, with the magnificent hardwood forests, is a good time to visit. The region's festivals bring in thousands to share in the fun.

Camping: Patoka Lake, Ferdinand State Forest, and Lake Rudolph Outdoor Resort in Santa Claus.

Services: There are services in Troy, St. Meinrad, Ferdinand, Jasper, and Huntingburg, as well as numerous spots along the route.

Nearby attractions: Patoka Lake, Holiday World and Splashin' Safari theme park, Lincoln Boyhood National Memorial and Lincoln State Park, Marengo Cave.

 The drive

In 1815 Virginian families platted Troy at the mouth of the Anderson River, one of the earliest towns below the Falls of the Ohio at Louisville. The small brick single-pen house that sits between Spring and Main Streets on Franklin (Indiana Highway 66) speaks of an Eastern esthetic sensibility. The Nestor House at 300 Water Street is a remnant of Troy's nineteenth-century commercial heyday along the riverfront. The rough-cut sandstone Greek Revival building dates back to 1863 and has served as a grocery, tavern, hotel, and now a private residence. Local lore has it that the basement served as a waystop on the Underground Railroad. A Greek Revival house on Market

Drive 4: Land of the Indiana Germans

Exploring the heartland of Indiana's German colonies

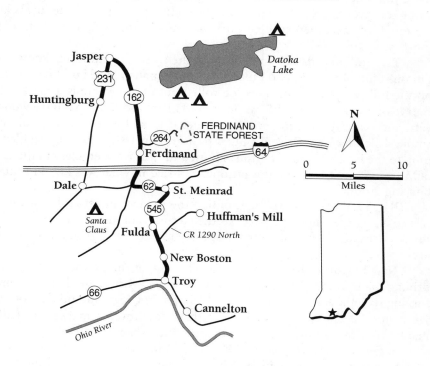

Street at Harrison was built in 1840, as was the gable-fronted Greek Revival in the next block east and I-house at 525 Walnut Street. Vintage structures ranging from Queen Anne to Craftsman are dotted throughout the tiny town. Fortwendel's Hardware Store on Market Street is a bustling general goods store with crafts among the chicken waterers and electrical supplies located in a well-maintained turn-of-the-century commercial structure.

Troy was Perry County's first seat, but when the county was reorganized in 1818 Troy lost the honor. The town continued to prosper through the nineteenth century as a port town for the road that ran north along the Anderson River into the German colonies. St. Pius Church with its 142-foot bell tower, is the most visible landmark in the town. Built 1881–84 to serve the area's German Catholics, the new church replaced one built in 1847 when the waves of German immigrants were arriving at the waterfront.

The eighteen-foot-high Christ of the Ohio statue is located a mile east of Troy along the river. It was fabricated by an ex-German prisoner of war, Herbert Jogerst, who returned to Indiana to practice his art after be-

27

ing incarcerated in Kentucky during World War II. He is responsible for religious monuments in the area. It has been a landmark for boaters on the Ohio since its dedication in 1957. There were once many potteries along the river, across the road from the statue. Potters used the local clay for much of the nineteenth century, manufacturing utilitarian Bennington-type pottery.

The bluff affords a 30-mile view of the river. The hilltop is known as Fulton's Bluff because Robert Fulton's brother Abraham died building a house on the hill, when an enormous log rolled onto him. There is a marker to Fulton on the west edge of Troy. He arrived in Troy in 1814 to build a wood-yard and manage his brother's coal mine. It is said when Robert Fulton's smoke-belching *New Orleans* puffed past Troy in 1811, the Troy residents took to the bushes in fear. Fulton is buried in the Troy Cemetery at the end of Washington Street, the first European buried in what was an old Indian burying ground.

IN 545 North follows the trail that the pioneer priest Father Kundek blazed along the Anderson River to the German colonies he founded. The towns of Fulda, Ferdinand, and Jasper were laid out a day's ox cart ride apart.

New Boston is 3 miles down IN 545, one of the prettiest biking and driving roads in the Midwest. The New Boston Tavern is an old roadhouse, serving regional fare like smoked pork chops, frog legs, and fiddlers on the weekends. At County Road 1290 North, follow the red markers to Huffman's Mill Covered Bridge, one of the few remaining in Indiana.

A few miles north on IN 545, the 150-foot steeple of the mid-nineteenth-century St. Bonifacius Kirche Catholic church rises from the landscape. The Romanesque interior has 16 stained glass windows and a 535-pipe organ dating from 1895. Come summertime, the parish puts on a renowned turtle soup dinner, with hundreds of gallons being served in a few hours. Louie's Bar in Fulda is another roadside attraction, regionally famous for their turtle soup.

The Archabbey of St. Meinrad, 5 miles north, appears to have been levitated from the Fatherland. The Benedictine monastery was begun in 1854, and the work continues today. In 1872, the monks began construction of the sandstone complex of buildings you see today. The church with its 168-foot steeples was built from 1899–1907. Local craftsmen and monks carved most of the stone with the sandstone coming from a local quarry.

The monastery at St. Meinrad remains one of the great centers for Gregorian chant, singing that dates back to the Middle Ages. The monks' daily singing of the medieval Gregorian chants rise into the lofts of the vaults. The monks' daily religious services, from 5:30 A.M. to Vespers at 6:00 P.M., are open to the public.

One half mile east of St. Meinrad on IN 62, the tiny sandstone chapel

The Monastery Immaculate Conception in Ferdinand reflects the strong German character of Spencer and Dubois counties. Photo courtesy of Dubois Country CVB.

at Monte Cassino is a paean to devotion, the site of an annual pilgrimage commemorating relief from an 1871–1872 smallpox epidemic. Each January since that date, hundreds of monks, seminarians, townspeople, and other devotees have climbed to the unheated chapel at the top of the hill to offer prayers of thanks for their miracle. The interior of the church is painted in a naive early Renaissance style by a German artist, Gerhard Lamers, in 1931.

The companion monastery of the Benedictine nuns, Monastery Immaculate Conception, is located about 10 miles away in Ferdinand. It can be reached by way of the scenic route down Old Ferdinand Road, or by driving west on IN 62 to IN 162, then north 3.7 miles to Ferdinand. The massive red-brick Romanesque has stood on the hill in Ferdinand since 1915, added to structures that were built in 1883–87. Trimmed in Bedford limestone and Italian terracotta, the building has an interior dome that rises 87 feet above the floor. The monastery and its grounds were listed as a National Historic District in 1983.

Ferdinand is among the more traditional towns in the region. *Indiana: A Guide to the Hoosier State,* written by the Works Project Administration's Indiana Writers Project (1941), notes, "Ferdinand is a German Catholic community retaining the language and customs of the Fatherland. English, of course, is understood and spoken, as is a strange admixture of the two languages. Rathskeller signs bear names such as Kunkler, Schnellenberger, and Hoppenjans. Many of the citizens carve and wear wooden shoes, or fashion wooden beer mugs and holders for pretzels."

The Dutchmen (as in "Deutsch") around here are fabled for their thriftiness. You'll go a long way to separate a Dutchman from a dollar. They expect value for their money and they expect to deliver it for the same. Turtle soup and brain sandwiches (a pork or beef brain flattened and fried) are still big, as is beer in giant schooners. Guys in the taverns play euchre and pound worn leather dice cups on the tables and bar, playing local favorites like three Horses, Crazy Trés, and Ship, Captain, Crew.

Jasper, the region's largest town, is 13 miles north on IN 162. It was laid out in 1830 as the county seat at a good mill site on the banks of the Patoka River. By 1841 there were a hundred German families in the vicinity of Jasper. The dense stands of oak that surrounded the town formed the basis of the town economy as Jasper became the nation's wood office furniture capital by the next century. The Jasper Desk Company began in the mid-1860s and is still the nation's oldest operating furniture factory. Kimball International, Inc., of piano and furniture fame is headquartered here, as are a number of other well-respected furniture manufacturers.

The heart of the town is St. Joseph's Church on Newton Street between Eleventh and Thirteenth streets. It is a tall, brooding, brown sandstone structure topped by a tower 235 feet high, built between 1867 and 1880 by the parishioners. The walls are 4 to 6 feet thick, and the foundation is ten feet deep. Swiss stained glass, Austrian mosaics, carved oak pews, and Italian marble altars grace the interior. To the south of the church, the first Deliverance Cross was erected in 1848 by George Bauman, who survived a raging ocean storm by promising to erect the statue in exchange for divine intercession. The original was destroyed by a lightning bolt in 1928, and the current cross was erected in 1932.

The Gramelspacher-Gutzweiler House on Eleventh Street between Newton and Main is the oldest house in town and listed on the National Register. Built in 1849, the Federal-style, two-story brick building was designated the state's most imposing Federal structure by the sagacious architectural historian Wilbur Peat. The stepped gables are a throwback to Jacobean and Flemish buildings, seldom seen on Federal-style buildings of this age and location.

The town square is the site of several Strassenfest activities, Jasper's frenetic German festival. Dubois County Courthouse on the square was built in 1909–10 to replace an 1845 structure. The John Opel House, built in 1850, also known as the Green Tree Inn on St. James Street at the south edge of town on IN 162, is another fine Federal brick building on the National Register. Green Tree Antiques, located in buildings on the premises, is one

Jasper's Strassenfest is a Teutonic Hoedown.
Photo courtesy of Dubois County CVB.

of the best shops in the region. Nearby on IN 162, on the Vincennes University regional campus, the Indiana Baseball Hall of Fame honors Hoosier baseball greats. The dedication in 1979 was attended by Yankee great, Mickey Mantle.

Another Jasper lodestone is the glockenspiel-topped Schnitzelbank Restaurant at 393 Third Avenue (IN 162). Since 1903 the Schnitzelbank has served southern German specialties like beef rolladen, sauerbraten, kassler rippchen, and turnip slaw and beer in goldfish bowl–sized glasses. It is the best in Indiana German cooking.

Huntingburg is 7 miles south on IN 231, another small German manufacturing town, specializing in furniture and decorative arts. The many brick homes date from the days when the town brickyards bustled with orders. The brick William Geiger Home, 511 Geiger Street, was built in 1854–55. The town's pride is the restored Italianate Huntingburg Town Hall, built in 1866, and Fire Engine House at 311 Geiger Street, scene of everything from civic business to wedding receptions. It was listed on the National Register in 1975.

The Victorian Fourth Street is the home of a number of well-stocked antique shops. The vintage architecture of the street has been an attraction in several movies including *A League of Their Own,* starring Madonna and Tom Hanks, that celebrated the women's baseball leagues of the 1940s. The filming of the baseball movie prompted an extensive restoration of Huntingburg's League Stadium, now the home field for the Dubois Dragons. The semi-pro games are held from late May to mid-August.

5

Hoosier Forest Loop
Along the scenic Ohio and into the rugged uplands

General description: The 138-mile loop courses through Perry and Crawford Counties' charming Ohio River towns and hamlets and then up through the Hoosier National Forest and the Crawford Upland, a region of forests, caves, and scenic rivers. A portion of the drive is along the Ohio River Scenic Route.

Special attractions: The historic Swiss-German town of Tell City; Cannelton, an early Industrial Revolution town with its famous cotton mill; historic southern Perry County; the Hoosier National Forest; Leavenworth's Overlook Restaurant; nationally renowned Wyandotte and Marengo Caves; scenic Blue River.

Location: Southern Indiana.

Drive route numbers and names: Indiana Highways 66, 166, 62, 37, and 64, and Interstate 64.

Travel season: The route is on curvy and hilly two-lane state highways through the most dramatic topography in the state. Winter snowstorms can make the trip a memorable one. The Hoosier National Forest offers great flowering tree displays in the spring and a phantasmagoria of fall color.

Camping: There is camping at Wyandotte Woods State Recreation Area, Leavenworth; Patoka Lake has several campgrounds around Indiana's second largest lake, including the Newton-Stewart State Recreational Area; Rocky Point Marina and Campground; German Ridge Recreation Area-Horsecamp and Indian-Celina Lakes Recreation Area in the Hoosier National Forest.

Services: Gas, food, and lodging are available in Tell City, Cannelton, Derby, and Leavenworth. There is gas and food at Rocky Point and Marengo and numerous places along the route.

Nearby attractions: Holiday World and Splashin' Safari; Spencer and Dubois Counties—German flavored towns and villages.

The drive

The drive starts in Tell City, founded in 1858 as a Swiss-German manufacturing community and named after the thirteenth-century Swiss hero, William Tell. In 1857 the cooperative land society purchased 4,154 acres of land between Corydon and Troy, which was the site of the first coal extraction west of the Appalachians.

In 1809, an associate of steamboat inventor Robert Fulton, Nicholas Roosevelt (great-uncle of President Theodore Roosevelt), spotted the coal seam while descending the Ohio by flatboat to scout out fuel for Fulton's maiden steamboat voyage down the river two years later. Roosevelt contracted with the locals to dig out the coal. The locals piled it on the riverbank where the coal remained until Robert Fulton's steamboat *New Orleans* chuffed down the stream on the way to New Orleans.

Tell City's 80-foot-wide, two-mile-long Main Street trumpets the ambitions of the Swiss settlers. The grand boulevard, wide enough to turn a horse team and wagon, was to be the main thoroughfare for a city of 90,000. The Swiss laid the city out into 400 town blocks with 7,600 residential and garden lots. Within five years of settlement, the town bustled with a flour and grain mill, a plow and wagon factory, and a brewery.

The Chamber of Commerce and the Visitor and Convention Bureau is located in the Southern Railroad Depot, built in 1915, at Main and Blum Streets. The Tell City Industrial Historic District encompasses most of the south end of the city's business district from Blum to Humbolt, and is a collection of industrial buildings from 1860 to the 1960s. The William Tell Woodcrafter building on Seventh Street has flood level marks painted on the northwest corner of the building, showing the levels of the 1883, 1884, 1907, 1913, and 1937 floods.

The brick-and-limestone City Hall, built in 1896, at Main and Mozart Streets was a tad large for a city hall, but Tell City anticipated wresting the county seat from next door Cannelton—which they did, but not until 100 years later. Parts of the building were used through the decades as a school, library, church, and town theater.

The Tell City Pretzel Company, at 632 Main Street has been hand-twisting traditional German pretzels since 1858. The Tell City pretzels are a teeth-challenging bit of yesteryear that are shipped all over the country. Most of the twisting is done in the morning, and you are welcome to stop by and see culinary history.

There are several fine examples of commercial architecture on Main Street including the neoclassical 1890 William Tell Hotel at Washington Street and the 1885 Italianate Tell City National Bank at Pestalozzi. The

Victorian flourishes of Main Street reflect the burst of affluence that followed the arrival of the railroad. The 1950s glass and stainless steel facades reflect the florescence of the Auto Era, as does the 1955 Frostop Drive-In at 947 Main.

Sitting obliquely on a rise above the uniformly level surroundings, the Old Stone House at 1239 Thirteenth Street predates the right-angle planning of the Swiss. It is the earliest house in town, a double-pen constructed of rough-cut sandstone. It served as an early meeting house and school.

Cannelton is a mile east of Tell City on Indiana Highway 66, founded

Drive 5: Hoosier Forest Loop
Along the scenic Ohio and into the rugged uplands

in 1837 to exploit the easily mined coal for steamboats and manufacturers. Cannelton prospered through the nineteenth century with coal mining, brick yards, and pottery and ceramic tile manufacturers. The most important industry, however, was the Cannelton Cotton Mill, founded in 1849. The austere sandstone building with 100-foot Italianate spires looms over the town yet today. The cotton mill was the largest industrial building in pre–Civil War Indiana. The mill is listed on the Registry of Historic American Engineering Records and the National Register of Historic Places. In 1990, it was listed as a National Historic Landmark as well.

The town still bears the mark of the early New Englanders. The Cannelton Historic District is bounded by Richardson, Fourth, Washington, and Adams Streets and includes examples of architecture from 1837 to 1936. The spare mill building and the fine ashlar stone houses on IN 66 (Seventh Street) speak of the esthetics and architectural traditions of New Hampshire. In use since 1869, the Free School is Indiana's oldest operating school building at the corner of Sixth and Taylor Streets. The congregation of the 1845 St. Lukes Church at 101 East Third Street were early recyclers. The windows are from a church in England, circa 1800, and the congregation salvaged the bell from the *Major Balfour* which sank off of Troy in 1848. The church is listed on the National Register of Historic Places.

The Perry County Courthouse was built in 1896 of yellow brick and Bedford limestone. Cannelton wrested the county seat from Rome in 1859, but lost it to archrival Tell City in 1994. The stately sandstone St. Michael's Church at Eighth and Washington Streets was started in 1858 for the German Catholics in the town and completed 12 years later. The 1937 Flood inundated the town, filling some of the buildings with water up to the second floor. At one point, a local man rowed through town, towing a pair of swimming 400-pound hogs behind him.

The Bob Cummings Bridge at the east edge of town is named after a Cannelton newspaperman. It leads to Hawesville, Kentucky's Riverview Restaurant on Old Highway 60 East that serves regional fare including quail, froglegs, and bumbleberry pie on an overlook over the Cannelton Locks and Dam.

Proceed east 1.1 miles on IN 66 from Cannelton to the Cannelton Locks and Dam. Replacing three smaller dams upstream, they were built between 1963 and 1974 for $99.6 million, taking as much concrete to build as 70 miles of Interstate highway. The high-lift dam created a vast, 114-mile-long, 87,000-acre lake that extends to Louisville, the longest on the Ohio.

The riverbanks begin to flatten in this section of the drive, and the bottoms are furrowed into rich corn and tobacco fields. Proceed east on IN 66 about 0.8 mile to the Lafayette Spring marker where the steamboat *Mechanic*, carrying Revolutionary War hero Marquis de Lafayette, snagged a floating tree and shipwrecked on a dark night in May 1825.

Marengo Cave is a natural wonder.
Photo courtesy of the Indiana Department of Commerce Tourism Division.

Indiana Highway 166, 1.6 miles farther east of the marker, runs down the Tobinsport Peninsula, the earliest settlement in the county, dating from 1802. In 1960, a Chicago-Miami flight carrying 63 people fell apart in mid-air and crashed into a hillside soybean field. The plane hit the ground at 600 mph, burying the nose 50 feet deep. Parts were strewn from German Ridge to Gatchel 10 miles north. Proceed 1.6 miles down IN 166 to Millstone Road, then turn east a mile to the Air Crash Memorial.

Rome, 3.6 miles east on IN 66 from the IN 166 turnoff, was Perry County's first seat of government, founded in 1818. The stately public square that surrounds the classical brick courthouse reflects the town's early importance. The Rome Courthouse was built between 1818 and 1822, a Federal-style building based on the new state capitol at Corydon. It is listed on the National Register of Historic Places and is considered the state's oldest existing courthouse.

The Connor and Shoemaker cemeteries dating from early in the nineteenth century have exceptional folk art–carved gravestones. The Conner cemetery is located at the end of the river road to the north of the village. The Shoemaker cemetery is 0.4 mile south of Rome.

Outside of town, German Ridge Road runs north 3.2 miles to the German Ridge Recreation Area in the Hoosier National Forest, a rugged landscape palisaded with spectacular cliffs. This was the first campground built by the Depression-era Civilian Conservation Corps (CCC) in the Hoosier National Forest. This county road to German Ridge follows the earliest Indian and pioneer trails in the region, running from Vincennes to the Sinking Creek in Kentucky across from Rome.

The farm of Nancy Alice Martin is 1.5 miles east. Martin returned home in 1929 after a celebrated career as Alice DiGarmo, circus trapeze artist. In 1934, hired-hand Ernest Wright argued with her over back wages of $2.75. Evidently, the employee conference was not to Wright's liking as he slit Martin's throat with a folding pocket knife and buried her in the barnyard, where her body was discovered a week later. Martin is buried in the Lower Cummings Cemetery 2 miles to the north.

Derby, 2 miles east, was laid out in 1835. Named after Derby, Ireland, it prospered as a river port, shipping lumber-related products such as barrels, chairs, and railroad ties. In the town's heyday, there were 103 people, 3 stores, 2 banks, and 2 saloons. A disastrous fire in 1893 ended its golden age. After that the town was a declining spot on the river until an influx of people building second homes began to have an impact in the 1970s and 1980s. Today, there are several pristine riverside cabins for rent and recreational facilities in the area.

The Hoosier National Forest surrounds the area, with 80 miles of hiking trails, five lakes, hundreds of camping spots, and eight mountain biking trails. The entire county is a bicyclist's haven with hundreds of miles of

An old-time excursion boat churning up the Ohio near Magnet.
Photo courtesy of Perry County CVB.

quiet country lanes and trails to tour. A fine bike touring map is available through the tourism information office in Tell City. The Mano Point Boat Ramp is in constant use, launching craft to cruise the river's 18,000-acre Cannelton Pool. Oil Creek is a bayoulike canoeing stream, a pristine home to thousands of waterfowl. The Mulzer County Park in Derby offer a shady riverside picnic area.

Magnet is a bucolic little spot on the river 5 miles east of Derby off IN 66. The Some Other Place tavern serves bar fare overlooking the Kentucky farmland across the river. The Magnet Overlook north of town is a nice picnic location, affording a long sweep down the river. It is a particularly good vantage point to watch the river traffic, including the giant excursion boats like the *Delta Queen* and *American Queen* when they make their regal way down the waterway.

A few miles upriver, the USDA Forest Service maintains Buzzard's Roost as a scenic overlook. In 1857, a slaughterhouse and commercial smokehouse were built nearby. Since only half of a carcass could be used for smoking, the balance became the provender for the flocks of buzzards who were attracted to the site. Today, it is a good place to spot bald eagles.

The site of Galey's Landing, an important shipping point for many years is 1.5 miles from Magnet. The Prather family, renowned horse thieves, lived nearby. The Prathers ran a ring in the 1850s that stole fine horses from

Kentucky, corraled them in several spots in the vicinity, and then moved them down the Rome-Vincennes Trace to Missouri for sale.

In August 1865 the steamship *Argosy III,* carrying home a roster of mustered-out Civil War veterans, ran aground in a storm, killing ten Union soldiers. Their ten white grave markers can be seen, along with a historical marker, 0.5 mile south of Magnet along the river.

Back on IN 66, 8 miles north through rich river bottoms, Oriole was originally named Chestnut City for the stand of trees that flourished there. It developed late in the nineteenth century as an archetypal rural town, with its grain elevator, post office, school, church, and town doctor. Today, the gable-fronted white clapboard Oriole Methodist Episcopal Church, built in 1870, still stands proudly. Nearby, the 1913 Oriole Grade School is still there, but in substantially rougher shape. Look for "Antique" signs for a quirky trove of diverse flea market finds.

The Crawford-Perry county line is 3.4 miles north of Oriole. The two counties have been among the poorest along the Ohio river shore from Pittsburgh down to Cairo. The lack of settlement across the river in Kentucky prevented the northward drift of southern uplanders that populated other stretches of the Indiana shore. However, the two counties are among the richest in the state in natural beauty, both above and below ground. Half of Crawford County's acreage is forested, with more than 30,000 acres in state and national forests; there are more than 60,000 acres of Hoosier National Forest land in neighboring Perry. Tourism is rapidly becoming an important part of the economy.

The ghost spa of Sulphur Springs is just north of the county line, one of the bustling mineral water spas that flourished in Crawford County at the turn of the century. The White Sulphur Spring Hotel, a three-story structure that served up to 250 health seekers at a time, prospered for years before burning in 1910. As late as the 1940s, Sulpher Springs was still a popular resort, with cabins and rooms in private homes. A stand pipe in a pavilion is all that remains.

Sulphur, 1.4 miles north, has a general store selling gas and refreshments and a never-open antique store that teases with intriguing window displays. Drive north to IN 62 and turn east.

The county road 3.6 miles east of the intersection turns south to Fredonia, Leavenworth's longtime rival for ascendancy in the county.

Tower's Orchard, Peach and Apple Shed at IN 66 North is a great place to stock up on munching material and take in the view.

Leavenworth basks high on an Ohio River bluff, a tidy town of frame houses, most dating from the construction in the 1930s and 1940s. Three antique and craft shops and Stephenson's General Store on the town square invite browsing. The Town Hall Gallery, open on the weekends through the warm months, offers the arts and crafts of dozens of the area's artists. The Overlook Restaurant at the west edge of town has become a landmark for many decades, offering Hoosier-style cooking with the best view on the Indiana shore.

Old Leavenworth is located down on the river at the eastern edge of Leavenworth. Look for the road sign for Old IN 62 or Bluff Road and follow the winding road down the bluff. Founded in 1818, the town was once one of the principal shipping ports along the Ohio, with nearly 2,000 residents.

Old Leavenworth continues to be occupied: a mixture of old, cobbled-together houses, some summer cottages along the river, and a grand old abandoned brick building that was once the water and electric company. In all, it's a place with the air of a slightly raffish yesteryear.

Wyandotte Caves State Recreation Area is 7 miles east, a 1,200-acre facility that includes the world-renowned Wyandotte Cave, home of some of America's largest subterranean rooms and columns. The park rangers offer six tours, from a short introductory tour to an all-day tour with the path leading through Worm Alley and Crawfish Springs. The Monument Mountain tour takes visitors past rare twisted and spiraled cave formations, to the world's largest underground mountain.

The Wyandotte Cave Recreational Area is part of the Indiana State Harrison-Crawford-Wyandotte Complex. Across the road from the caves, the Wyandotte Woods Recreational Area is a 2,100-acre facility with 100 miles of horse trails and ten hiking trails. Campgrounds and cabins are available for rent, including the old CCC Camp for large group camping. The recreational area extends 1 mile along the Ohio shoreline and 2 miles along the Blue River.

Named for its clear blue, spring-fed water, the Blue River is a meandering canoeing river that courses through the hill country, past caves and bluffs and wooded glades, foremost among Indiana's Natural and Scenic River System. "The Blue is the most natural stream of its size in Indiana," the renowned ecologist Alton Lindsey wrote in the 1960s, and it remains so today. To add a mild touch of danger, the stream remains the only habitat of the hellbender, a giant poisonous salamander that can reach 15 to 20 inches in length. The hellbender is a flabby, wrinkled specimen with a wide head that is among the largest salamanders in the world.

Return to IN 66 North at the west edge of Leavenworth and drive 12 miles north to Marengo, home of another famous Indiana cave. Discovered in 1883, Marengo Cave, with enormous cavern rooms like the Queen's Palace and the Crystal Palace, is one of the nation's most beautiful. There are several tours through the cave, and the cave operators recently added a digitized historical presentation in one of the caverns. The cave facility also offers canoeing, horseback trail riding, hiking, fishing, and a picnic area.

The Outdoor Center features courses on cave exploration, a cave simulator, gemstone mining, and a climbing tower.

Milltown on the Blue River is 4 miles east of Marengo on IN 64. Cave Country Canoes rents hundreds of canoes and kayaks for trips down the limestone-bluffed valley. The Blue River Cafe is a gastronomic find, offering gourmet fare in an unlikely setting.

Proceeding west 17.7 miles from Marengo on IN 64 will take you to IN 145 and the highland region of 8,800-acre Patoka Lake, Indiana's second largest lake. The $65-million multipurpose facility was dedicated in 1980. Besides the lake itself, there are four state recreational areas around the lake covering an additional 8,880 acres and 7,900 acres devoted to wildlife. The Newton-Stewart State Recreation Area on IN 164 north of Eckerty offers nature interpretation in its solar-heated center, along with camping, swimming, boat launching, and diverse amusements.

At Taswell, you can proceed west under the railroad trestle and proceed to the Yellow Birch Nature Preserve, the only place in Indiana where yellow birch, hemlock, and mountain laurel occur together. Continue south 4 miles to Hemlock Cliffs, an exceptional natural site of deeply cut sandstone cliffs, waterfalls, and caves of archaeological interest. The nature preserve is particularly magical in the spring when the enchanter's nightshade and jack-in-the-pulpits are in bloom. Continue south 5 miles to IN 37 at Grantsburg; then turn south on IN 37.

Drive 10.5 miles south to Interstate 64 and take the interstate 6 miles west to the continuation of IN 37 South. Tell City is 27 miles south. There are three Hoosier Forest lakes, Lakes Celina and Tipsaw, and Saddle Lake off of IN 37, all offering a pleasant break from the road. The turnoff for the French-Belgium hamlet of Leopold, named after King Leopold of Belgium, is 8 miles south of the intersection with US 64.

The Gothic Revival St. Augustinius Church was built between 1866 and 1873. A statue of the Virgin Mary holding the Jesus child was carved in Luxemburg and still stands in the church.

Proceed south on IN 37 to the loop conclusion at Tell City.

6

The Road to Utopia

Urban Evansville to romantic New Harmony

General description: The 38-mile drive courses through the lowlands of southwestern Indiana, from the bustling city of Evansville through the Victorian river port of Mt. Vernon to the renowned wetlands of Hovey Lake. The tour concludes in the early nineteenth-century Utopian town of New Harmony.

Special attractions: Angel Mounds State Historic Site, Mesker Park Zoo, Casino Aztar riverboat, Evansville Museum of Arts and Science, Reitz Home, Hovey Lake cypress bogs, and the nationally celebrated historic town of New Harmony.

Location: Extreme southwestern Indiana.

Drive route numbers and names: Indiana Highways 62 and 69.

Travel season: Except for inclement winter weather, the roads are negotiable in all seasons. The attractions at New Harmony are open year-round.

Camping: Harmonie State Park south of New Harmony.

Services: There are full services in Evansville, Mt. Vernon, and New Harmony, and food and gas at numerous places along the route.

 ## The drive

The drive begins at the east edge of Evansville on Indiana Highway 164 a mile south of IN 66 at Angel Mounds State Historic Site—*really* one of Indiana's beginnings: a 103-acre Middle Missisippian village that prospered in the fourteenth and fifteenth centuries on a palisaded bluff above the Ohio. One thousand Native Americans erected 11 significant earthen mounds, the largest rising 44 feet high and covering 4 acres. Angel Mounds was declared a National Historic Landmark in 1966, the nation's highest designation. An interpretation center offers exhibits, an informational slide show, and a simulated archeological excavation. A replica village gives the visitor a sense of urban life in America while Europe was still in the Medieval Ages.

Thanks to excellent rail connections, progressive business, and civic leaders, Evansville is the pre-eminent city in the tri-state region. Indeed, Evansville is the largest city on Indiana's entire Ohio River shore (126,000 people in 1990) and the third largest city in Indiana. The city has several outstanding parks, as well as the vintage Ellis Park horse racing track. The calendar is crowded with festivals, from the thrilling Thunder on the Ohio hydroplane racing festival to the Teutonic charm of the Volksfest at the 150-year-old Germania Maennerchor, from Native American Days at Angel Mounds to the West Side Nut Club Days, second only to Mardi Gras in attendance. There are six historic districts and 86 individual structures on the National Register of Historic Places. It's a prosperous place with industrial parks, large manufacturing facilities, regional shopping centers, and affluent suburban neighborhoods.

Evansville has never turned her back on the Ohio, celebrating her river heritage with a riverfront promenade along the levee built after the 1937 flood. The Evansville Convention Center and Visitors Bureau is located in a whimsical 1913-tile-roofed Japanese-styled pagoda overlooking the Ohio and the Casino Aztar gambling boat. The Casino Aztar was Indiana's first gambling boat and offers 1,300 slot machines and 48 blackjack tables along with a plethora of gaming options. Nearby, the Evansville Museum of Arts and Science at 411 S.E. Riverside Drive is a cultural mainstay of southwestern Indiana, showcasing more than 25 exhibits annually, along with a fine permanent collection that covers everything from a cabinet that Abe Lincoln built to sixteenth-century paintings to a collection of locomotives and train cars.

Drive 6: The Road to Utopia
Urban Evansville to romantic New Harmony

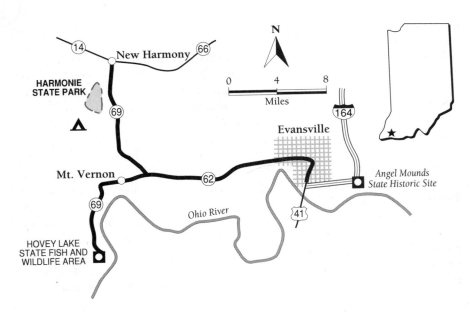

Across Riverside Drive, nineteenth-century timber barons' mansions rise like giant wedding cakes in the Riverside Historic District, with the 1871 Reitz Home Museum at 224 S.E. First Street as the centerpiece of the neighborhood. The Reitz home is open for tours.

Evansville's downtown has an outstanding collection of historical architecture from the neo-Baroque treasure of the Old Courthouse at Fourth and Vine to the 1930s Art Deco sleekness of the Greyhound Bus Terminal at Third and Sycamore Streets, with the only running neon dog left in the country. The 1913 Alhambra Theatre at 50 Adams Avenue is a Moorish Revival fantasy, while the Old Vanderburgh County Jail and Sheriff's residence are a crenelated Gothic Revival interpretation of Lichtenstein Castle. The Old Post Office Place at 100 N.W. Second Street housed the Federal offices and the customs office as well as the post office when it was built in 1875–79. After an extensive restoration, it now houses the Evansville Chamber of Commerce, offices, and a restaurant.

Wesselman Woods Nature Preserve is a unique urban forest at 551 Boeke Road. It encompasses a National Landmark forest and a recreation area offering tennis, ballparks, picnic grounds, and a playground. The Mesker Park Zoo, on Bement Road, was Indiana's first when it started in the late 1920s with a few small animals, a couple of ragtag lions retired from the circus, and Kay, the elephant purchased in 1929 after a citywide fund drive. Today, more than 700 animals cavort and congregate on the zoo's 70 acres, making it one of the state's largest. It is in the early stages of a major long-term renovation that will place it in the forefront of American zoos.

Evansville and Vanderburgh counties have embarked on a remarkable outdoor project that encompasses recreation and healthy living. The Pigeon Creek Greenway Project will eventually include more than 40 miles of walking, biking, and nature trails that will link parks and neighborhoods through the city in a linear park. Eventually, the greenway will encircle Evansville and connect to the American Discovery Trail, an interstate system of trails that crosses America. The first phase of the greenway begins near the Heidelbach Avenue canoe launch.

Down in the bottoms on the Old Henderson Road on the west edge of Evansville, catfish fiddlers are the specialty of the old wooden Dogtown Tavern. The place was built in 1889 as the Cypress post office, situated on the Red Banks Trail, an early buffalo trace.

Drive west on IN 62 out of Evansville across the Posey county line. "Everything is near the river in Posey County," state tourism official and Posey County native Marianna Weinzapfel said, "We've got two to pick from." The Ohio curls along the southern border and the Wabash (that's pronounced "Wall'-bash" by the locals, with the accent most distinctly on the first syllable) wiggles down the western side. The road is through a flat lowland with

Evansville's sprawl alternating with prosperous farms tilling the rich soil, dotted with perpetually pumping oil wells.

There are several prehistoric archeological sites scattered along the route, none open to the public. There are four archeological sites in Posey County listed on the National Register of Historic Places, including the Mann site just east of Mt. Vernon, which was the largest Hopewell town in Indiana, probably a satellite town of Angel Mounds to the east.

Mt. Vernon, 20 miles west of Evansville, is a throwback to the Hoosier small town of yesteryear with a courthouse square surrounded by rococo Victoriana and its turn-of-the-century neighborhoods. Founded in 1805, the town grew rapidly after it was named the county seat in 1825. The Courthouse Square and its 1876 courthouse is a historic district on the National Register of Historic Places, as is the Welborn Historic District bounded by Ninth, Locust, and Second Streets, and the alley between Walnut and Main Streets. The 1895 William Gonnerman house at 521 W. Second is on the National Register of Historic Places, a fine example of the period.

At the foot of Main Street, Shelburne Park provides public access to the Ohio River. The town is also the home of the Southwind Maritime Center, Indiana's second largest port, dedicated in 1979 to handle cargo traveling the inland waterway system from the Great Lakes to the Gulf of Mexico. The center includes a mile of riverfront designed to handle mooring, fleet assembly, and drydock repair.

At the west edge of town is IN 69. Proceed 5.7 miles south to Hovey Lake State Fish and Wildlife Area. The Nature Conservancy calls the pristine environment one of the "Last Great Places." The enormous wetland in the pocket of southern Posey County where the Ohio joins the meandering Wabash is a slurry of sloughs and swamps reminiscent of the Deep South. Bald cypress trees poke their bony knees from the swamp water as blue herons stalk among the water lilies. Turtles bask on their favorite log as warblers and gnatcatchers flit through the wild grapes. Deer peer from behind the moss hanging on the cottonwoods and wild pecans. The refuge is a nesting place for bald eagles, along with double-breasted cormorants and great blue herons.

The nearby Twin Swamps Nature Preserve and Gray's Woods complex is an unsullied 890-acre wetland with some of the Midwest's most intriguing flora and fauna, including America's northernmost stand of bald cypress. Some of the old stand remains—massive trees, hundreds of years old, stately among the buttonbush and swamp rose. Moonseed, chanterelles, rare featherfoil, and spider lily are scattered though the swamp, with wild blue orchids flaring here and there. More than 50,000 visitors come yearly to witness the spectacular arrival of the migratory birds and recreate amidst the quiet beauty.

Thrall's Opera House in New Harmony remains a civic center.
Photo courtesy of John Eicher.

Hovey Lake is also a magnet for hunters—6,000 hunters, the majority waterfowl hunters, used the park in 1996.

Three miles farther down IN 69, the Uniontown Locks and Dam is at the lowest point in Indiana. The first boat passed through the locks in 1970. This is considered a high-lift dam, raising vessels an average of 18 feet. Four to five million tons of cargo move through the locks monthly.

Return to IN 62 and drive east to IN 69 North. The famous Utopian community of New Harmony is 10.9 miles north. Early in the nineteenth century when most of Indiana was still a vast untamed forest, New Harmony was the site of two remarkable Utopian experiments. New Harmony was unique in that it harbored both sacred and secular communal societies. The first, the Harmonists, were waiting for the Second Coming of Christ. The second, the Owenites, rejected religion completely. The Harmonists' legacy is New Harmony's magnificent historic buildings and town layout dating from 1814. In turn, the Owenites' left a remarkable scientific and intellectual legacy a decade later.

Jane Blaffer Owen, married to a descendant of Owenites' founder, Robert Owen, arrived in New Harmony in 1949. She immediately recognized the extraordinary possibilities of the sleepy little town. Inspired by the town's intellectual and spiritual history, she set up the Robert Lee Blaffer Trust in 1959 and embarked on the next Utopian journey, the longest to date.

She envisioned New Harmony as a place of spiritual awakening, where the mystical and spiritual could commune with a well-nurtured built environment. The town became the destination for assorted clergy, writers, and artists, co-evolving in an atmosphere of seminars, think tanks, liturgical ceremony, and secular expression.

The road to New Harmony, IN 69 North, courses past hay fields and green hillsides of corn, with old Greek Revival structures along the way. New Harmony founder Robert Owen proposed a 30-acre Agricultural and Manufacturing Village of Mutual Co-operation that transfixed the young American republic is just north of Solitude, about 5 miles from Mt. Vernon. Except for a few loads of brick, construction on the project was never started.

Harmonie State Park is another 5 miles down the road. The park stretches along a series of rapids in the Wabash, which gave the original Harmonie the reason for its location.

New Harmony is 2.5 miles north of the park. Architect Richard Meier's Atheneum visitor center at Arthur and North Streets is the starting point for most tours. Visitors can orient themselves with an informational film and pick up maps and literature. The multilevel building offers New Harmony visitors exhibits, and great vistas of the Wabash and the town.

Across North Street from the visitor center, Cathedral Labyrinth and Sacred Garden is based on the sacred geometries of Charles Cathedral in France. The brick wall next to the labyrinth encloses the Harmonist Cemetery, where 230 Harmonists are buried in unmarked graves alongside a ninth-century Hopewell burial mound. The wall was built by Harmonists who returned in 1874 to raze the original Harmonist church that had deteriorated and used the bricks to build the wall. Proceed down North Street past austere frame houses that the Harmonists left unpainted, since the Second Coming was eminent. The David Lenz house at West and North Streets is typical of the Harmonist period. A cluster of log cabins across the street speak of the structures lived in by Harmonists' neighbors in the hinterland. They are not original to the site but were moved in from the county. The Barrett-Gate house at Main and North Streets is one of only two existing log-and-frame Harmonist structures.

Across from the Barrett-Gate house, the Roofless Church is modernist architect Phillip Johnson's interdenominational paean to spirituality, designed with the thought that only the sky is a big enough roof to shelter all faiths. The church includes sculptures and gates by Jacques Lipchitz and the recently installed *Pieta* by Stephen de Staebler. Next door to the church on North Street, the small white building is the Richard Meier–designed Pottery Studio, completed in 1978. New Harmony's premier restaurant, the Red Geranium, and the New Harmony Inn are farther to the east on North Street.

One block south at Granary and Brewery Streets, the 1823 Salmon Wolf house contains an entrancing diorama of New Harmony as it appeared in 1824. The house was moved from another site in 1975, and the original bricks were rotated so the unweathered side was exposed. Nearby, the fieldstone Harmonist Granary is in a state of intense reconstruction. Because the upper windows were mistakenly thought of as gunports, old accounts of New Harmony call it the "Rappite Fort." David Dale Owen used it as his geology laboratory and museum. It was the headquarters for the U.S. Geological Survey during his tenure as chief geologist.

On Main between Church and Granary Streets, the mammoth brick Dormitory No. Two was built in 1822 by the Harmonists to communally house both men and women. During the Owenite period, the building housed a Pestalozzian school and a tavern. It later served as a newspaper office for the *New Harmony Register*.

The greensward on Church Street is the site of the two Harmonist churches. The brick church that later formed the cemetery wall was built in 1822 and was a marvel to travelers of the day. The Workingman's Institute at Tavern and West Streets is a remarkable holdover from the era of endowed public libraries, before Andrew Carnegie dispersed his library buildings throughout the land in the twentieth century. It is Indiana's oldest public library. Today, it is a repository of manuscripts and artifacts relating to the communalist days, as well as a quirky town museum.

The gingerbreaded brick house across the street is the Schnee-Ribeyre-Elliott house, built in 1867 by a saddle maker who made his fortune in the Civil War. The corner of Tavern and Brewery Streets has a clutch of historic houses, including the brick Georgian 1830 Owen house. The other three corners include a National Register Harmonist shoemaker's house, now used for historic exhibits, and the Keppler house, now used for geology exhibits.

New Harmony's Main Street reflects Indiana's boom time in the Victorian era. There are several interesting shops, galleries, and cafes along the tidy street. The New Harmony Maximillian-Bodmer Collection in the Lichtenberger Building on Main Street showcases artist Karl Bodmer's depiction of zoologist Prince Maximillian's exploration of the still-wild Upper Missouri in 1832 to 1834 when the traditional life of Native Americans was still intact. On Church Street, Thrall's Opera House was important to New

Harmony through the decades. Originally built by the Harmonists as Dormitory No. Four, it served as a singles dorm and boarding house during the Owen period. In 1828, the building began its life as a theater. In 1888 the facade was given an up-to-date look and operated as a theater and cinema until 1914, when it became a garage. The state of Indiana bought the opera house in 1964 and restored the structure to its 1888 splendor. It reopened as a theater in 1968 and operates today under the management of the University of Southern Indiana.

7

Southern Indiana Amish

Amish settlements and into Washington and Orange Counties

General description: The 68-mile route traverses several areas of Amish settlement from Montgomery in Daviess County through the Amish farms of Orange County and Washington County.

Special attractions: Gasthof Amish Restaurant, Raber Wheel Works, Southern Indiana Horse Collar Shop for traditional Amish horse collar construction, Wagler Amish Woodworking, Wagler Quilts and Crafts, Stoll's Lakeview Restaurant, Lost River, Gus Grissom Memorial, Spring Mill State Park, Washington County Amish furniture makers.

Location: Southern Indiana.

Drive route numbers and names: U.S. Highway 50/150; Indiana Highways 60, 37, and 56.

Travel season: Except for inclement winter weather, the roads are negotiable in all seasons. Spring, with the birth of young farm animals, is a nice time to visit.

Camping: There is camping at Spring Mill State Park in Mitchell, and Delany Park in Salem.

Services: Gas and food at Montgomery, Loogootee, Shoals, Mitchell, Orleans, Paoli, and Salem, and many other places along the route. Lodging at Loogootee, Mitchell, Paoli, and Salem.

Nearby attractions: French Lick Springs Resort and West Baden Springs Hotel; Blue Springs Cavern and Antique Auto and Race Car Museum in Bedford.

 The drive

Montgomery was founded in 1818 with St. Peter's Catholic Church as the locus. The town is still clustered around the stone building. In 1841, church pastor Father Edward Sorin planned to build a great Catholic university in the tiny town. Instead, the bishop at Vincennes deeded him the land near South Bend that became Notre Dame University. The eastern half of Daviess County is known for rich farmland along with extensive coal reserves. A compromise was reached between the two when legislation required the coal companies to be responsible for land reclamation for three years following the surface mining. Examples of virgin farmland, mining, and prosperous reclaimed land can be seen throughout the area.

The Amish have long had a strong presence in the area, arriving in the mid-nineteenth century from Pennsylvania. Their settlement area was 64 square miles in the 1930s and has expanded to almost 170 square miles—13 by 13 miles—as the families have grown. Today there are 525 Old Order families—approximately 3,500 Amish people in eastern Daviess County.

The Amish are the spiritual descendants of the followers of Jacob Ammann, a seventeenth-century German minister who preached a belief in a focused Christianity dedicated to a simple piety and strong community. The beliefs included a wariness of technology and cultural change. Today Old Order Amish still forswear automobiles and electricity, depending on their horses for transportation and windmills for power.

Most of the Amish settlement is north of Indiana Highway 50, stretching to IN 58 around Odon. The western edge is IN 57 near Washington, and the eastern border is IN 231. Plain people in their black buggies can be seen throughout the rolling countryside. Their many austere farms are distinctive with windmills and pristine, unadorned houses. Stolid farm horses graze in the pastures or pull vintage plows through the fields. Don't look for Amish churches as they don't believe in them, choosing to worship in their homes in a round-robin fashion. There are a number of white clapboard schools, however, serving the children up to eighth grade. German is still the first language in most of the homes, though the language has evolved in isolation to the point where Daviess County Amish can't understand the German of their northern Indiana brethren and have to resort to English to converse.

Because of their skilled craftsmanship and strong work ethic, dozens of Amish owned businesses thrive in the region. They include the Southern Indiana Horse Collar Shop on County Road 525 East, northwest of Montgomery, and Raber Wheel Works on CR 300 North that makes wooden buggy wheels. There are several Amish construction companies around Montgomery and Cannelburg, 2.5 miles east, specializing in farm and metal buildings. Crews of Daviess County Amish men radiate out all over southern Indiana daily on projects. Amish women run candy kitchens and quilt shops around the settlement. Each spring and fall, buyers from all over the country arrive at Henry Knepp's farm for his draft horse auctions. Knepp's is north of Cannelburg on CR 500 North, half mile north of 900 East.

The Gasthof in Montgomery is a good spot to pick up information and maps of the area. Beyond serving groaning tables of Amish-style fare, the country complex also has a hotel and gift shops. Dillon Amish Country Tours (see appendix for more information) also arranges excellent, respect-

Drive 7: Southern Indiana Amish

Amish settlements and into Washington and Orange Counties

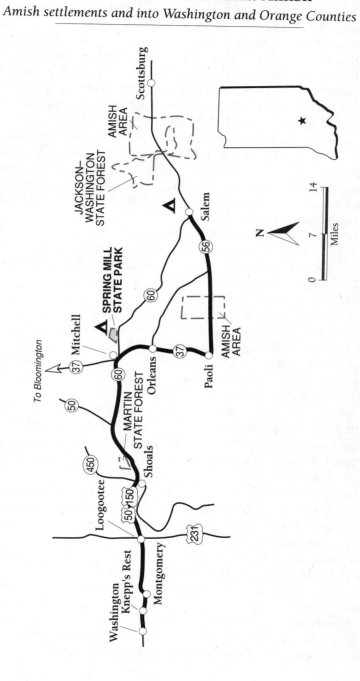

ful tours for groups of 15 or more. Their tours can include farm dinners in Amish homes, with the family singing traditional capella hymns.

Knepp's Restaurant, 4 miles west of Montgomery on IN 50, serves authentic Amish food with conscientious service provided by young Amish women. Scattered throughout the Amish settlement area are 20 or so Amish general stores, providing wares that seem almost antique by modern standards—lamp oil and bulk baking yeast, for instance. Enos Graber Furniture, located on CR 1200 East, north of CR 600, is a hybrid—a family furniture factory, farm, and Amish store.

Loogootee, 4.6 miles east of Montgomery, is the only incorporated city in Martin County. (Drive 1 has additional information about the town.) About 6 miles from Loogootee, the road abruptly leaves the Southern Bottoms to rise into the Crawford Upland, the most rugged scenery in Indiana. During Prohibition, the Crawford County hills were the bailiwick of moonshiners and bootleggers.

Shoals, 8.1 mile east of Loogootee, is the seventh county seat of Martin County. The vintage courthouse is south of the highway and west of the East Fork of the White River in west Shoals. Bo-Mac's Drive-In in east Shoals is a bit of Roadside Americana. Jug Rock, a sandstone formation, teeters to the west of the town just off the highway.

Martin State Forest, 5.1 miles east of Shoals, was a Depression-era project—eroded farmland planted with thousands of pine trees by CCC laborers. Drive 6.1 miles east to the junction of IN 60. Proceed 8.8 miles east to Mitchell. Lawrence County is the birthplace of three astronauts, Gus Grissom, Charlie Walker, and Ken Bowersox. A monument to Grissom is on South Sixth Street 4 blocks south of Main Street in Mitchell.

Spring Mill State Park, the second most popular state park with accommodations and amenities, is 2 miles east of Mitchell on IN 60. It is a 1,319-acre park with a historic grist mill and restored pioneer village as the centerpiece. Donaldson's Woods Nature Preserve in the park is an 80-acre stand of virgin forest.

South of Mitchell 2 miles on IN 37 is a cemetery on the east side of the road with several early gravestones as well as a stunningly well-carved log cabin in the southwest corner as a grave marker. Lawrence County is part of the Oolitic limestone belt that stretches from Bloomington 50 miles south, a band of fine-grained building stone that has clad everything from the Empire State building to the Pentagon. It engendered a tradition of fine stone carvers that graced the area's cemeteries and buildings with extraordinary carving.

Orleans is 4.7 miles south of Mitchell, another town with a growing Amish population in the hinterland around it. The area is attracting Amish from other regions like Ohio, Pennsylvania, and upstate New York, who are drawn to southern Indiana by relatively low-priced farmland. Orange County's topography ranges from the flatter limestone area in the north to rumpled hill land. It predisposes farms to be small by agribusiness standards, but fine for the Amish with their horse-powered economy.

Amish people with their buggies and shy children can often be seen on the town square (also called Congress Square and Seminary Square after an academy that stood there for 60 years) selling prepared foods and crafts. The main area of settlement is southwest of town off of the Vincennes Road, stretching toward Orangeville. Watch for slow-moving buggies. There were 27 families living in the area in 1998.

Orleans is the oldest town in the county, platted in 1815. It is famous for its springtime Dogwood Festival when hundreds of pink and white dogwood that the town planted in the 1960s burst into bloom. At the east edge of town on Washington Street just past Stetson Street, a green-shuttered home has an association with Elizabeth Shindler, who was the heir to the Stetson hat fortune. Her doting husband had the house constructed in Philadelphia in 1894 and shipped to Elizabeth's parents, making it one of the first pre-fab homes.

The dry streambed of the Lost River is 3.6 miles south of Orleans. The mysterious river rises in neighboring Washington County and travels 22 miles above and below ground before entering the East Fork of the White River in Martin County. The highway passes over part of an 8-mile stretch where the stream is underground except in periods of high water when it rises to flow in the channel. It resurfaces at the Orangeville Rise 6 miles west near the town of Orangeville.

The Lost River is part of the region's karst geology which features underground streams, sinkholes, and caverns. The southern hill country of Indiana that stretches across the bottom third of the state is physiographically composed of three hilly upland belts, two limestone plateaus, and two lowlands. Traversing west across southern Indiana from the Ohio state border, the traveler passes through the sprawling ridges and deep branching valleys of the Dearborn Upland. At Laughery Creek on the Dearborn-Ohio county line, he descends to the Muscatatuck Regional Slope, a tilted limestone plateau with walled canyons and damp, crawfish-rich flatlands, dropping farther into the Scottsburg Lowland, dominated by the wide alluvial plains of the Muscatatuck and White Rivers' drainages.

Proceeding west, the geology begins its ascent again, as if it's climbing a flight of tilted stairsteps. First there is the Knobstone Escarpment, the most prominent physiographic feature in Indiana, more than 600 feet above the Ohio at New Albany. The Knobs are the transition to the Norman Upland, plateaulike here in the south, but rumpling into the steep-sided canyons of Brown County further north. The slice of the Norman Uplands is followed by the pocked limestone karst geology and red clay soils of the Mitchell Plain that the road has been passing through since Mitchell. It extends north toward Bloomington.

The Knobs, the Mitchell Plain, and the Brown County Hills to the north are some of America's most rugged terrain east of the Rocky Mountains, acting as a highland rim above most of the surrounding landscape. It is a biologically rich, topographically challenged region—part of the nation's Interior Low Plateaus Physiographic Region that runs from North Alabama all the way to Morgan County south of Indianapolis.

Paoli, 7.8 miles south of Orleans (see Drive 1 for more information on the town), has a sizable Amish population east of town along IN 56. Ironically, many Amish emigrated out of the country to Central America in the 1960s when Indiana legislated the orange-triangled slow-moving vehicle signs. Many of the more conservative Amish thought carrying the sign violated their rules concerning decoration and ornamentation. As around Mitchell, the area has become a new colonization spot for Amish from around the country, most arriving in the last five years. There are two bishops in the area as compared to ten in the Montgomery area and none around Orleans.

Take IN 56 east of Paoli 6.7 miles to the Pumpkin Center turnoff, which is 2.6 miles north of IN 56. There are several Amish farms in the area along with Pumpkin Center, an idiosyncratic folk art environment with a jumble of collections and hand-painted homilies.

Return to IN 56 and proceed 13 miles east to Salem. Founded in 1814, Salem was the site of a short fight during Confederate John Hunt Morgan's invasion. A marker on the courthouse lawn commemorates the skirmish where the town's tiny, 18-inch-long cannon failed to ignite because the gunner dropped his match. Morgan and his men burned the town's depot, water tank, and bridges, pillaging like "boys in an orchard." As the raiders rode out of Salem, they unrolled bolts of calico and gave them to the women and girls of the town.

The John Hay Center at 307 E. Market Street is a small, well-run complex consisting of a county museum (with a strong genealogical library), a pioneer village, and the John Hay House. Hay a nineteenth-century author and diplomat, served as Abraham Lincoln's private secretary and as secretary of state in the McKinley and Theodore Roosevelt administrations.

The primary Amish areas in Washington County are east of the county seat of Salem on county roads around New Philadelphia and Little York. The settlement is primarily Amish who arrived in the last ten years from older settlements in Delaware and Ohio. Look for signs for Amish furniture and picnic tables. Rocking chairs are one of their specialties.

South Central Indiana

8

Brown County Loop
A loop around the hills and hamlets of Brown County

General description: The 49-mile drive is through the dramatic hills and valleys of Brown County, nationally known for its scenery and artist colony.

Special attractions: Picturesque scenery throughout; The Story Inn in Story; The Brown County Historical Society Museum Complex in Nashville; shopping.

Location: South Central Indiana.

Drive route numbers and names: Indiana Highways 46, 45, and 135; county roads, Carr Hill Road, 150 South, Whitehorse Road, Bellesville Pike, Christiansburg Road, Plum Creek Road, South Shore Road, Indian Hill Road, Someron Road, and Owl Creek Road.

Travel season: This is a rumpled landscape with some precipitous hills, best avoided in snowy weather. The autumn brings staggering amounts of traffic into Nashville and Brown County State Park, but the back roads can still be enjoyable driving. Avoid the state highways into Nashville and the park on peak leaf-season weekends unless you enjoy sitting in traffic jams.

Camping: There is camping at Brown County State Park, as well as private campgrounds at Nashville: The Last Resort, Westward Ho, and Valley Branch Retreat. Columbus has Columbus Woods-N-Waters.

Services: There are full services at Columbus and Nashville. There is gas and food en route including Pikes Peak and Beanblossom.

Nearby attractions: The architectural haven of Columbus begins the route, and the university town of Bloomington is 15 miles west of Nashville.

 The drive

Brown County is as much an idea as a place, an icon of bygone days that's been merchandised and packaged a thousand different ways. Yet in spite of all the hype, the county remains an extraordinary destination for scenic driving, a roller-coaster ride of dramatic hills and serpentine roads, charming hamlets and beautiful vistas.

The spectacular scenery for today's visitor was an anathema to the early settlers. The hilly, rocky terrain made all but subsistence farming impossible. Roads and place names speak of poverty and isolation: Scarce o'Fat Road, Gnaw Bone, Milk Sick Bottom, Needmore, Stoney Lonesome. Scarce o'Fat was said to have soil so poor the starving cows had to lean against the fence to bawl. Timbering, salt collection, and gold-mining activities were the main occupations until urban artists began filtering into the hills after the turn of the twentieth century.

The Brown County School of Art became nationally known, a regionalist outgrowth of the Impressionist movement. The "Hoosier Group"— T. C. Steele, Marie Goth, Adolph Shulz, C. Curry Bohm, Genevieve and Carl Graf, V. J. Carriani, and others—found Brown County to be "an authentic American landscape," in Shulz' words, and they spent their careers rendering the soft light and hazy air in thousands of romantic canvases. By the late 1920s, Brown County was a locale at the confluence of art and commerce. Up to 20 painters were full-time residents with twice that working seasonally. Nashville enjoyed a national reputation, and the artists bustled to keep up with demand, with the results sometimes speaking of creativity and sometimes of business realities.

Tourists followed soon after, and the county has depended on tourism since. Millions today still trundle down the two-lanes into the hilly county to enjoy the combination of rusticity and sophistication that Brown County has been known for since Model T days.

The uplands and steep ravines of the area are part of the limestone karst topography of the Mitchell Plain. The Mitchell Plain is in turn part of the Interior Low Plateaus Physiographic Region that extends northward from northern Alabama to south of Indianapolis, some of the nation's most rugged terrain east of the Rockies. The complex erosion patterns of the V-shaped valleys and high "knob" hills are courtesy of the glacial ice sheets that slid down to the northern edge of the county, the runoff cutting through to the shale and siltstone beneath the limestone. Southern Brown County was never glaciated, and it is where the most dramatic scenery is found.

Black walnut, wild cherry, and sycamore line the stream banks, and oak, beech, sugar maple, and hickory thrive on the hilltops and slopes. Wildflowers and berry bushes light up the understory. Painted sedge, a grasslike plant that is rare in the rest of the state, covers most of Brown County's dry slopes.

The drive begins in Columbus. Proceed west on Indiana Highway 46, 0.8 mile from the junction with IN 11 to Carr Hill Road and turn south. It is the only road on the left before the highway reaches the junction with Interstate 65. The road traverses a tongue of flat field that is a remnant of the

Drive 8: Brown County Loop

A loop around the hills and hamlets of Brown County

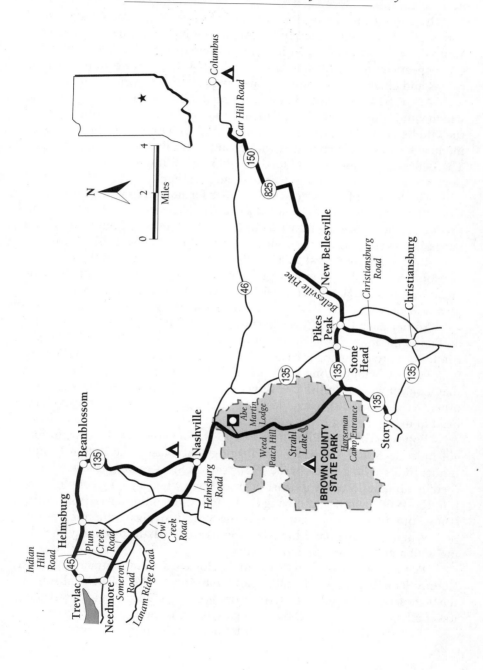

glacier before twisting into the hills 0.5 mile later. The road passes through an upscale suburban neighborhood that has crept into the hills from industrial Columbus.

In 2 miles the candy ribbon road descends to become County Road 150 South. Hulking forested hills loom at the horizon. The road becomes Youth Camp Road and the youth camp with a two-story Greek Revival structure appears on the north side of the road. At Wolf Creek Road, the first log cabins and chicken yards appear, a harbinger of the Brown County hills.

At CR 825 West, turn left and proceed 0.2 mile to Whitehorse Road which winds down through a ravined, sun-dappled forest into the valley of the Middle Fork of Salt Creek. Turn right (south) onto Bellesville Pike. New modular homes are interspersed with abandoned cabins and vintage houses. The Bellesville Cemetery, founded in 1853, is 2.8 miles from the intersection. It has some fine early gravestones and markers.

The hamlet of Pikes Peak is 1.8 miles farther southwest. A frustrated Gold Rusher, James Ward, founded the town. He traveled to California but became so homesick he returned to the hills of Brown County to start a general store. In jest, the customers began calling the place Pikes Peak.

Turn south on Christiansburg Road. The crossroads hamlet of Christiansburg is 1.6 miles over a ridgetop with an artist's studio near the peak and down into the Hamilton Creek valley. Another 1853 cemetery is located on a hillside with a lovely view 0.2 mile before the village.

Slither back down Christiansburg Road to Pikes Peak and turn west on Bellesville Pike. Stone Head is 4 miles west on the valley road. The reason for crossroads' name is easily seen at the junction of IN 135 and Bellesville Pike. A benign stone head presides there over a road marker noting that Columbus is 17 miles one direction and Fairfax and Sparks Ferry the other. "H. Cross 1851" reads the sign as it has since Henry Cross carved the head in lieu of paying his road tax.

Follow Bellesville Pike onto IN 135 South and drive the hairpin road 4.4 miles to Story. The same overlogging that caused the Brown County timber industry to go bust in the 1930s caused Story to lose its several hundred inhabitants. Story was nearly a ghost town when a young couple found it in the 1960s and began buying it up. Today, the old grocery store with a couple of vintage pumps out front is the Story Inn, a gastronomic destination. When all the bed-and-breakfast rooms are filled, the town may be bulging with a population of nearly twenty.

Return 2 miles north on IN 135 to the Horseman Camp entrance to Brown County State Park. Proceed 6 miles past Strahl Lake to Weed Patch Hill, one of the highest points in Indiana offering a dramatic view. The fire and observation tower offers a fine vista for those who have the vim and vigor.

The Abe Martin Lodge is 1.5 miles north. It is another Depression-Era construction, named after cartoonist Kin Hubbard's character. For nearly 25 years, Hubbard's nationally syndicated cartoon spread Abe Martin's wry country wisdoms around the nation, helping to publicize Brown County as the home of rustic philosophers.

Drive through the park to the west park entrance and turn north on IN 46 to Nashville, the epicenter of the Brown County tourist industry. Nashville is the county's governmental seat, largest town, and home to more than 300 shops, selling bric-a-brac and fine art from corn-husk brooms to handcrafted birdhouses to original oil paintings, candles, quilts, wrought iron, stained glass, toys and dolls, and enough salt-water taffy and fudge to fuel you far down the road. This and much, much more—it's all here for the dedicated shopper.

The 1874 red brick courthouse at Main and Van Buren Streets has several "Liars' Benches," replicas of the one in the famous 1923 Frank Hohenberger photograph that captured a lineup of town storytellers swapping yarns. Catty-corner from the courthouse, the worn wooden floors of the Hob Nob Corner Restaurant have seen a lot of traffic since it was built in 1870. It's the county's oldest commercial structure. One block east of Van Buren, the Brown County Historical Society Museum Complex at Gould Street and Old School Way has among other things, an 1840s log barn, an old log jail, a pioneer cabin, an early doctor's office, and an 1820s blacksmith shop. Interpreters help re-create the nineteenth-century lifestyle.

Drive north 5 miles on IN 135 to Beanblossom. The Beanblossom Overlook provides a stirring panorama of the hills. Just north of here, both the Illinoisan and Wisconsinan glaciers ground to a halt. The town is 1 mile farther. Beanblossom is renowned for the annual Beanblossom Bluegrass Festival made famous by Bluegrass music pioneer Bill Monroe. Thousands make the pilgrimage yearly to the Bill and James Monroe Campground to hear the plangent chords and high plaintive notes of Bluegrass music. The 1880 Beanblossom Covered Bridge, the only one ever built in the county, is located 0.5 mile southwest of the hamlet's main crossroads.

Turn west on IN 45. Helmsburg, 3 miles west was once a bustling railroad town. Trevlac, 2.7 miles father west, also thrived during the railroad's heyday. One mile south is the little railroad burg of Needmore, site of the colorful hippie Needmore Commune in the 1960s and 70s. The South Shore Road in Needmore leads in 2.5 miles to Lake Lemon and the Riddle Point Park.

Turn east on Plum Creek Road. Quirky surviving examples of houses that reflect the '60s-era woodbutchers' art are still scattered along the road. A few miles of the road is gravel but returns to pavement for the balance of the drive.

Drive 2 miles through the intersection of Indian Hill Road and Someron

Road to Lanam Ridge Road and turn left. Drive 0.1 mile and turn right on Owl Creek Road. The road down to the valley is a green tunnel of trees past vintage log cabins and prosperous new homes. In 2.2 miles turn right onto Helmsburg Road. The road leads through a green valley and then climbs upward. Nashville is 2.3 miles farther. The road leads directly to the courthouse square.

9

Sweet Owen

A tour from Cataract to Bloomington

General description: The 32-mile drive runs from Cataract with the state's highest waterfall through the rugged scenery of Owen and Monroe Counties to Bloomington.

Special attractions: Cataract Falls; the picturesque town of Spencer; McCormick's Creek State Park and the college town of Bloomington.

Location: South Central Indiana.

Drive route numbers and names: U.S. Highway 231; Indiana Highways 43 and 48.

Travel season: These are all-weather two-lane roads, though winter weather can bring lots of drifting snow.

Camping: Blackhawk Campground and campgrounds at Cloverdale and Cloverdale RV Park. Leiber State Park and McCormick's Creek State Park both have camping.

Services: There are full services at Cloverdale, Spencer, and Bloomington, and gas and food at Cataract and near Whitehall at the junction of IN 43 and 48.

Nearby attractions: Leiber State Park.

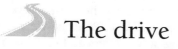 The drive

There is a soothing sound as the water falls over the shoals at Cataract Falls. Trees line burbling Mill Creek, and a faded red covered bridge dating to 1876 crosses the stream like a barely recalled memory. The tiny village of Cataract with its upright frame houses and old general store looks like something out of Norman Rockwell's New England.

The pair of falls at Cataract are Indiana's highest; the upper one drops 45 feet over striated bands of limestone and a little farther downstream the lower one falls 30 feet. The falls stand at the cusp of two dramatically different natural regions. To the north the glaciated prairies stretch in a fertile swath all the way to the Great Lakes. To the south, the rugged upland limestone belts rumple their way down to the Appalachians. The falls drop between them.

The town of Cataract began in the 1820s when Issac Teale erected a small mill. In 1842 Governor Jonathan Jennings' brother, Theodore, began the tiny town's mercantile boomlet when he erected a sawmill, flour and woolen mill, blacksmith shop, and general store. For decades the town buzzed with lumbering and flour milling, selling to locales as far away as Louisville. At its peak in the last quarter of the nineteenth century, Cataract had three groceries, a hotel, and a drugstore. When the forests were depleted and the lumber mill closed, the other enterprises lost their customer base and the town devolved into the sleepy place you see today.

The Cataract General Store began in 1860. Outside the barn-red building, old Texaco Fire Chief gas pumps stand waiting. A pair of battered red wooden doors swing open to an establishment lost in time. The shelves and walls are lined with a serendipitous collection of antiques and modern goods, potato chips beside the horse collar, old thread cases beside ones with new Case knives, wooden crank phones above the detergent. Soft drinks come out of a vintage Coca Cola case. Scythes and wooden rakes are there along with Ding-dongs and Twinkies.

Take North Cataract Road 2.3 miles across the flat prairie to U.S. Highway 231 and turn south. The tiny town of Carp boasts little but Russell's Plantation House Antiques Shop, long a hidden treasure of regional antique mavens. A few miles south the road begins to descend into the Hoosier uplands where the limestone bones of the land become more pronounced.

Two miles south of Carp, you can take a side trip by turning east on Indiana Highway 67 and driving 4 miles to Gosport. About 0.3 mile north of Gosport, there are two highway markers denoting the 10 o'clock line, the 1809 treaty boundary negotiated by William Henry Harrison and Chief Little Turtle that brought almost 3 million acres into United States government control at a cost of about 3 cents an acre. The town of Gosport began in 1829 as a flatboat shipping port on the White River. For many years an odd hybrid bridge crossed the White River between Owen and Monroe County; half of the bridge was steel girders and half was a wooden covered bridge, each county following its own style.

While the town still retains a historic air, fires and thoughtless demolition have robbed it of many of its landmarks. One that still remains is the curious Chivalry Trough, a 4 x 8-foot spring-fed concrete bath. In previous days, the town's grooms grimly awaited the traditional late-night dunking in the trough on their wedding eves. The trough is located near the remains of the Brewer Flour Mill, often hidden in the weeds. Take Main west to Fifth Street, turn north and proceed to East North Street, turn back east and the mill and trough are about 4 blocks.

Return west on IN 67 to US 231/IN 67 and turn south to Spencer. Founded in 1820, the town was incorporated in 1866 and the coming of the railroad two years later gave the town a boost.

Owen County itself was organized in 1818. In 1976, only 1.5 percent of the county was developed; the balance was divided between farm and

Drive 9: Sweet Owen

A tour from Cataract to Bloomington

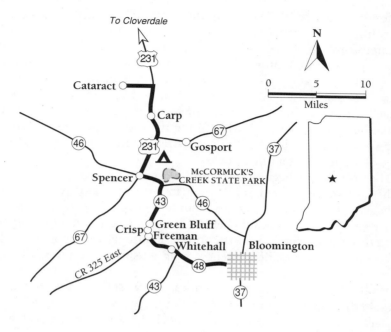

forest. The county has experienced some development since then, but it is still among the state's most rural in character.

The present courthouse dates to 1911, and its copper dome was recently recovered with a new $225,000 skin. The "Spirit of the Doughboy" statue on the courthouse lawn is by Spencer native Ernest Visquesney, a renowned early-twentieth-century sculptor.

The John Robinson House at Franklin and Montgomery Streets was built prior to 1850. It is currently the home of the Spencer-Owen Civic League where visitor information can be obtained. Continue north on Montgomery Street to Hillside Avenue. The street is a gracious residential street with a number of sprawling turn-of-the-century homes.

Return to the junction of IN 67 and IN 46 and proceed east across the White River 1.8 miles to McCormick's Creek State Park. The park is the state's oldest, dating back to 1916, chosen for its extraordinary natural beauty and unique features. Tongues of the glacier crept across the present White River and climbed the bluffs in and around the park. A badly eroded ridge that represents an ancient glacial moraine tops the bluff there. Ancient lake beds formed by the runoff are a few miles east near Ellettsville, creating a formation known as flatwoods. Within the park, a 1-mile-long 100-foot-high canyon is a dramatic remnant of glacial melt.

The park is the site of an early limestone quarry that furnished the stone for the state capitol. There are numerous recreational facilities and the Canyon Inn is a cozy WPA-era inn with rustic comfort.

The turnoff for IN 43 is just past the park entrance. Proceed south. The road goes through another flat glaciated area for 3 miles until new forestry industries along the road announce the remainder of old Owen County Poor Farm. In recent years the county has sold off much of the original 395 acres for industrial development. The hulking red-brick County Home building on the right side of the road is one of Indiana's last remaining homes for indigents. Built in 1878, it remains the home for an average of 16 people at a time.

The road quickly begins a serpentine twist through deep ravined woods. It is the land of the upland South yeoman farmers, many descendants of nineteenth-century North Carolina mountain people who settled the hills in the 1840s. Not many decades before that, there were still hunter-gatherers wresting their livings from the forests. Ginseng-gathering—"sang"—is still a lucrative local sideline, and spring mushroom hunting a fevered pastime.

South of the county farm, 2.5 miles, turn west on County Road 525 South (Sherfield Road) to the Nature Conservancy's nature preserve, Green's Bluff. The area is a refuge for eastern Hemlock that thrive in the cool, moist environment of Raccoon Creek's sandstone bluffs. Other rare plants include species of ferns, goldenseal, and spleenwort. Drive 2 miles to the "T" which is CR 75 East. Turn left and proceed half a mile to the Hedding Cemetery and a parking lot.

Return to IN 43 and proceed 0.5 mile. Crisp, Indiana, is a tiny ridge-top hamlet with a restored one-room schoolhouse that is still used for local gatherings.

The road snakes out of Crisp, down to Freeman, and into the Raccoon Creek valley. It is still a traditional valley in spite of the new homes mixed in with vernacular double-pen structures. The Little Flock Church 0.1 mile down CR 325 East looks like it belongs in the hills of Elmer Gantry's rural south. As recently as 25 years ago, some of the farms were still worked with draft horses.

The road continues into Whitehall, a modest hamlet strung along the roadside. The road at the top of the hill is State Ferry Road, named for the free Farmer's Ferry crossing across the White River many miles away in Greene County, operated by the state from the 1870s till its passing in 1989.

The Monroe County line is 0.2 mile from Whitehall and there are gas and groceries available at the junction of Indiana Highway 48. Indiana Highway 48 parallels Richland Creek in another bucolic valley. The jumbled two-story Victorian house on the left announces the piles of organic matter that form a private compost farm. Monroe County residents deliver hundreds of tons of organic debris to the farm where it is slowly rebuilding the fertility of the "corned-out" acreage. A rustic Gothic-style home is on the left side 0.1 mile past the compost farm and the picturesque Richland Church is on the left.

The large structure on the right at Garrison Chapel Road, 0.2 mile farther, is Mary's Children Retreat Center for pilgrims coming to the site of a vision of the Virgin Mary in the early 1990s. A trail leads to a chapel and the pilgrimage site at the top of the hill.

The road bounds over two humpy hills and the industrial underbelly of Bloomington appears. The local airport, industrial parks, raw new subdivisions, strip malls, and the detritus of the Automobile Age form the gateway to the city. (Bloomington is covered in Drive 10.)

10

Culture to Culture
A drive from Bloomington to Columbus

General description: The 60-mile drive is through the rumpled hills of Monroe, Brown, and Bartholomew Counties between the culturally diverse college town of Bloomington and the architectural wonder of Columbus.
Special attractions: In Bloomington: Courthouse Square, Indiana University Campus, Tibetan Cultural Center. In Columbus: modernist and vintage architecture.
Location: South Central Indiana.
Drive route numbers and names: Indiana Highways 46 and 446.
Travel season: The roads traverse a very hilly region and are treacherous in snowy weather. Fall weekends bring out foliage fans in amazing numbers, clogging the roads coming into Nashville.
Camping: There is camping at Brown County State Park, as well as private campgrounds. In Nashville: The Last Resort, Westward Ho, and Valley Branch Retreat. In Columbus: Columbus Woods-N-Waters.
Services: There are full services in Bloomington, Nashville, and Columbus, and numerous opportunities for gas and food en route.
Nearby attractions: Indianapolis is 50 miles north.

 The drive

The tour begins on the courthouse square in Bloomington, home of Indiana University (IU). The 1908 courthouse and the surrounding square reflect Bloomington's polyglot population and quirky mix of lifestyles and esthetics. Around the square, ethnic clothing stores sit next to abstract companies and local attorneys. Shoppers peruse fine designer jewelry made of ancient fossils, Peruvian folk art, and cutting-edge computer games, before toddling off for a cappuccino or a loaf of European bread. The cafes and restaurants of the downtown area offer fare from Moroccan to Afghani, Japanese to Hoosier.

Given the diversity, it's not that surprising that Bloomington is considered a Little Tibet. In a town better known for basketball, John Mellencamp, and the Kinsey Institute for Sex Research, this link to the traditional culture of the high Himalayas seems incongruous. But an enormous Buddhist

Drive 10: Culture to Culture

A drive from Bloomington to Columbus

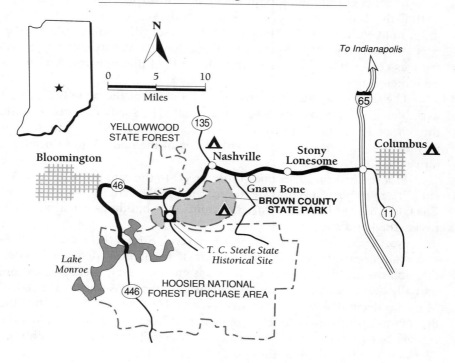

stupa, a massive spire-topped cylindrical shrine, glints gold and white on the town's outskirts, surrounded by fluttering prayer flags. It is the focus of the Tibetan Cultural Center located at 3655 Snoddy Road on the southeast side of town. Visited four times by the Dalai Lama, the 90-acre site is dedicated to teaching Tibet's history, culture, and art with ceremonies, festivals, and workshops.

Bloomington has two Tibetan restaurants. Cars with "Free Tibet" bumper stickers announce Tibetan supporters. Shaven-headed monks dressed in maroon are a common sight in town, leading meditation groups, giving concerts of their remarkable chanting, and visiting their countrymen.

Since their foundings early in the nineteenth century, Bloomington and Indiana University have been connected whole and part. The town's first settlers moved into what President James Madison named as "Seminary Township," designated for the location of a state university. It was located on the highest ground in the region to protect the townsfolk from ravaging floods and the malaria of the more fertile lowlands.

A nascent university began in 1825, but teetered along for 60 years, barely alive. The town itself, strangled by the endemic water shortage, also limped along. Given the water problem, it's not surprising that it was a fire in 1883 that finally got the place going. After the science building burned to the ground with President David Starr Jordan's scientific collections (Jordan later served as the revered president of Stanford University), he convinced the trustees to rebuild in the countryside east of Bloomington, and it has been there since.

The limestone industry fortuitously boomed at the same time, and a world-famous limestone campus is the result. The shady campus with the tiny Jordan River running through it, ennobled with Gothic and contemporary architecture, has long been ranked one of the nation's most beautiful universities.

Proceed east on Kirkwood (Fifth Street) to the campus at Indiana Avenue. The Sample Gates provide the entrance to the earliest part of campus. The Old Crescent Historic District contains nine buildings constructed between 1884 and 1908.

Northeast of the Beck Chapel on Seventh Street, the Fine Arts Plaza surrounding the Showalter "Birth of Venus" Fountain is dedicated to culture and the arts. The IU Auditorium was erected in the Great Depression, partially funded and built under the auspices of the WPA. Inside, the Hall of Murals is decorated with Regionalist Thomas Hart Benton's bodice-busting depictions of Indiana's economic and social evolution. Benton painted the murals for Chicago's 1933–34 Century of Progress International Exhibition. The state installed them in the auditorium in 1940.

Designed by architect I. M. Pei, the wedge-shaped IU Art Museum is an evolution (or devolution, depending on the critic) of the East Wing of the National Gallery. It houses IU's outstanding collections of Mediterranean, Asian, African, Oceana, and American art, as well as a collection of twentieth-century Western European art. The Lilly Library across the plaza is one of the country's great repositories of rare books, with an original Gutenberg Bible.

Return to Jordan Avenue and continue north to 17th Street to Assembly Hall, the "House that Knight Built," a 17,000-seat basketball arena for Bobby Knight–coached teams. Farther north on 17th Street, the Little 500 Stadium is the scene of the yearly bicycle race that inspired the cult-classic movie, "Breaking Away." The neighboring Bill Armstrong Soccer Stadium is considered one of the nation's finest facilities, home to Indiana's perennial powerhouse teams.

Turn east on Indiana Highway 46 and proceed east 4 miles to IN 446 South. The Lake Monroe Visitor Center and the Paynetown State Recreation Area is 6.4 miles south, part of the complex at Indiana's largest lake. A

The bell tower of Indiana University is a beloved landmark.
Photo courtesy of Gene Howard.

mile farther south, the highway curls down to the dramatic causeway that spans the lake with a vista of water and forested hills on either side of the bridge. A pull-off is located on the south end of the causeway. The Hardin Ridge Recreational Area is 3.6 miles south on IN 446.

Return to IN 46 East, which twists the rough terrain of Brown County to the east. Turn south at Steele Road to Belmont. The T. C. Steele State Historic Site is 1.5 miles farther. The limestone arches, surrounded by acres of daffodils in spring, lead to the former home of Indiana's most beloved painter and the founder of the Brown County Art Colony. In 1945 his widow donated the 211 acres, the house, the 900-volume library, and 300 paintings to the state. The two studios and the Trailside Museum are open for visitors, as well as several walking trails that inspired Steele's Impressionist canvases.

Return to IN 46 East. Yellowwood State Forest is 2.1 miles east. The 22,508-acre forest is land that the federal government bought in the Depression when the hill people fled the rugged, unfriendly hills and the eroded fields stood idle. The government paid an average of $9.19 an acre. CCC workers reforested the land, and in 1953 the federal government turned over the woodlands to the state. There are three lakes and numerous trails and primitive campsites.

Ski World is 1.7 miles east, a surprising feature of Indiana. It opened in the 1980s, suffered through mild winters too warm even for manmade snow, but now appears to be a faux Alpine opportunity for southern Hoosiers. It offers several slopes of varying degrees of difficulty, and summertime slope activities. The road climbs precipitously, offering a stirring panorama at the top of the surrounding Norman Upland. The entrance to Brown County State Park is just beyond.

The park opened in 1929, and with 15,547 acres is the state's largest. Runoff from the Illinois-period glacier formed the streambeds of Beanblossom and Salt Creeks and the ravined hills between them. The park has extensive recreational facilities including two lakes, horseback and hiking trails, a nature center, and the Abe Martin Lodge.

Little Nashville Opry, 3.4 miles east, hosts some of the best country music stars on the planet. (Nashville is 1 mile east. See Drive 11 for information on Nashville.)

At the junction of IN 135, turn east on IN 46. Because of the difficult terrain, settlers came late to Brown County. Once they learned farming was a bad deal, they turned to timber, salt, and gold for economic development, although no significant gold reserves were ever found.

Since the 1930s, tourism has formed the backbone of the economy. Each year, millions converge on the county's little towns and hamlets to partake in a bit of nostalgic visitation. On fall weekends, it's said that the fastest way to get into Nashville on either IN 46 or 135 is to walk on the hoods of cars that are lined up for miles trying to get into the tourist town.

*The Tibetan Cultural Center's chorten in Bloomington is a taste of central Asia
in southern Indiana.* Photo courtesy of Lorraine Merriman Farrell.

The north entrance to Brown County State Park is 2 miles east. Gnaw
Bone is 2 miles west, a flea market haven. Mounds of gourd art and a giant
cut-out woodpecker sign tell you that you are there. According to local lore,
one early settler, when asked the whereabouts of another, replied, "I seed
him a-settin' on a log above the sawmill a-gnawin' on a bone," and the name
stuck. Most likely the original settlers' French name of Narbonne was Hoo-
siered.

Bartholomew County is the home of Columbus, an internationally renowned architectural mecca. Driving past silos and barns and near-iconic
rows of deep green corn, you'll spot the twin red arches rising incongruously from the prairie at the edge of Columbus. It's the first sign you are entering a very unusual town. By the time you see the Victorian county courthouse,
all belfries and widow's walks and looming red-brick rectitude, with a forest
of 25 towering stone monoliths erupting from its lawn, you'll know this
isn't your standard Indiana town.

Columbus people like to say they're different—different by design. And
they are. Since the 1940s, Columbus citizens have engaged in a remarkable
experiment in modern living, hiring the top international architects to design their public buildings and meld them into the fabric of their nineteenth-
century town of 35,000. There are more than 50 buildings representing an
honor roll of modern architects, including Cesar Pelli, both Saarinens,
Harry Weese, Kevin Roche, I. M. Pei, Robert Venturi, Deborah Berke, and

Richard Meier. The American Institute of Architects named Columbus the sixth most architecturally significant city in the United States, behind only New York, Chicago, Los Angeles, Boston, and Washington, D.C. It has become a cultural tourism shrine.

Downtown, the visitor center at Fifth and Franklin Streets is an ideal spot to pick up maps, literature, and information. Nearby at 531 Fifth Street, the austere geometric First Christian Church—designed by Finland's foremost architect Eilel Saarinen, is a striking counterpoint to the common Gothic and Georgian churches of the Midwest. The piazza in front of the church centers on Henry Moore's bronze sculpture "Large Arch," a 20-foot-high primal paean to Stonehenge, I. M. Pei's town library, and the Commons, a glass-boxed downtown shopping center designed by Cesar Pelli, where kids sit under surrealist Jean Tinguely's enormous "Chaos I" sculpture with its scavenged gears and levers.

The last work by architect Eero Saarinen (of St. Louis Arch fame) is the North Christian Church, which stands on the north edge of town along IN 46 East at 850 Tipton Lane. Hexagonal walls leap from the bermed earth with one dynamic pulse into a needle-thin spire that etches the sky—a bold, modern, timeless design.

Columbus is an architectural petrie dish, where the idea that good architecture improves the human condition is still being tested—with an almost naive faith. Robert Venturi designed one of the fire stations, Robert A. M. Stern the hospital. Pritzker Prize–winner Kevin Roche, who created the Metropolitan Museum of Art's master plan, designed the sleek post office at 450 Jackson on the tidy Victorian main street, across from Zaharakos Confectionery, where ice cream is still sold at the rococo 1890s onyx soda fountain bought at the 1890s Columbian Exposition.

The folks still love their old buildings here in spite of all the modernist architecture. In fact, many buildings and some districts are on the National Register of Historic Places. Small wonder that the first Post-modernist architect, Harry Weese, found Columbus an ideal place to explore the value of folk architecture, blending it into his buildings and the Columbus neighborhoods in the 1950s.

11

Autumn Loop I

An autumn ride through Southern Indiana near Bedford

General description: The 80-mile loop courses through the southern Indiana hills from Bedford through Shoals, West Baden, Paoli, and back to Bedford.

Special attractions: Spring Mill State Park, Blue Springs Caverns, Paoli Square, West Baden Springs Hotel.

Location: South Central Indiana.

Drive route numbers and names: U.S. Highways 50 and 150; Indiana Highways 37 and 450; and County Road 500.

Travel season: The roads are all blacktop and fine for fall driving.

Camping: There is camping at Spring Mill State Park and Patoka Lake.

Services: There are full services at Bedford, Shoals, and French Lick–West Baden. Food and gas is available in Orleans and several places en route.

Nearby attractions: Bloomington and Indiana University are 25 miles north of Bedford. Patoka Lake is 5 miles south of French Lick, and the German communities of Jasper and Huntingburg are 20 miles southwest of French Lick and West Baden.

 ## The drive

The loops begin in Bedford, center of the Indiana limestone industry. About 340 million years ago, the ground we call Indiana was down by the equator covered by a shallow ocean. It was a comparatively calm sea where trillions of tiny animals—crinoids and gastropods and other slithery sea creatures—lived out their lives. As they came to their natural ends, their carcasses piled atop one another for eons on end, till shoals of the bodies lay on the ocean floor. Where the sea bottom and currents coalesced in optimal ways, the shoals rose to great heights.

As time moved on, so did the continent, migrating north to place Indiana where it is today. The vast shoals, now compressed into rock by the weight of water and earth and endless time, awaited the next great geologic moment. A million years ago, give or take a few millennia, the great glaciers ground down from the North. While the glaciers stopped short of scouring southern Indiana, the meltwater from the mile-high glaciers eroded most of the rock shoals. Only a slender band of the ancient reefs wiggling through southern Indiana escaped erosion, leaving outcrops of pristine limestone—the best in an area only 30 miles long by 2 miles wide—barely 28,000 acres. And Bedford is in the middle of that band.

Many dozens of stone companies have worked the limestone belt since the beginning of the limestone industry in the nineteenth century. More than three-quarters of all the stone buildings in the United States are constructed with Indiana limestone.

The influence of the limestone culture can be seen around Bedford's downtown square. The Lawrence County Courthouse is a neo-classic design that dates to 1930, though it has the esthetics of a building half a century older. The square retains several exceptional examples of the stonecutters' art, though some of the structures are in poor shape.

At 18th and L Streets, the Green Hill Cemetery is a veritable gallery of the stone carving art, a rich repository of formal and folk monuments. In the southwest corner of the cemetery, a full-sized craftsman stands to memorialize the Journeymen Stonecutters Association. Nearby, the gravestone of carver Louis Baker is an extraordinary sculpture done by his co-workers. Other impressive and uniquely carved limestone markers can be found throughout the cemetery.

Proceed south on U.S. Highway 50. The Antique Auto and Race Car Museum is located in the Stone City Mall at the intersection of US 50 and Indiana Highway 37. It has over a hundred antique roadsters, sprint cars, midgets, and Indy 500 race cars as well as a collection of antique stoves, washing machines, and sewing machines.

Continue south on US 50. The road to Blue Springs Cavern is 5 miles south of the intersection with IN 37. The cavern is 0.5 mile from the highway via a well-marked road. It is a commercial show cave with boat tours on the underground Myst'ry River. The cave was formed by the White River cutting through the soft limestone bedrock and forming an underground channel. The cave was hidden until the 1940s when a large farm pond disappeared overnight after a heavy rain, revealing the entrance to the cave. The cave has more than 20 miles of passages, making it one of the longest in Indiana.

Return toward Bedford to the turnoff to IN 450. It is a twisty ride along the East Fork of the White River. Williams is 5 miles southwest. The small town boasts one of the state's longest covered bridges, 368 feet long. The 100-year-old structure uses a Howe Truss design first patented in 1840. The town dam was built in 1912 for one of the state's first hydroelectric power plants. The river as it flows through Williams is a prime mussel-gathering site, which are used in Japanese cultured–pearl production.

Continue southwest 4.2 miles to Trinity Springs, a non-defunct mineral springs resort. At its turn-of-the-century peak, Trinity Springs had two large hotels and a bustle of activity surrounding the two mineral water wells at the north end of the village.

Proceed another 2 miles down IN 450. McBride's Bluffs along the White River to the south allegedly hold a fortune in Indian treasure. According to the legends, Choctaw Indians captured early settler Absalom Fields and took him blindfolded to their cave hideout along the river. There they showed him a mound of silver molded into bricks (they probably just wanted to show *someone*) and then returned him to his home. The Indians left the area soon after. Fields spent the balance of his days trying to retrace his steps and

Drive 11: Autumn Loop I

An autumn ride through Southern Indiana near Bedford

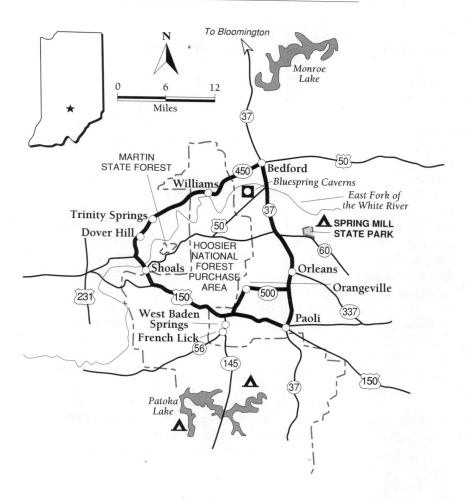

find the fortune. Twice since then bars of silver that fit the description have been found in the fields, so the tale goes.

Dover Hill is 1.5 miles farther, a disappearing little hamlet strung along the road. It was the Martin County seat from 1848 to 1857. Proceed 1 mile to US 150 East.

Shoals is 0.6 mile east on US 150. Shoals is the seventh town to be Martin County's governmental seat, wresting the honor in 1877. The Jug Rock west of town on US 150 is the only free-standing "stand-rock" west of the Mississippi. (See Drive 1 for more information on Shoals.)

Proceed 13 miles south on US 150 to IN 56 and turn south to West Baden and French Lick. The two communities share the Springs Valley, noted since pioneer days for the sulfurous smells. Since early in the days of human habitation, the valley was noted for its salt springs.

Indians hunted the abundant game drawn to the salt licks, including the bison herds that pounded down Indiana's first highway, or "trace," as they migrated from the Illinois prairies to the Falls of the Ohio near present-day Louisville, Kentucky. The first Europeans followed suit, using the buffalo trace to travel between the two areas of early settlement on the Wabash and the Ohio Rivers. In the eighteenth century, French fur trappers and Jesuit priests visited the area.

Given the importance of salt in food preservation, the young state of Indiana carefully reserved all saline springs in the state for common use, including "French Lick," as the area was known. Following the failure of state-sponsored salt wells due to the weakness of the saline waters, Dr. William A. Bowles bought the French Lick springs and started the first hotel in the valley in the mid-nineteenth century.

The venture prospered, due to the advantageous location midway on the state's main highway, and the increasing consumption of medicinal mineral water. In 1855, Dr. John A. Lane opened a competing hotel a mile to the east, initially calling it the Mile Lick Hotel. Later, the name was changed to the West Baden Springs Hotel, to capitalize on the cachet of the renowned European baths at Wiesbaden, Germany.

When the Monon Railroad finished a 17.7-mile branch line from Orleans, the hotel's clientele traveled in the newest steam-driven trains to take to the healing waters, and the valley boomed.

With its magnificent dome, the West Baden Springs Hotel was one of the world's top watering holes. The mineral water resorts offered their wealthy clientele the latest in physical therapies and mental rejuvenation. Sprudel water, as the spa's water was known, was reputed to cure more than 50 diseases including sprains, cancer, sterility, rheumatism and asthma, constipation, diabetes, gout, insomnia, and urinary afflictions.

The resort offered an array of activities for the guests: an opera house brought in Broadway stars and a sparkling lineup of seasonal shows, bowling lanes, billiards, an enclosed natatorium, a shooting range, and handball courts. A 300-foot-long, two-story turreted causeway linked the hotel to a gambling casino, one of dozens in the valley.

The immense hotel shut its doors in the Depression, and it served as a Jesuit College and private business college for decades. After a sad decline, the structure went through a remarkable restoration and is again open for tours. The neighboring French Lick Springs Resort is another Roaring 20s spa. It has remained open and offers a full resort experience including championship golf courses and tennis courts.

Return to US 150 and turn southeast. Proceed 8 miles through a rustic valley. Paoli Peaks, Indiana's first ski resort, is south of the highway on the high hills overlooking the valley. Its unique snow-making machines continue to spew out snow for the slopes in all but the warmest of winters.

Paoli has the quintessential town square, with its Greek Revival courthouse. Built in 1848–50, the brick and stone structure has outside iron staircases to save interior room for the workings of the law. North Carolina Quakers settled the town in 1811, part of the Great Quaker Migration out of the slave-holding South. This part of Orange County was strongly abolitionist, with a fugitive slave community known as Lick Creek, 3 miles south of town.

The Landmark Hotel on the south side of the square is yet another mineral springs resort. The hotel opened in 1896 after drillers hit a sulfur spring on the banks of nearby Lick Creek.

Turn north on IN 37. The road passes through the Mitchell Plain, a region of porous karst topography and thousands of sink holes. In 6 miles the road crosses the most-often dry bed of the Lost River, a unique sinking stream that rises and falls across its 22-mile watershed, sometimes above ground, sometimes below. In heavy rains, the river emerges and runs in the above-ground bed. Turn west on County Road 500 North to Orangeville, 4.1 miles. The river emerges in a fern-draped grotto called the Orangeville Rise after traveling 8 miles underground.

Return to IN 37 North and drive 4 miles to Orleans. Orleans, the first town in Orange County, was founded two months after Andrew Jackson's victory at the Battle of New Orleans, hence, the name. The square, with its gazebo, is called Seminary Square after an academy that stood on the square from the 1870s to 1963. In 1966, hundreds of flowering dogwoods were planted in the town's yards, parks, and streetsides, and now it is known as the "Dogwood Capital of Indiana."

Proceed north 4.2 miles to IN 60 and turn east. Spring Mill State Park began in 1815 when a very adrift Canadian seaman built a mill in the deep valley. It hung on as a small mill village until the arrival of the Ohio and

Mississippi Railroad in the 1850s spurred the growth of nearby Mitchell. The county bought the derelict mill in 1916 and convinced the state to turn it into a state park. Today, with a host of different recreational options including caves, swimming, trail riding, and boating, the park is one of the most popular in the state. A restored village serves as a reminder of pioneer days, and the nearby Donaldson's Woods Nature Preserve is an 80-acre stand of virgin forest. Vintage Spring Mill Inn offers rustic charm and Hoosier homestyle cooking.

The park also has the Grissom Memorial, dedicated to Gus Grissom, Lawrence County's first astronaut. Three American astronauts called the small rural county their birthplace: Gus Grissom, Charlie Walker, and Ken Bowersox.

Nearby Mitchell has a wide Victorian main street that has blossomed with antique shops and malls. Return to IN 37 and proceed to Bedford, 7 miles north.

12

Autumn Loop II

Southern Indiana: Bloomington
through eastern Greene County

General description: The drive is through the rugged hills of eastern Greene County on back roads, some of which are gravel, through hill villages to a remarkable 1906 viaduct that leaps across the Richland Valley.
Special attractions: Indiana Railroad trestle at Tulip; scenic countryside.
Location: South central Indiana.
Drive route numbers and names: Indiana Highways 48 and 43; County Roads 420 North, 400 North, 375 North, 475 East, 515 North, 460 North, 575 North, 760 North, 735 North, and 985 East.
Travel season: The gravel roads should be fine most of the year, but winter weather will make them difficult to get around on without four-wheel drive.
Camping: There is private camping near Bloomington at Lake Monroe Village Resort and state-owned camping at the Lake Monroe Reservoir.
Services: There are full services in Bloomington, and gas and food at the junction of IN 48 and 43.
Nearby attractions: McCormick's Creek State Park is near Spencer north of the loop.

 # The drive

The loop begins at the junction of Indiana Highways 37 and 48 in Bloomington. (Bloomington is covered in Drive 10.) Proceed west on IN 48. Mary's Children Retreat Center is 4.3 miles west, a Catholic pilgrimage site relating to a vision of the Virgin Mary in the early 1990s. A trail leads to a chapel and the pilgrimage site at the top of the hill. A large hostel retreat center is in the process of construction, in spite of official ecclesiastic disapproval.

The road follows the Richland Creek Valley. After traveling 1.2 miles west, IN 48 ends. Bear left on IN 43 South and follow a snaky road along a rim of the valley. The Greene County line is 0.5 mile farther. Greene County is the state's fourth largest in land area, stretching from the rich coalfields in the western part of the county to the chaotic hills and small ridgetop pastureland farther east. The White River bisects the sprawling county, and roughly divides the rugged forest land from the rolling farmland and coalfields of the western half.

Rosie's Diner, 2.1 miles farther, is a local hangout. The sign reads "You've got to be tough to eat here," but it relates more to one's ability to handle heavy down-home cooking. Basketball Coach Bobby Knight has been sighted here on occasion.

The town of Hendricksville is 0.2 mile past Rosie's. The sleepy appearance belies the bustle that was once here. The big business was the Hendricksville pottery shop. Five potters spun out utilitarian ware for over half a century, the wheels powered by a water wheel that also powered the local grist mill. A two-story general store served the area for many years until the pull of Bloomington merchants shut it down in the 1970s. The building serves a woodworker today.

After Hendricksville, the road ramps up and down past modest little houses perched on the ridge sides. The Union Church was an early place of worship for the settlers, and retains a devout and determined congregation. A mile farther the road opens into one of the rare broad open valleys tucked in the hills, before climbing a steep hill. There is a sharp right turn at the top of the hill with broad hilltop pastures around. To the left, a large old cemetery shares the field with several giant hay rolls parked beside it.

The Indiana Railroad underpass is 1.6 miles farther, the village of Solsberry is 0.4 mile beyond. Solsberry dates back to 1846 when the town's namesake, Solomon Wilkerson, laid out 16 lots on top of the watershed between Beech and Richland creeks. The conflict over slavery wracked the town's early years. An anti-slavery Wesleyan Methodist church was burned to the ground in the 1850s by slavery proponents, and the congregation was forced to meet in homes until long after the Civil War.

The village and surrounding hill farms subsisted on cattle, grain, and timbering until the Illinois Central came through town in 1906. With a railroad siding, the town prospered. A grain mill was built beside the tracks. Lumberyards stored the fine hardwoods for shipment to the burgeoning city markets. Buyers roamed the hills buying up cattle to ship from the stock pens beside the tracks.

Take County Road 420 North to the left of the Yoho Grocery, proceeding past the post office. The road passes over the railroad on a humpbacked wooden bridge 1 mile farther. The railroad cut down below is clue to the travails the railroad men had trying to lay a track through the hill country. The road crosses a high open ridge where the soil is more fertile than the rough surrounding ground.

The road twists for 3.6 miles, becoming CR 400 North and CR 375 North—same road, just different geopositions. A lovely ravined glade at the

Drive 12: Autumn Loop II

Southern Indiana: Bloomington through eastern Greene County

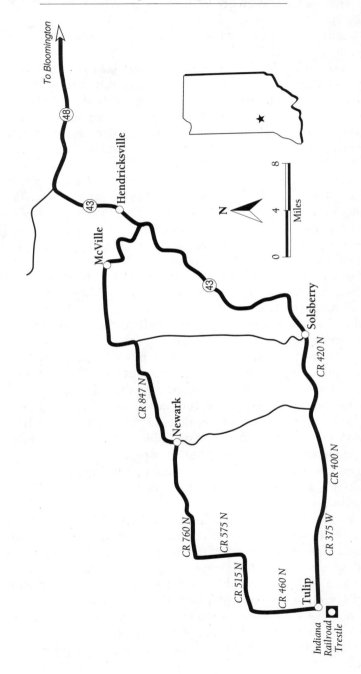

junction of CR 375 North and CR 580 East offers a glimpse into the sylvan beauty of the forested hill.

The road makes an abrupt turn 0.6 mile farther at CR 475 East. Stay on the blacktop.

Continue down the hill into the Richland Creek valley, crossing an old iron bridge.

Look to the left for the remarkable Indiana Railroad trestle. Built in 1906 by Italian laborers, the 2,295-foot-long trestle rises 157 feet over the stream. The 18 daddy-long-legs supporting steel columns rest on steel-reinforced concrete foundations that are 8 feet wide at the base. More than 167,000 board-feet of pine was used for the decking. Even with the steel workers making 30 cents an hour, and laborers half that, the viaduct cost the Illinois Central Railroad $1.5 million.

Return back up the road to the gravel road at CR 475 East and turn left onto it. Drive 0.9 mile after the turnoff to an intersection. Turn right on County Road 460 North and drive along forest glades choked with springtime mayapples and spreads of trout lilies. Continue on through a small valley 1.4 miles past the last intersection and bear right up CR 515 North.

An early oral history of this part of Greene County noted that one of the first weddings among the settlers was between Miss Mouren Martin and Big Issac Stalcup, who was described as a drinking man and a widower. According to the tale, he sold his first wife for a fur hat and 10 gallons of whiskey, and she and her new betrothed floated down the White River on a water craft.

A Christmas tree farm and a flock of well-tended sheep 0.7 mile farther connote better land. The road becomes CR 575 North in another 0.8 mile, and a few rustic hill farms appear on the ridgetop.

At the intersection of CR 760 East and CR 575 North, turn left onto the blacktop. The hamlet of Newark is 1.4 miles ahead. Newark (pronounced New Ark) was named after Newark, Ohio, at its founding in 1859. At one time, there were three grocery stores, a post office, a telephone exchange, and two churches. The churches remain, but the falling down buildings and the payday cash advance loan store are evidence that the good times are behind them.

Turn right at the intersection of CR 735 East and CR 760 North toward the New Ark Pentecostal Church. A tidy hilltop farm with a country Gothic farmhouse and a small family cemetery is 0.5 mile farther. The road passes second-growth forest and a large derelict barn, a vivid memory that at the turn of the century all of the forest land was tilled and enough fodder and provender were raised to justify the size of the barn.

At the intersection of CR 985 East and CR 840 North, 2.8 miles from Newark, bear to the right. Deep woods are on either side of the road. The tall green McVille water tower and a newly painted red barn announce the former town. McVille, named after founder Henry McHaley, stood at the junction of the State Ferry Road that leads down to White River to the right of the intersection. Little has been left of the town for many decades.

Twist along a ridgetop and curl back down 2.6 miles to the Richland Creek valley at Hendricksville. Liberty Church of Christ dates back to 1850. The current 1985 church replaces one built in 1868. Turn left on IN 43 and drive 2.8 miles back to the IN 48 junction and bear right back to Bloomington, which is another 8 miles.

Eastern Indiana

13

Early Indiana: The Whitewater Valley
New Trenton through the Whitewater River Valleys

General description: The 65-mile tour loops through the region of some of Indiana's earliest regions of settlement in the valleys of the state's swiftest and steepest stream.

Special attractions: In Brookville: historic architecture and canoe rentals. In Metamora: Whitewater Canal State Historic Site. In Oldenburg: historic architecture.

Location: Southeastern Indiana.

Drive route numbers and names: U.S. Highway 52, Indiana highways 121, 229, 46, and 101 (St. Mary's Road).

Travel season: The good all-weather blacktops should allow travel in all but periods of deep snow. Canal Days in Metamora bring many thousands to the old canal town, making visits a crowded festival event.

Camping: There are state campgrounds at Whitewater Memorial State Park and Brookville Lake. There are private facilities at Brookville's Scenic Campground, Metamora's MacLyn Campground, and Batesville's Indian Lakes.

Services: There are full services in Brookville, Metamora, Connersville and Batesville. Gas and food are available in Cambridge City, Knightstown, and other small towns en route.

Nearby attractions: Whitewater Memorial State Park, Brookville Lake, Richmond.

 The drive

The drive begins at the south end of U.S. Highway 52 near New Trenton, the gateway to the scenic Whitewater Valley. While Indians long inhabited the valley, leaving their pre-Columbian mounds on heights above the river and its tributaries, New Trenton is one of the earliest European-American towns, settled by those who made their way up from the Ohio and nearby Cincinnati. The first pioneers arrived in 1803, platting the town in 1816.

The Whitewater River is the state's steepest and swiftest, dropping from the highest point in the state in two forks that rush southward in valleys that parallel one another until they join at Brookville. The river continues south in a shallow rock-filled stream to the Miami River near Cincinnati. Big-shouldered hills hulk over much of the narrow valley.

When the state of Indiana embarked on the Mammoth Internal Improvement Program of turnpike, railroad, and canal building in 1836, the Whitewater Canal was the first project, since the valley had a quarter of the state's citizens and the most political clout. Indiana finished 20 miles of the canal, until the vast expansion's voodoo economics did the state in, and

Drive 13: Early Indiana: The Whitewater Valley
New Trenton through the Whitewater River Valleys

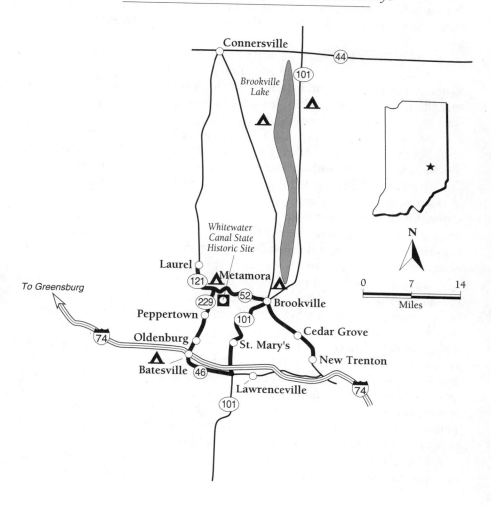

bankruptcy was declared. A private corporation finished the balance of the canal up to Cambridge City on the National Road in 1846, and Hagerstown a few miles north dug their own channel to join it in Cambridge City.

Floods roaring down the steep valley in 1847 and 1848, washed out major sections of the channel, as well as aqueducts and locks, causing $200,000 of damage. But the ultimate problem was the arrival of the railroad that offered dependable all-season transport of goods and passengers. Eventually the canal company collapsed and the railroads took over the towpath for their roadbed. U.S. Highway 52 parallels the river and the path of the Whitewater Canal for 31 miles northwest.

New Trenton's two taverns, the Rockafellar and the Manwarring were popular stops for the canal workers. Thomas Manwarring double-tasked with his tavern, dispensing hard liquor through the week and preaching to the assembled pioneers on Sunday from the steps of the tavern. The two-story brick tavern was located on the left side of New Trenton's only side street.

Cedar Grove is 11.6 miles north on US 52. Little Cedar Grove Baptist Church is the state's oldest, and is still on its original foundation. It is constructed of hand-hewn timbers with a brick exterior. Rows of slots in the second-story exterior speak of its early history. The parishioners used the slots as rifle ports in pioneering days.

Brookville, the county seat for picturesque Franklin County, sits on a bluff at the junction of the east and west forks of the Whitewater River. It was founded in 1808 and became the county seat in 1811. The location of the Federal land office fueled the town's growth as settlers flocked into the territory following the signing of the Indian treaties. When the land office moved north to Indianapolis in 1825, a number of town luminaries, including several future governors, went with it. The site is at 766 Main Street. Nearby, between Sixth and Seventh Streets on the west side of Main Street, a plaque notes the site of an early Indian trading post.

For the most part, Brookville has basked gently in the valley air for the last half-century, with enough money to maintain its canal-days' structures, but not enough to build anew, giving the town today an ambient nineteenth-century feel.

The Whitewater Valley emerged as one of Indiana's art colonies at the turn of the century. While the "Richmond School" became dominant, Brookville was the home of a number of celebrated artists, including some who later came to fame in Brown County. T. C. Steele, Indiana's preeminent Impressionist, owned the Hermitage on Eighth Street with J. Ottis Adams. Fellow artists William Forsyth and Otto Stark were frequent visitors.

The site of the Brookville College, established in 1852, is at Tenth and Franklin, a block east of Main Street. It originally was organized as a female academy and several of the state's notable women were graduates.

The Governor Ray House at 210 East Tenth was the home of James Brown Ray, Indiana's governor from 1825 to 1831. The ornate Palladium-style window almost cost him the election, as opponents said it proved he was too high-faluting to be governor of the state. Ray was elected as a proponent of the Mammoth Internal Improvement bill, but broke with the group over the Wabash and Erie Canal. Ray correctly foresaw the advantages of railroads, though the fight destroyed his political career. Not a shy fellow, he is said to have always signed hotel registers, "J. Brown Ray, Governor of Indiana and Commander-in-Chief of the Army and Navy thereof."

Proceed 8 miles west on US 52 to Metamora, an old canal town. In its heyday in the 1840s, several gristmills and factories were located here. When the canal company lapsed and the railroad took over the towpath, the town grittily hung on. But the discontinuation of passenger service in the 1930s and the relocation of US 52 outside of town sent it into a decline.

The state jump-started the town in the 1940s with the establishment of the Whitewater Canal State Historic Site, which rebuilt 14 miles of canal from Metamora to the dam at Laurel and took over the Metamora Grist and Roller Mill. The 14-ton, 44-foot-long *Ben Franklin* plies the waterway, drawn by horses down the old towpath. The Duck Creek Aqueduct is a rare surviving example of what was once common on the canals—a long water-filled covered bridge that allowed the canal boats to pass over the streams they encountered. The 60-foot-long bridge originally built in 1846, levitates 16 feet over Duck Creek.

A number of vintage structures remain in the little tourist town. The Banes House a block east of the mill is a Federal-style house built in the 1840s. Across the street, the three-story building is the 1853 Odd Fellows Lodge. Farther east, the Martindale Hotel dates back to 1838, built by a shipping agent for the canal boats.

Proceed west 3 miles to IN 121 North. A tall red barn on a green hillock, stands just north of the intersection. Drive 3.7 miles past manicured fields and soft hills along the river valley to Laurel, another canal town with a feeder dam and an enormous turning basin that can be seen beside the new bridge over the Whitewater. The canal that arrived in 1843 was the late-comer to the town's transportation. The Whetzel Trace began at Laurel and blazed across the country to the White River Bluffs near Waverly in Morgan County in 1819. It was an important east-west trail for the settlers. A pre-Columbian Indian mound at the north edge of town indicates even earlier pioneers.

A building boom erupted when the canal arrived in 1843. Remnants can still be seen, including the Federal-style White Hall Tavern that sits above the old turning basin at Baltimore and Franklin Streets. The 1850 Laurel Hotel at Franklin and Pearl Streets is the only east-facing building in town.

Return to US 52 and drive east for 1.7 miles to IN 229 South. The road is a roller coaster through sycamores and old hemlock. Cupp's Chapel, 2 miles later, is a simple board-and-batten country church ennobled by a Greek Revival cornice. Peppertown is 4.4 miles south of US 52. The red-brick St. Nicholas Lutheran Church anchors the town, and the rustic limestone buildings tell of the Peppertown masons' skill. It was founded in 1851 when August Pepper began a store and tavern in his limestone house on Beacon Road. The lane has other 1830s and 1840s examples of primitive rubble-stone masonry. The two-story limestone building at the corner of IN 229 and Beacon Road is a Federal-style structure built in 1860.

Five miles south of Peppertown, the many spires of Oldenburg rise from a bucolic landscape. German immigrants flooded into surrounding southeastern Franklin County in a great migration in 1832 and 1833, fleeing the economic chaos of post–Napoleonic War Europe. The emigrants, known as *auswanderers,* platted Oldenburg in 1837. The devout settlers built so many massive churches that the town became known as the "Village of Spires."

The huge barn on the left coming into town is known as the Sisters' Cow Barn as it is owned by the Convent of the Immaculate Conception. A Franciscan monastery flourished here from 1894 untill 1981. Today the town is still a Teutonic throwback, with many of the old rubble–stone houses still standing and the street signs in German.

The enormous, brooding Holy Family Church was built in 1861, the third church erected by the indefatigable Father Josef Rudolph, the pastor of Oldenburg from 1844 to 1866. The Franciscan convent and monastery surrounded the massive brick structure until the monastery was razed in 1984.

The elaborate tin-work of the King's Tavern on Pearl Street is a fine example of Prussian-born tinsmith Casper Gaupel, who worked in town in the 1860s. The Oldenburg Flower Shop at Hauptstrasse and Fernending (Main and Pearl) Streets was the old Hackman's General Store. It has Gaupel's ornate tin fancies in the eaves and cornices.

The stone Town Hall between the tavern and Schweineschwanz Gasse (Pigtail Alley) was built in 1878 as a fire station. Next door, the 1845 Huegal Tavern has a well-carved sun and moon above the lintel. The Waechter House on Wasser Strasse (Water Street) has a remarkable carved and curlicued balcony that cantilevers from the brick house. Wasser Strasse has the earliest houses in town, clapboard structures that include medieval European wattle-and-daub construction. The house and blacksmith shop at IN 229 and Wasser Strasse are both of this type, though the shop dates to 1880 and the house to 1836, a testimony to the enduring customs of the town.

Batesville is 2.6 miles south on IN 229. It's a johnny-come-lately town for the area, laid out in 1852 when the railroad arrived. The dense hardwood forests attracted German craftsmen and timber buyers, primarily from the industrial boomtown of Cincinnati. The Hillenbrand family was one of the leaders of the town, as they are now, the scions of the family industries which include casket, hospital-equipment, insurance, and furniture companies.

The Sherman House at Main and George Streets dates from the town founding and has been a favorite stop since. The hotel escaped one of the town's periodic infernos in 1872 by the piling of salt bags on the roof. Today it is decorated in a faux Bavarian-Viennese style, but the food is still renowned.

The Weberding Carving Shop is a throwback to the days of artisanal carving, producing still elaborate wood statues and industrial models by hand. It is located 1 mile east on IN 46. They welcome visitors.

Proceed east on IN 46 to IN 101 North. The town of Lawrenceville is 3.2 miles farther east on IN 46. Turn right on Lawrenceville Road to the Schoettelkotte Bros. Grocery Store, which has served the area's German farm families since 1922 in a rustic old white Italianate building. Return to IN 101 North.

Proceeding north on IN 101 over the Interstate, the road becomes St. Marys Road. Bear left at the Y, 1 mile farther north where a small hand-painted sign points the way to St. Marys. The road that leads to Brookville begins in a ravined woodland and suddenly opens up into a land of hills and dales as lovely as the Yorkshire hills. Prosperous farm buildings peek from tidy fields.

St. Marys' prim Victorian Gothic steeple emerges from the green hills and forests. It is another mid-nineteenth-century German village with fine masonry rubblestone and brick homes. Most of the town's structures were built from 1850 to 1870. Oak Forest, 2 miles east, has a general store and St. Cecilla of Rome Catholic Church with a white striped steeple like St. Marys. Log cabins and upright brick homes intersperse as the road drops down to a sycamore-lined stream. A historic marker notes the boundary lines of the 1795 Treaty of Greenville, Ohio, and the 1805 Treaty of Grouseland.

Running along the valley, the road leads across the Whitewater onto Brookville's West Sixth Street which intersects US 52.

Drive 14: The Old National Road
Richmond to Indianapolis

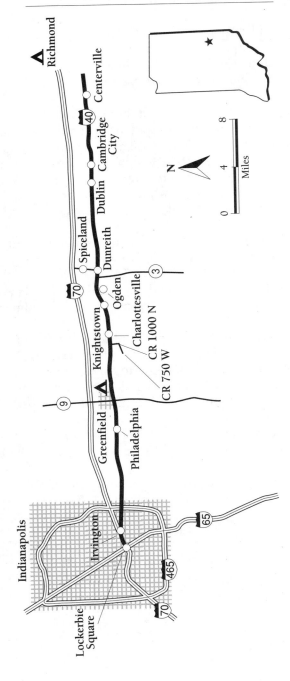

14

The Old National Road
Richmond to Indianapolis

General description: The 70-mile drive courses along the route of the first road from the eastern seaboard into the heartland of the United States.

Special attractions: In Richmond: Madonna of the Trail Statue. In Centerville: Federal-era buildings and Antique Alley. In Cambridge City: Whitewater Canal architecture. In Knightstown: Knightstown Academy. In Greenfield: James Whitcomb Riley Birthplace. In Indianapolis: Irvington, James Whitcomb Riley Home.

Location: Eastern and central Indiana.

Drive route numbers and names: U.S. Highway 40, County Roads 1000 North and 985 East.

Travel season: The highway is fine for travel in all seasons barring heavy, unplowed snow. For the most part, US 40 parallels the truck-clogged Interstate 70. Driving time on the National Road from the state line to the edge of Indianapolis is almost the same and much less nerve-racking.

Camping: In Richmond: Deer Ridge Camping Resort and Richmond KOA; In Greenfield: Heartland Resort, Indianapolis KOA, and S&H Campground; In Indianapolis: Indiana State Fairgrounds Campground and Raceview Family Campground.

Services: There are full services, hotels, restaurants, shopping, movies, etc. in Richmond, Greenfield, and Indianapolis. Gas and food are available in Cambridge City, Knightstown, and other small towns en route.

Nearby attractions: Whitewater Memorial State Park, Brookville Lake, Metamora Canal State Historic Site, and Indianapolis attractions.

 The drive

The National Road was authorized by an act of Congress in 1806 to stimulate settlement of public lands in the West, as the heartland was known in the early days of the Republic. Leaders dating back to George Washington saw the need to connect the populous East with the lands newly opened to settlement.

Crews moving westward from the terminus at Cumberland, Maryland, surveyed and graveled to the Ohio at Wheeling, West Virginia, by 1818 and reached Columbus, Ohio, in 1835. When the federal government turned over the road to the states in 1839, Indiana, still smarting from the canal bust, leased the Hoosier section to a private company who paved it with thick planks, making one of the best wagon roads in the world—until the planks rotted, that is.

By 1850, Irish laborers and local farmers paved the Indiana road in the most modern means available, macadamization. The process, invented by a Scottish engineer, consisted of layers of stone starting with 7-inch rocks laid a foot below the surface and graded up with smaller stones mixed with soil and crowned for drainage.

Down the road through the 1840s and '50s, stage coaches thundered to the inns that dotted the road every 5 miles or so. Mail coaches announced their imminent arrival with blasts of their trumpets; postmasters raced out to throw the bag. Looking like an odd land-bound craft, settlers' and pikemen's canvas-covered Conestoga wagons sailed across the prairie, pulled by solid teams of six horses. Whole towns in the East pulled up stakes and moved West, drawn by the lure of cheap land and a new life, passing through the little pike towns of Indiana which grew properous on the trade.

The drive begins at the Ohio-Indiana state line 0.6 mile east of Richmond. (Richmond is covered in depth in Drive 15.) The two-lane–covered National Bridge across the Whitewater Gorge was considered one of the engineering marvels of the age—the finest span from Maryland to St. Louis. Building commenced in 1833 and finished in 1835. It was an elegant entrance into Richmond until it closed in 1893.

The Madonna of the Trail Statue in Richmond at the entrance to Glen Miller Park at 22nd and East Main Streets is a 10-foot-high, 5-ton statue of a pioneer woman striding forward. Looking stolidly off into the future, she holds one babe to her breast while her young son clutches at the hem of her dress. One of the four plaques on the base notes that Indiana's first tollgate was located nearby.

Gray Gables, a large gray-painted stucco structure on the south side of the road 2 miles from the edge of Richmond, was a National Road tavern and inn and later a private home for the county's mentally retarded citizens. Two derelict two-story I-houses just past the Gray Gables are reputed to have been Underground Railroad stops.

Centerville is 3.9 miles west of downtown Richmond. The town was platted in 1814 and became a major town on the National Road. As many as 40,000 wagons passed through the town in the pre–Civil War heyday of the National Road.

Centerville is an architectural restatement of Eastern sensibilities, more resonant to Maryland Federal styles than the Hoosier state's. Brick row houses with shared sidewalls walled off the back spaces from egress, so the old tidewater habit of arched passageways were added. Today seven of the original eleven remain. The Lantz House Inn Bed and Breakfast at 214 West

The Huddleston Farm House Inn Museum is a restored stop along the Old National Road.
Photo courtesy of Wayne County CVB.

Main is an excellent example—the arch leading into what was a nineteenth-century version of a well-equipped truck stop: a wagon-making and blacksmith business that could repair any wagon or horse ill you might have, or sell you a new one. The space above was the local Oddfellows lodge.

The Mansion House Inn, 214 East Main Street, is an 1840 Greek Revival former stagecoach stop. Today it is the home of Historic Centerville, Inc.

The old Sheriff's House at East Main and First Streets bears the mark of Centerville's last hurrah as the County seat. When two men from Centerville heard the news that the court records were to be moved to Richmond, they fired a cannon load of iron scraps from an archway across the way from the mouth of locally celebrated Black Betty. It scared off the jailer, but the state militiamen restored order and conveyed the ledgers to Richmond. The scars of the last battle can still be seen in the brickwork above the door.

Today, the town center feels much as it did when the republic was young and Indiana was still the West. Over a 100 buildings are on the National Register of Historic Places. The two-story Federal-style home at 214 West Main Street was the home of Israel Abram, Jewish pioneer and merchant. The first floor was a wagon shop and the Masonic Lodge met in the room above. The Morton Home at the southeast corner of West Main and Willow Grove was the one-time home of Civil War Governor Oliver P. Morton.

Antique dealers discovered the town in the 1960s, and now Centerville is known as the beginning of "Antique Alley of Indiana"—a 33-mile stretch of U.S. Highway 40 where more than 900 antique dealers offer their wares.

Pennville and East Germantown, 6 and 7.6 miles west, respectively, have sprinklings of early architecture, some uninhabited, most down at the heels.

The old Whitewater Canal town of Cambridge City differs from other Wayne County towns both in ethnic make-up (it has few Quakers and is mainly German) and age. The town was incorporated in 1841 to take advantage of the coming Whitewater Canal, which arrived in 1846. The old Vinton Hotel at 22 West Main Street was a stagecoach and canal boat stop, beginning in the late 1840s. One sidewall was angled for a canal-side location. The Bertschland Family Practice building at East Church and South Center Streets was once an 1853 canal boat repair shop.

At 520 East Church Street in Cambridge City, the Lackey-Overbeck House is the oldest and perhaps most illustrious house in town. The Federal-style house was built in the late 1830s and was the home—from 1911 to 1955—to the six Overbeck Sisters who produced the highly collectable Arts and Crafts Overbeck Pottery. The kiln was just west of the house. The Museum of Overbeck Art Pottery at 33 West Main Street preserves the memory of Cambridge City's most famous artists and has examples of their wares.

The Huddleston Farmhouse Inn Museum is a period restoration of the National Road enterprise built in the road's heyday. Unlike most inns of the day that readily served "strong waters to relieve the inhabitants," the temperate Quaker Huddlestons didn't serve liquor.

While the road declined with the advent of the railroad, the Huddlestons continued to prosper with their rich farmland and business dealings. Accordingly, the next generations of Huddlestons spiffed up the austere three-story Federal structure with the Victorian trappings of the day, which include the louvered Italianate cupolas on the barn. The Historic Landmark Foundation of Indiana, a preservation organization, now operates the house as a museum and community center.

Dublin is just down the road. While the name may relate to Ireland, locals say the teamster's habit of adding another team of horses at this point—"doublin"—because the next stretch of road was exceptionally rough is more likely the origin. An early tavern, the Maples, stood at the corner of US 40 and Middletown Road. In the boom years, 12 stagecoach lines operated over the pike.

At Dublin, US 40 becomes a four-lane highway and Dunreith is 11 miles west. The original name of Coffin's Station, named after town founder Emery Dunreith Coffin, thankfully gave way to Dunreith in 1865.

Centerville on the National Road is a redoubt of eastern-style Federal architecture.
Photo courtesy of Wayne County CVB.

A two-lane remnant of the original National Road connects Dunreith and Knightstown. Turn south on Water Street in Dunreith and follow the contours of the land through woods and fields as nineteenth-century travelers did.

North 2.2 miles on IN 3 is Spiceland, home of the former Quaker Spiceland Academy, which began in 1827 and was a renowned educational institution. The eminent American historian, Charles A. Beard, was a graduate of the academy. Return to US 40.

A bowl of blue sky hangs over a slender line of soothing landscape. The highway runs across what appears to be the distinctly flat Tipton Till, though in reality it is gently undulating swells and swales, the result of the Wisconsinan Age glaciers that left rich black soil reaching as much as 40 feet deep, one of the earth's most fertile places.

Knightstown, 4 miles west, was named for the government engineer responsible for this section of the National Road. A rest stop spring at the east end of town has quenched travelers on the road since the 1830s. While the state board of health advises against using the water, it appears locals are ignoring the warning.

Turn north on Washington Street, past the mini mall built in 1976 to honor the bicentennial. A proud vestige of the Automobile Age sits shining on the corner of Washington and Brown, a vintage Spanish Revival Texaco station in perfect condition, replete with vintage pumps, tiled roof, and glazed cream brick.

Proceed 0.3 mile to Cary Street, then turn right to Adams Street. The three-story, Second Empire–style Knightstown Academy was built in 1876 and served as a luminary private school for many years. The city converted it into a public school when the private school folded. The 40-foot-high twin towers have immense models of a globe and a telescope at their peaks, symbolizing education and science.

Return to US 40 and drive west 0.5 mile to 517 West Main, the former home of John J. Lehmanowski, a French-Polish clergyman who also served as a colonel in Napoleon's Imperial Guard and saw action in Spain, Russia, and at Waterloo.

Charlottesville, 4.3 miles west, is on Rush County's northern line. It is another fertile, well-watered agricultural county, with more than 90 percent of the county under cultivation. Turn south in falling-down little Charlottesville and drive 2 miles to County Road 1000 North. Turn left and drive 1.7 miles to CR 725 West. A long lane 0.3 mile later leads to Beech Church, which served a congregation of free African Americans who migrated to the area in the 1830s at the behest of local Quakers. The congregation voted in 1832 to merge their affiliations and join the African Methodist Church (AME). The Indiana AME was organized here in 1840. The present white clapboard structure was erected in 1860 to replace an 1838 log church. Yearly homecomings have taken place since 1914.

Return to US 40 and continue west. Cleveland, 1 mile farther west of Charlottesville, is more farm country with healthy looking cattle and horses with glistening coats. Prosperous farms line the road.

The Hoosier Poet Motel is the harbinger of Greenfield, birthplace of famous Hoosier poet James Whitcomb Riley. The motel itself speaks of passing days, an example of roadside architecture that stretches back to the 1950s when ones like it lined the highways coast-to-coast.

The James Whitcomb Riley Home at 250 West Main Street resonates the cozy family life that suffuses so much of Riley's poetry. Built in 1849–50 by Riley's father, Reuben, the house is a two-story clapboard house with Italianate styling. The interior with period Victoriana and warm walnut trim exudes a homey charm. Since 1937 the house has been a historic site.

The Hancock County Courthouse statue of Riley presents him in academic robes and his fusty pince-nez, somewhat inappropriate for a poet of the uneducated populace. It represents his honorary doctorate he received from Indiana University in 1907. The courthouse itself was built in 1896–1898 in a Gothic-Romanesque blend.

The James Whitcomb Riley Memorial Park was dedicated in 1925. The Old Log Jail Museum is the mid-nineteenth-century county lockup. The 1865 Old Chapel next to the jail is a white frame United Methodist church, relocated from nearby Philadelphia in 1980.

Philadelphia is 3.6 miles west, formerly an important stage stop for National Road travelers. It was also the former home of Mrs. Mary Alice Gray, the childhood playmate of Riley and the model for his famous poem "Little Orphan Annie." To see her house, proceed west 0.8 mile from Philadephia on US 40 to Spring Lake Road and turn south 0.8 mile. The white frame house is on the right.

Modern America rapidly replaced heritage landscapes as the exurban bulge of Indianapolis reached out into the prairie. Cumberland, named after the eastern terminus of the National Road, is primarily a modest bedroom community of Indianapolis. The mammoth Washington Square Mall is soon after, the first of the capital city's necklace of suburban shopping malls.

Proceeding west into Indianapolis on Washington Avenue (US 40) is a trip backward in time from the postmodern shopping malls. The tiny turn-of-the-century neighborhood of Irvington is a quiet residential place dotted with low-scale tile-roofed shopping arcades. In 1987 the entire community of some 2,000 structures was put on the National Register of Historic Places. The styles range from Second Empire, Classical, and Queen Anne to Arts and Crafts and Prairie Style. Walking tour maps can be purchased from the Irvington Landmarks Foundation at 312 South Downey Street.

The campus of Butler University was on Downey Street along with the nationally renowned School of Missions that trained Protestant missionaries to carry the gospel into far-flung lands. For many years, it was the only place in the country where languages like Tibetan were taught.

Return to Washington Street and drive west through a gauntlet of ramshackle pawn shops, used car lots, car repair places, small ethnic cafes, rough looking bars, and vintage commercial buildings. A pair of cowled stone gnomes clutch books beside the front doors of the Marion County library on the north side of Washington at Rural Streets.

At Park Avenue, turn north to Lockerbie Street and turn west again to the center of Lockerbie Square and back into the mid-nineteenth century. Lockerbie Square was settled in 1830, and in the 1860s the more substantial homes of the well-to-do began to be interspersed with the cottages of local artisans.

The area owes its survival to James Whitcomb Riley's last home which is located at 528 Lockerbie Street. He moved into the home of his friends, the Holsteins, in 1893 and spent the last 23 years of his life there. Following his death in 1916 (and the subsequent death of the Holsteins), a group of his influential friends arranged to purchase the home and turn it into a museum, and it has been a tourist destination since. All of the furnishings and art that accompanied Riley in his last years are still there, along with his top hat, piano, and the painting of his beloved dog, Lockerbie. The house was placed on the National Register of Historic Places in 1963 and it formed the anchor of Lockerbie Square.

Beginning in the 1960s, the neighborhood underwent a startling renaissance from a low-end rental area with moldering and collapsing houses to one of Indianapolis's most prestigious residential areas.

15

Underground Railroad
Through Wayne County exploring the Quaker Heritage and the Underground Railroad

General description: The 55-mile drive explores Richmond and Fountain City with their Quaker traditions and a loop through Wayne County and a bit of Randolph.

Special attractions: In Richmond: Earlham College, Samuel Charles Home, Wayne County Historical Museum, Gennett Records Site, Old Richmond and Starr Historic Districts. In Fountain City: the Levi Coffin State Historic Site.

Location: Eastern Indiana.

Drive route numbers and names: U.S. Highways 40, 27, and 36; Indiana Highways 227, 35, and 1; Arba Pike; County Roads 600 South, 800 East, and 850 East.

Travel season: The roads are fine for travel in all seasons barring heavy unplowed snow.

Camping: There are campgrounds at Richmond: Deer Ridge Camping Resort and Richmond KOA. The state has campgrounds at Whitewater Memorial State Park and Brookville Lake.

Services: There are full services, hotels, restaurants, shopping, movies, etc., in Richmond. Gas and food are available in Fountain City, Hagerstown, and Cambridge City.

Nearby attractions: Whitewater Memorial State Park, Brookville Lake, Metamora Canal State Historic Site, and Centerville.

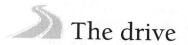 The drive

The Great Quaker Migration into Wayne County began in 1806 when North Carolina Quakers settled in former Indian hunting and fishing grounds at the Whitewater River Gorge. They were the first of a vast flow of southern Quakers who escaped the South's "peculiar institution" of slavery to help pioneer the free state of Indiana. So many Quakers moved north through western Virginia and Ohio that it became known as "the Quaker Trace."

By 1821 the Whitewater Friends Meeting had grown to become the Indiana Yearly Meeting with jurisdiction that stretched to the Pacific, encompassing more than 14,000 Quakers. Richmond and Wayne County became the country's second largest concentration of Quakers behind only Philadelphia—a distinction the area still holds.

The large aggregate of Quakers naturally made Wayne County a hot bed of abolitionism in the decades before the Civil War, though the region was by no means unanimous in the tactics to be used. There were several wings of the anti-slavery movement, which ranged from gradualists who argued slavery could be eliminated over time to lessen the economic blow to the South, to anti-slavery groups who argued for immediate manumission without compensation to the slave owners.

The Quakers entered their feelings in the national debate in 1842 when slave-owning Henry Clay addressed a crowd of 20,000 at the corner of Seventh and A streets in Richmond. A local businessman gave Clay a petition signed by 2,000 Richmond Quakers asking him to free his slaves. Clay snorted that his 50 slaves were worth $15,000 and asked his hecklers if he were to free them would they raise the money for recompense. He concluded by suggesting that the petitioner should go home and mind his own business. The local Quakers have long suggested that resulting national uproar cost Clay his presidential contest with Polk, though historians have had to dissuade them of the idea.

The Underground Railroad, the shadowy organization which helped spirit fugitive slaves from the South to freedom in Canada, was the extreme wing of the Abolitionist movement. There were several main routes north to Canada. A major route from the Upper South slave states of Kentucky and Tennessee drove north through Ohio and Indiana. Slaves moved at night, always keeping the North Star as their guide. Once they negotiated the Ohio River, often with the help of Freemen who lived in the northern border towns, the fugitives were helped northward by a network of Underground Railroaders.

The various fugitive slave laws that culminated in the particularly onerous Fugitive Slave Law of 1850 made cooperation with the Underground Railroad strictly illegal and subject to severe punishment and confiscation. In Wayne County, the anti-slavery controversy and other sectarian fights tore the Quaker community apart. From the late 1820s, there were competing meetinghouses in town, each certain of their beliefs. In Fountain City (known as Newport then), the leaders of the Underground Railroad, including Levi Coffin who was termed the President of the railroad, were expelled from the New Garden Meeting, the oldest Quaker meeting, for what was perceived as illegal and extremist activities.

The drive begins in Richmond, home of Earlham College, which was founded in 1847. The college is located in the 1000 block of West National Road (US 40). It is the third largest Quaker college after Friends House in

Drive 15: Underground Railroad

*Through Wayne County exploring the Quaker Heritage
and the Underground Railroad*

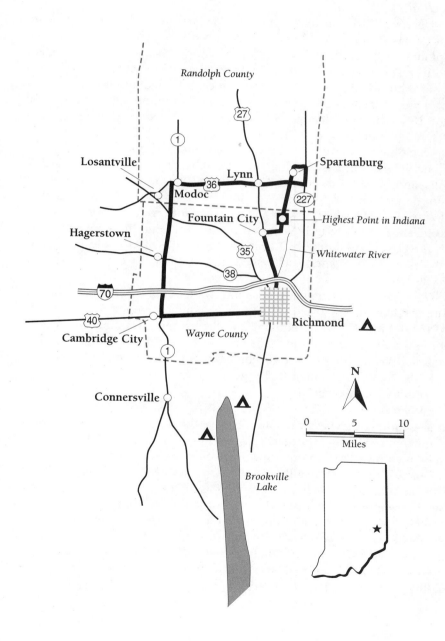

Randolph County

Losantville

Lynn

Spartanburg

Modoc

Fountain City

Highest Point in Indiana

Hagerstown

Whitewater River

Richmond

Cambridge City

Wayne County

Connersville

N

0   5   10
Miles

Brookville
Lake

London and Haverford College in Philadelphia. There are currently 1,200 students and 60 pastoral students with a particular concentration in peace studies and the sciences. The Joseph Moore Museum of Natural History on the south side of the campus holds a packrat's dream of diverse items, from a 15,000-year-old Mastodon skeleton to an Egyptian mummy to a live snake collection.

Nearby at 1150 North A Street, the Wayne County Historical Museum holds the other mummy in town, as well as airplanes, jazz recording exhibits, pioneering roller skates, exotic bikes, and fine early autos. It's a giant curiosity case of Wayne County's early entrepreneurial activities and the collections of the resulting nabobs. A thirteenth-century Buddha head graces the front lawn, serenely meditating on the passing Richmond scene. It is housed in the 1865 Hicksite Meeting Houses, one of the sectarian congregations that sprang up before the Civil War.

The Starr Historic District which surrounds the museum is on the National Register of Historic Places. It stretches from North A to North E Streets, and from North 10th to North 16th. It has long been the home of the local elite. The Andrew F. Scott Home was built in 1858, an Italianate structure at 126 North 10th which is now an annex to the county museum, an excellent example of early Victorian architecture. High Tower at 326 North 10th Street was the home of Elizabeth Starr, wife of an early Richmond promoter. Her son, James, established the Starr Piano Company and also lived in the house.

The Starr Piano Company was long-lived, but one of their smaller enterprises remains one of Richmond's claims to fame. Gennett Records began in 1916, and in 1922 was producing 3 million records annually. From 1916 to 1934 the Richmond studio made jazz history, recording luminaries like Jelly Roll Morton, King Oliver's Creole Jazz Band with a young Louis Armstrong, the New Orleans Rhythm Kings, and Tommy Dorsey with Bix Beiderbeck and his Jazz Wolverines.

When trains rumbled by on the nearby tracks, recording would have to cease, though a few early recordings have the tremor of passing boxcars. A fragment of the last of the Starr's 31 buildings, which still has the Gennett sign painted on it, can be seen by going south on South First Street at the east end of East Main Street Bridge.

The Whitewater Valley Gorge Park is at the bottom of the Ice Age canyon where the Whitewater River has cut through the ancient limestone and shale. It is renowned as a fossil-hunters' haven, a great source of trilobites, brachiads, and corals. The rubble piles in the park are free game for collectors. The gorge was originally the site of early industrial Richmond, and remains of a woolen mill, an electric power dam, and a remnant Starr Building are in the valley.

A young visitor peeks from the hidden passage where escaped slaves once waited at the Levi Coffin House in Fountain City. Photo courtesy of Wayne County CVB.

Another early neighborhood, the Old Richmond Historic District between South A and South East Streets and South 11th Street and the railroad is a mixed commercial, residential, and industrial neighborhood. The upright homes and buildings speak of the German immigrants who migrated to Richmond in the 1840s and 1850s. Their stern rectitude and lack of ostentation fit well with the Quakers' simple esthetics and lifestyle.

The Gaar Mansion at 2411 Pleasant View Road reflects another esthetic entirely. It is an opulent, mansard-roofed mansion with a remarkable collection of elaborate turn-of-the-century furnishings. The tiles on the roof modestly spell out "A. Gaar," the proprietor's name. The Gaars were steam-thresher tycoons who were benefactors of Richmond. The house with many of its original furnishings is now a museum.

The Pennsylvania Railroad Depot on North E Street between Nineth and 10th Streets is one of Daniel Burnham's masterpieces (famous for his

Washington D.C. Union Station design), a 1902 Roman Renaissance fancy. The two-story, red-brick classical columns are particularly rare.

The Richmond Art Association dates back to 1898 when a local group organized to encourage popular appreciation in art. The McGuire Memorial Hall was opened in 1941 as an addition to Richmond High School, 350 Whitewater Boulevard, in the hopes it will kindle a love of art in the malleable students. Since then the association and the museum have been stalwarts in art appreciation for a wide swath of Indiana and neighboring Ohio. The curvilinear tiled space has four galleries filled with diverse art, with particular strengths in Indiana Impressionists and Overbeck art pottery.

East of downtown, the Glen Miller Park is a 194-acre urban grove with picnic grounds and recreational facilities as well as an award-winning rose garden. Farther east, the E. G. Hill Memorial Rose Garden is a blooming wonder, with more than 70 rose varieties.

The Samuel Charles Home directly behind the garden was built in 1813 of gray stone and stucco by a North Carolina Quaker. Reportedly the parlor's flagstone fireplace had a removable section that led to hidden cellar steps where fugitive slaves could hide.

Proceed from Richmond on U.S. Highway 27 North, 8.9 miles to Fountain City. It was originally named New Garden City in 1818 when it was laid out by North Carolina. The tidy brick church just south of Fountain City at New Garden Road is one of the earliest in the county and is still used for worship.

During the national upheaval over slavery prior to the Civil War, the small town was called the "Grand Central Station of the Underground Railroad," with local storekeeper Levi Coffin its president. As many as 2,000 fleeing slaves made their way from Cincinnati, Madison, and Jeffersonville through Fountain City on their way farther north, most finding refuge in Coffin's small home at the corner of Mill Street and US 27.

Coffin moved to Fountain City in 1826 from North Carolina and founded a general store and mill. He said he "knew the horrors of slavery firsthand." Almost immediately he embarked on his life work of shepherding ex-slaves to safety farther north. He built a taut two-story, red-brick house in 1839 and made sure it was designed to assist him in his work.

From the time it was erected, fugitives were hidden in the house, one, two, three at a time, sometimes more. Once a farm wagon pulled in front to the house in the dark of night, and Coffin's wife Catharine opened the door. "How many?" she asked. "All of Kentucky," the driver answered, as 17 weary refugees filed in.

Five years after Coffin built his home, he started a Free Labor store, dedicated to selling only goods made with non-slave hands. In the 1840s, it was very difficult to purchase southern goods such as cotton and sugar without it being worked with slaves. In 1847, at the behest of abolitionists, Coffin moved to Cincinnati to run a wholesale version of a Free Labor store, to supply other retailers with Free Labor material. During the Civil War, he became the general agent for the Western Freedmens's that raised funds for freed slaves. It is often said that the protagonists of Harriet Beecher Stowe's *Uncle Tom's Cabin* were based on the Coffin couple.

The next stop northward for the fugitive was most often Cabin Creek, a community of African-American freemen in Randolph County. While the Underground Railroad is often celebrated as an organization of right-thinking white folk, it was often the African Americans who bore the greatest risk and took the most dangerous jobs of the railroad.

Cabin Creek has long since moldered into the earth, though the noble memory lives on.

The Coffin house passed through a variety of owners, but was purchased by the state and leased to the Wayne County Historical Society for a museum in 1967. The house is now furnished with period furniture true to the austere style of a Quaker. The attic hiding spot is open for those who want to crawl into the warren and experience a few moments of a fugitive slave on the run.

Return to the caution light in Fountain City and turn east on Fountain City Pike. Drive 2.5 miles to Arba Pike, then drive north to the Wayne-Randolph county line. Arba Pike was the early trail known as the Quaker Trace that settlers established by running along the east fork of the Whitewater in 1817 to the Miami trading post at Fort Kekionga at today's Fort Wayne.

A mile east on the county line road is the state's highest point at 1,257 feet. The headwaters of eight major rivers including the White, Whitewater, Wabash, and Big Miami flow from this spot, causing local farmers to note that the streams hereabouts run downhill a number of ways. The Whitewater that runs through Wayne County and the center of Richmond is the state's steepest and swiftest, dropping 800 feet from this point to its junction with the Miami near Cincinnati.

Just over the county line on Arba Road, Arba was the first settlement in Randolph County. For many years it was the largest town in the county. North of Arba on Arba Pike, bear right 0.6 mile past the new Quaker meeting-house. Spartanburg is 3.5 miles north. Proceed north 1.2 miles to County Road 600 South and turn east. The remains of the brick, two-story Union Literary Institute is 2 miles farther, southeast of the intersection of CR 850 East. It was a Quaker school established in 1845 to provide elementary and secondary education to both white and African-American students.

Return west 0.5 mile to CR 800 East (Indiana Highway 227) and turn left. Drive 2 miles south to US 36 and go west 6 miles to Lynn, which suffered a horrendous 1986 tornado that damaged 284 buildings and destroyed

24 houses. Amazingly enough, there were no casualties. Continue west to Modoc and turn south on IN 1. Hagerstown is 9.5 miles south.

German Baptists or Dunkards arrived in the area around 1820, joining New Jersey migrants who had come in 1815. In 1836, an influx of settlers coming down the National Road caused a name change from Elizabethtown to Hagerstown, presumably after their home place in Hagerstown, Maryland, the jumping-off point for the National Road.

Hagerstown was a brief boomtown when the Whitewater Canal terminated there in 1847. Within six years it was kaput and it has been a small sleepy burb since, except when crowds surge into the buffet at Welliver's Restaurant or hit the three-generation Abbott's Candy Shop. The Nettle Creek Valley Museum at 96 1/2 Main Street is dedicated to the town's past, housed in an 1880s public hall graced with 1913 murals painted by local artist Charles Newcomb.

Drive 6.8 miles south on IN 1 to Cambridge City and proceed 12 miles back to Richmond on US 40. See "Drive 14" for information on US 40 and Cambridge City.

Central Indiana

16

Mansions to Barns

Hamilton County

General description: The 55-mile drive explores Hamilton County from the pioneer past to the rustic farm towns to the upscale neighborhoods near Geist Reservoir.

Special attractions: In Fishers: Conner Prairie Living History Museum and sumptuous residential neighborhoods surrounding Geist Reservoir. In Noblesville: Courthouse Square; and Indiana Transportation Museum. In Cicero: Morse Reservoir.

Location: Central Indiana.

Drive route numbers and names: U.S. Highways 32 and 31. Various city and county roads.

Travel season: Heavy winter snows can cover the country roads with drifts, but otherwise it is smooth sailing across the prairie.

Camping: Arcadia at Overdorf Lake and White River Campground in Cicero.

Services: There are full services in Fishers and Noblesville: hotels, restaurants, shopping, movies, etc. Gas and food are available in Westfield, Cicero, and Atlanta.

Nearby attractions: Marion County and Indianapolis are just south.

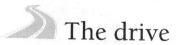 The drive

The tour begins at Conner Prairie Living History Museum, a re-created 1836 pioneer settlement located at 13400 Allisonville Road in Fishers. In many ways Conner Prairie mirrors Hamilton County from its beginnings on the frontier, through the booming days of settlement and farming, to its decline and then rejuvenation as part of the industrial heartland.

William Conner arrived on the frontier in 1800, migrating from Ohio. He served as a trader and as a liaison between the European settlers and the Delaware Indians who lived along the White River.

He later married Mekinges, daughter of a prominent Delaware chief, and had six children with her. One of his duties as liaison was to translate during the 1818 Treaty of St. Mary's which required the Delaware to move west of the Mississippi. Accordingly, Mekinges and their children went west with their kinsmen, while Conner stayed behind.

He quickly remarried, to Elizabeth Chapman, a young white woman, and produced another large brood. After his remarriage, he built a large brick home to replace his cabin. Following the removal of the Delaware, Conner took his place as a patriarch of the frontier.

Conner successfully developed towns, stores, and mills, and invested in canals and railroads. He served as state representative from 1829 to 1832 and from 1836 to 1837. Like most successful country boys, he headed for the city when he made his fortune—in this case Noblesville, where he died in 1855.

The Conner house and farm slowly declined, until the place was bought by industrialist Eli Lilly in 1934. After some restoration, Lilly opened the house to visitation and turned the surrounding 1,000-plus acres into a model farm.

Lilly donated the farm to Earlham College in 1964, and the college has operated it as a museum and living history farm since 1973. Today a variety of buildings from across Indiana are clustered together on the farm to re-create an 1836 settler village. Costumed interpreters bring history to life with vivid portrayals of pioneer people. The 65,000-square-foot Museum Center contains galleries, cafes, a library, gift shop, and administrative offices. Earlham's Quaker heritage is being incorporated into Conner Prairie as they have added a Quaker cabin and a stirring living history depiction of the life of a fugitive slave on the Underground Railroad.

Noblesville is 4 miles north on Allisonville Road. William Conner and Josiah Polk platted the town in 1823 as the county seat. The county slumbered as a farming region for many years, but beginning in the 1970s, the county became a bedroom community of Indianapolis with the population jumping more than 300 percent in a few decades.

Turn west on Conner Street to the courthouse square. The courthouse is a French-Renaissance structure dating to 1878, though the tower is from 1968. The lurid murder trial of Ku Klux Klan Grand Dragon and state kingpin D. C. Stephenson was held in the courthouse in 1925. The jury convicted Stephenson and he was given a life sentence. The Hamilton County Jail southwest of the courthouse is where Stephenson was jailed during the trial. The wedding-cake sheriff's residence is now a historical museum.

The Victorian square has experienced a revival as an upscale shopping and eating destination. There are fine restaurants and antique shops and malls scattered in with the attorneys and hardware store.

At the north edge of town on Indiana Highway 19 in Forest Park, the Indiana Transportation Museum has an excellent collection of antique

Drive 16: Mansions to Barns
Hamilton County

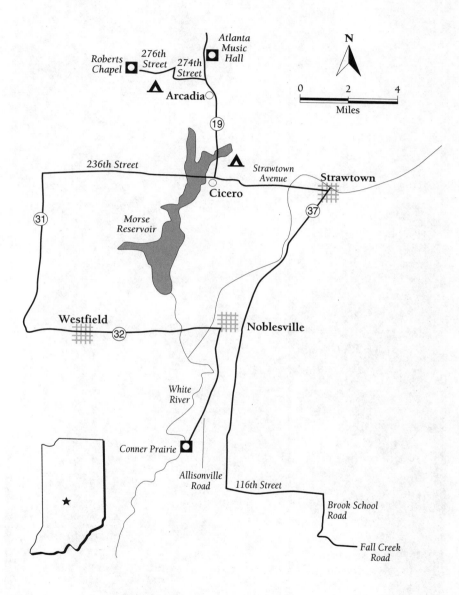

Indiana courthouses are often the pride of the county.
Photo courtesy of Hamilton County CVB.

equipment, from locomotives and trolleys to rare old vehicles like a 1921 Stutz fire truck.

Return to IN 32 and drive 5 miles west across the prairie to Westfield where new suburban developments along the road supplant the collapsing barns. From its beginnings in 1836 as a Quaker settlement, Westfield was active in the Underground Railroad. A weathered white wooden sign at the edge of town still advertises the Westfield Friends Meeting. North on Westfield Boulevard (Union Street) 0.3 mile, the Union Bible Seminary was a Quaker academy dating to 1861. In the twentieth century, it became a fundamentalist school for the training of Christian missionaries.

Turn north on U.S. Highway 31 and drive 7 miles across the flat land past sprawling corporate headquarters and office buildings to 236th Street and turn east. Cicero and Morse Reservoir is 6.2 miles west of US 31. A cemetery at the edge of town has an exceptional carved limestone, Victorian gravestone. The marker, rendered as a lifelike dead tree with severed limbs is meant to represent a person dead before their time, cut off in the prime of life.

Cicero is a nineteenth-century brick and limestone railroad town, named after a Delaware chief who inexplicably carried a classical Roman moniker. Seventh Day Adventists settled the town, and their Indiana Academy is still a major employer in town. The other major attraction in Cicero is Morse Reservoir, a water source for Indianapolis and a modest holiday getaway for central Indianans. Lakefront lots have become another choice location for Indianapolis McMansions.

Turn north on IN 19 and drive across the swells and swales of the Tipton Till prairie land. Arcadia, another railroad town, is 2.9 miles north. In its heyday, it was a glassblowing town, fueled by central Indiana's gas boom at the turn of the century.

Atlanta is 3 miles north of Arcadia at the edge of the county. The Main Street dead-ends at both ends and the railroad doesn't stop there anymore. The old-time Atlanta Hardware seems to be hanging in there, as does the Carnegie Library and the gaily painted Queen Anne Bed and Breakfast. The downtown was bought up by an entrepreneurial couple in the 1970s who attempted to turn it into a tourist attraction. The dogs sleepily ambling across Main Street give a clue to their success.

Return to IN 19 South and drive south 2.4 miles to 274th Street. Proceed west 1.1 miles to Gwin Street and drive 0.2 mile to 276th Street. Turn left and drive 3.8 miles to Roberts Chapel, the remains of a unique settlement of people with mixed white, black, and Cherokee blood, established in 1838 by Hansen Roberts, a descendant of a black valet who inherited a wealthy English plantation owner's fortune when he died in North Carolina. When community pressure forced them from North Carolina, they settled in the prairie of Indiana. The community prospered until the 1890s when

Antiques abound in Hamilton County. Photo courtesy of Hamilton County CVB

the Roberts's descendants decided the land was too overcrowded and wouldn't support them. Accordingly, many moved to eastern and midwestern cities to pursue professional careers.

Return to IN 19 and drive south to Cicero. Take 235th Street east which becomes 234th Street. Proceed 2.5 miles to Strawtown on the White River, site of the village of Chief Straw of the Delaware tribe. Strawtown offers a fine view of the White River and perhaps offering some understanding of the state's solons who chose the site of Indianapolis on the White as the state capital.

Though not a sailing river, the White still does its job: Four of Indiana's ten largest cities are on its banks. The entire watershed of the river drains more than a third of Indiana before joining the Wabash. Where Americans now manufacture a host of industrial products, ancient moundbuilders did their work. Anderson's monumental mounds upsteam remain a penultimate example of the earliest Americans' industry.

Proceed 12 miles south on IN 37 to 116th Street (Exit 5). Go east on 116th through a gauntlet of office parks and new developments with wishful nautical names like Spyglass and Sawgrass. Go south on Brook School Road to Fall Creek Road. Turn east to peruse the many affluent homes that surround Geist Reservoir—faux Tudors mingled with Louis XV hunting-lodge reproductions next to curiously overdeveloped Frank Lloyd Wright–inspired mansions.

Because of the growth in upscale suburbs and the availability of farm-land, Hamilton County has become known as a premier golfing destination. There are 15 golf courses in the county and 2 golf schools. The county boasts a number of championship courses, designed by some of America's best golf-course designers such as Pete Dye and Robert Trent Jones, Jr.

Drive 17: The Big Empty

A drive across the Hoosier prairie from Greencastle to Lafayette

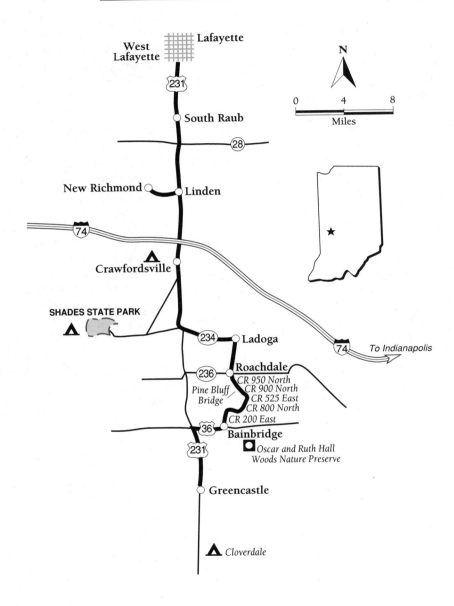

17

The Big Empty

A drive across the Hoosier prairie from Greencastle to Lafayette

General description: The 60-mile drive explores the Indiana prairie through the college towns of Greencastle, Crawfordsville, and Lafayette.

Special attractions: In Greencastle and Putnam County: Depauw University and covered bridges. In Crawfordsville and Montgomery County: Ben Hur Museum, Old Jail Museum, the Lane Place and Linden Railroad Museum. In Lafayette and Tippecanoe County: Purdue University and Fort Ouiatenon.

Location: Western Indiana.

Drive route numbers and names: U.S. Higways 231 and 36; Indiana Highway 234; and County Roads 200 East, 800 North, 525 East, 900 North, 950 North, and 250 East.

Travel season: Except when heavy snow can drift into huge banks covering the highway, the roads are fine year-round. The covered-bridge section of the drive is particularly scenic in the fall leaf season.

Camping: There are campgrounds 10 miles south of Greencastle at Cloverdale, Blackhawk Campground, and Cloverdale RV Park. Crawfordsville has the KOA Kampground and there is camping at Shades State Park.

Services: There are services in Greencastle, Crawfordsville, and Lafayette; hotels, restaurants, shopping, movies, etc. Gas and food are available in Cloverdale, Linden, and the US 74 interchange.

Nearby attractions: Parke County, famous covered-bridge country, is just to the east; Shades State Park is in the southeast corner of Montgomery County.

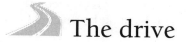 The drive

Greencastle is Putnam County's seat of government, established in 1821. The courthouse square centers around the 1904 limestone Greek Revival structure with a World War II V-1 German buzz bomb that terrorized London on the corner. Local citizens erected the war memorial on Memorial Day in 1947. It is one of only two buzz bomb missiles located in America, the other being in storage at the Smithsonian.

The courthouse square was also the site of pharmaceutical king Eli Lilly's first drugstore. At Washington and Indiana Streets, the Fleenor Building stands on the location of Lilly's 1861 apothecary. There is a plaque on the east side of the building. The store lasted but a short while before he enlisted in the Union Army. After serving in several battles, he relocated to Indianapolis where he commenced his career as an industrial giant.

John Dillinger visited the Central National Bank building at 20–24 West Washington in 1933, before it was converted to the retail and office space you see today. When he left, the bank was short several thousand dollars (his biggest haul) as Dillinger scooted for his hideout in southern Parke County.

Depauw University is 6 blocks south of the square, a liberal arts school founded by Methodists in 1837. It was known as Indiana Asbury College until Washington Depauw, a New Albany tycoon, decided to underwrite the failing school in 1884. Their best-known alumnus is former Vice President Dan Quayle.

East College at Locust and Simpson Streets is the oldest campus building, an 1871 belfried and turreted structure that soars four elaborate stories high in Gothic excess. It was magnificently restored in 1981, and the original interior with extraordinary woodwork and original furniture is lovingly maintained.

Behind the Gobin Memorial United Methodist Church and Charter House at Simpson and Locust Streets, the Old Bethel Church stands. Built in 1807 near the Ohio River at Charlestown for circuit riders' services, the church is believed to be the oldest Methodist church in Indiana. It was moved three times before coming to its current roost in 1953. The area east of the campus is a historic neighborhood that boasts many well-ordered Victorian homes including those of several past college presidents.

Return to the courthouse square and continue north on U.S. Highway 231. The Monon Restaurant at the railroad tracks on the north edge of town is a popular breakfast and lunch place, decorated with a mare's nest of railroad and Hollywood kitsch and memorabilia.

With nine covered bridges, Putnam County has the state's second largest collection after Parke County. North of Greencastle, the road crosses Big Walnut Creek which cuts diagonally across the county through the rumpled remnants of the glacial melt. Most of the covered bridges are along this creek and Raccoon Creek.

The road traverses the melt line of the glaciers, where the flat land of the glacial scour meets the unglaciated woodlands. Proceed 8.9 miles to US 36, through the aptly named country hamlet of Brick Chapel with an imposing brick church on the knoll.

Turn east on US 36 and drive 3.9 miles to Bainbridge in the wooded valley of Raccoon Creek. East of town, look for signs to the Oscar and Ruth

Hall Woods Nature Preserve, a fine wildlife viewing location, which is south of US 36 along Raccoon Creek. Return to the center of the village and head north out of Bainbridge on Washington Street which becomes County Road 200 East. (The county has laid out a twisty path of covered bridges through the countryside that is well marked with signs. Should you become intrigued to investigate more than is laid out here, just make your way back west till you hit US 231 and proceed north on this route.)

Turn east on CR 800 North and drive 0.5 mile to Rolling Stone Bridge, then snake through the woods to CR 525 East, drive 0.5 mile to CR 900 North, and turn west to Pine Bluff Bridge. The Big Walnut Natural Area Conservation District, one of the state's loveliest, is along the country road. The gravelly roads weave in and out of the rugged valley, a land of a few down-at-the-heels farms, soaring hawks and peering deer, with gaggles of wild turkeys at the roadside. After reintroduction in the 1970s, the wild turkeys have procreated with zest; it is not unusual to see flocks of a few dozen feeding beside the roadsides in rural.

County Road 900 North becomes CR 950 North which Ts at CR 250 East. Turn north and drive 5 miles across a landscape of totemic silos and big skies through Roachdale to Ladoga across the Montgomery county line.

The town was laid out in 1836 on the former Shawnee hunting grounds along the Raccoon Creek. The town was named after a birch-lined lake in Russia by a group of students who chose it from a geography book. The village was clustered around a four-story sawmill on the creek, and the local brickyard produced the material for several fine homes and buildings that are still standing.

In 1855, Baptists established the Ladoga Female Seminary that operated until the Civil War. The building still stands on a hill in the center of town. The Central Indiana Normal School and Business Institute took over the building in 1876. The open-door institute offered education to students unable to afford it elsewhere.

In 1878, the school moved to Danville, Indiana. The old Normal School served as the public high school for more than 70 years until it became the American Legion Home in the 1970s.

Proceed 7.8 miles across the prairie on Indiana Highway 234 to US 231. Parkersburg is 3.7 miles south, near the site of Chief Cornstalk's Village along Cornstalk Creek 3 miles east. From 1774 to 1820 the Eel River tribe of the Miami lived peaceably with the early settlers before being moved out to a reservation at Thorntown to the northeast.

Crawfordsville, another college town, is 11 miles north on US 231. Sometimes known as the "Athens of Indiana" because of its strong cultural interests and institutions, the town is famed as the home of Major General Lew Wallace, hero of the Mexican War and author of the wildly successful nineteenth-century novel *Ben Hur*.

On Pike Street, east of US 231, the Lew Wallace Library and Ben Hur Museum stand surrounded by a brick wall, built by Wallace with the enormous profits from his book. The unique structure is an austere brick cube with a Greek-style portico, a Romanesque turret with an English-style fireplace, and an ornate Moorish central room that incorporates Wallace's interest in ancient architecture—Byzantine, Greek, Roman, Turkish, and Art Nouveau motifs and styles. Built in 1896, the structure houses 77 years of Wallace's memorabilia that includes his military career in the Mexican and Civil Wars, vice presidency of the Lincoln assassination trials, governor of the New Mexico Territory, and U.S. Minister to Turkey. There are oil paintings, objects d'art, military uniforms, gifts of the Sultan of Turkey, and Wallace's collection of over a thousand volumes.

Nearby, the Lane Place is a fine Greek-Revival antebellum house, operated by the Montgomery County Historical Society. Built in 1845, it was the home of Henry Lane, congressman and confidant of Abraham Lincoln. The house is the centerpiece of Elston Grove, a neighborhood listed on the National Register of Historic Places. Examples of domestic architecture dating to the 1830s line the leafy streets, from Greek Revival and Tudor to Prairie Style and Arts and Crafts. The district is bounded at the north and south by Water Street and Wabash Avenue.

Wabash College, a four-year liberal arts college for men, is west of the library and Lane Place across US 231 on Wabash Avenue. Founded in 1832 as a high school, it became the Wabash Manual Labor College and Teacher's Seminary a few years later. The name was shortened in 1839.

The northwest corner of the campus has three early buildings. The 1838 Caleb Mills house was the home of the college's first president. Hovey Cottage was the 1837 home of one of the college's first teachers, Presbyterian minister Edmund Hovey. The 1833 Forest Hall is the oldest structure on campus. The two-story frame building was the first classroom and dormitory building.

The architectural rigor of New England resonates throughout the campus. Several other Federal-style buildings line Wabash Avenue, and even the twentieth-century buildings are built in Georgian style. Center Hall anchors a landscaped mall in the center of campus. Built in several stages in the mid-nineteenth century, the hall contained numerous "recitation rooms," lecture halls, and a laboratory.

The whimsical Herron House at 406 West Wabash Avenue was the home of William Herron, a friend of Lew Wallace. The neo-Jacobean house was built in 1890.

The 1882 Old Jail Museum at 225 N. Washington Street features the remarkable rotary jail, a pie-shaped double-decker cell block that rotates to a single opening on each floor. The jail was one of seven built in the country and the only one still in operable condition.

The Tippecanoe Battlefield Monument near Lafayette commemorates the 1811 battle between William Henry Harrison's United States Army and the Indians of Tecumseh's tribal alliance. Photo courtesy of Great Lafayette CVB.

The Montgomery County Courthouse at Main and Washington Streets was built in the Neoclassical style in 1875. A 155-foot clocktower used to stand alongside the structure, but parsimonious commissioners had it removed in the 1940s.

Proceed north on US 231. Sugar Creek, one of the state's most scenic streams, courses by the highway. The road climbs from the Sugar Creek's valley onto the tableland of the vast prairie. Enormous silos and inflatable grain storage structures hug the rail line. A giant dome of sky overhangs the empty vista. The only swells in the landscape are manmade—railroad overpasses and highway exit ramps.

The small railroad town of Linden is 10 miles north. The Linden Railroad Museum sits beside the mainline of the old Monon and Nickel Plate line. Today the CSX Railroad still thunders down the line between Indianapolis and Chicago. The 1907 depot is the oldest intact junction depot in the state, housing a museum with a collection, including the gleaming red Nickel Plate Caboose No. 497 that rests on an adjacent track.

The Lindy Freeze on the highway is the place for ice cream and sodas. Just down the road, the Trackside Bar and Grill promises mountain oysters should that be your taste. New Richmond is 5 miles west of Linden on a well-marked road through a flat pale landscape with utility lines punctuated by patient hawks. At the edge of town, a sign welcomes you to New Richmond. Under it, another, rustier one welcomes you to Hickory.

New Richmond gained Indiana fame when it was chosen for the movie *Hoosiers* that celebrated Indiana's basketball obsession. Set in the early 1950s, the film used New Richmond as the set, as it needed almost nothing to have a vintage look. Gene Hackman, Dennis Hopper, and Barbara Hershey starred in the basketball epic—the tale of small-town "Hickory" boys rising to the state championship.

A cheerful blue water tower overlooks the decaying grain elevator and empty railbed that stretches to the horizon. A faded sign painted on an old brick commercial building promises a fine selection of buggies and harnesses. The prairie fields lap up to the backyards where children play baseball beside the old maples.

Return to US 231 and turn north. The railroad town of South Raub, 7.8 miles to the north, has the Purdue Throck-Morton Ag Center experimental farm, a harbinger that Lafayette, home of the Purdue Boilermakers, is nearby. Lafayette is 6 miles north.

Lafayette sits at what was the head of the Wabash River's navigable water during the steamboat era. The town's founder, raffish Wabash River boatman William Digby, had the sense to purchase the land there. The fine central convinced the county commissioners to choose the town as the seat of Tippecanoe County.

The current courthouse dates to 1885, a limestone wedding cake of Second Empire, Baroque, Gothic, Georgian, Beaux Arts, and Neoclassic styles. Four statues representing the four seasons surround the dome, which is topped by the Goddess of Liberty, who lost her sword and shield somewhere along the way.

While the town prospered with increasing steamboat traffic (60 arrived in 1832 alone), it got little respect. "Laugh-at" is the name the haughty Crawfordsville citizens preferred to use for the small market town. Lafayette boomed when the Wabash and Erie Canal arrived in 1843. From 1843 to 1850, the population jumped from 2,600 to 6,129. Manufacturing, beginning with pork-packing, added to the agricultural products of the region, increasingly transported by the railroads that arrived in 1852. Today the economic base is split between manufacturing and Purdue University.

The Fowler House at 909 S. Street is an 1852 English Gothic mansion that is currently the home of the Tippecanoe County Historical Society, a good place to begin a visit to the area. It houses numerous exhibits of local memorabilia, artifacts, and the "grandma's attic" items that seem to proliferate in local museums.

The Purdue Block at Eight N. Second Street is the oldest surviving commercial structure, built in 1845 by John Purdue, the school's namesake. It is a Federal-style red-brick building that currently houses offices and a restaurant. The Samuel Johnson House at 608 Ferry Street is the oldest house, built in 1845 for the first Episcopal pastor. The Perrin Historic District on Perrin Avenue between Main and 18th streets is a nineteenth-century upper-middle-class neighborhood. The streets wind along the hilly landscape with a variety of Victorian styles still gracing the lanes.

European history in the area goes back to 1717 when the governor of New France assigned an ensign to fur trade among the Wea, part of the Miami tribe who camped at Wea Creek on the Wabash. It became Fort Ouiatenon, the first permanent European settlement in Indiana. By the late eighteenth century, the fort was no longer used.

The reconstructed blockhouses were built in the 1920s by a local physician and are the focal point for the annual autumn Feast of the Hunter's Moon that re-creates the life of a French fur trading fort with modern mountain men and period foods and crafts. The fort is located in West Lafayette, 3.8 miles southwest of State Street.

Return to West Lafayette, formerly known as Chauncey. Turn west on State Street into the town. State legislators chose the village of Chauncey in 1869 as the site of the new state agricultural college after a rancorous four-year conflict. As was the common case among early educational institutions, leaders named the school after John Purdue and donated $150,000 to the college.

Today it is a world-class educational and research institution, with its agricultural and engineering schools particularly revered. The school nickname of Boilermaker comes from their early engineering focus. In general, Purdue is a red-brick campus, more noted for no-nonsense academic structures than architectural beauty. The Purdue Union, however, opened in 1924 and retains a neo-Gothic flavor with vintage woodwork and furnishings.

Amelia Earhart was part of the Purdue faculty when she took off in March 1937 from the Purdue Airport, the world's first university airport, in her Lockheed Electra for her fateful round-the-world trip. The Purdue Research Foundation funded the plane's construction. From this early involvement with flight, the university has nurtured their aeronautical engineering schools and other technical programs relating to flight.

So many American astronauts have come from Purdue that it is known as the "Mother of Astronauts." More than two dozen graduates of Purdue have been selected for space flight, Gus Grissom being the first. The first man on the moon, Neil Armstrong, was a Boilermaker, as was the last, Eugene Cernan.

Western Indiana
18

Economic Meditation
Terre Haute to Williamsport

General description: The 65-mile drive follows the path of the fabled river and the nineteenth-century Wabash and Erie Canal, from the gritty industrial town of Terre Haute through the northern Italian coal mining town of Clinton to the old canal town of Williamsport.

Special attractions: In Terre Haute: Historical Museum of the Wabash Valley, Inland Aquatics, Farrington's Grove Historic District, Paul Dresser Home, Hippodrome Theatre, Indiana State University, Big Shoe's Barbecue and St. Mary's-of-the-Woods. In Clinton: Immigrant Square, Four Seasons Fountain on the Wabash. In Dana: Ernie Pyle State Historic Site. In Williamsport: Williamsport Falls and historic architecture.

Location: Western Indiana.

Drive route numbers and names: U.S. Highways 36 and 41, Indiana Highway 63, 136, and 28.

Travel season: The roads are drivable in all but the worst of winter weather.

Camping: The Thousand Trails–Horseshoe Lakes Campground is at Clinton. Summers-Carroll Campground at Attica is just east of Williamsport.

Services: There are services in Terre Haute: hotels, restaurants, shopping, movies, etc. Gas and food are available in Clinton, Dana, Williamsport, and Newport.

Nearby attractions: Parke County, famous covered-bridge country, is just to the east.

 The drive

The Wabash River is not really so big a river, only 475 miles long from its start as a prairie ditch just a few miles east of the state line in Ohio. Nor does the Wabash ever become a sprawling inland sea like the Amazon or Hudson as it curls across northern Indiana and swoops south down the western border, disgorging muddy and full into the Ohio at the southern toe of the state. It's just a comfortable Midwestern river of willows and islands and muddy banks with stalking herons and scooting ducks.

But the river looms large in the mind of Indiana. The Wabash drains 33,000 square miles, most of them Hoosier. More than four-fifths of Indiana's counties lie in its watershed, and it washes the banks of 11 county seats, forming an almost archetypal patterning in the state's consciousness.

Importantly, the Wabash was Indiana's historical connection to the world outside the mid-continent. Through a few strategic portages, it connects the Great Lakes, the St. Lawrence, and the Atlantic to the Mississippi and the Gulf of Mexico. In the days of French *voyageurs* and unconquered Indian tribes, the Wabash was the great canoeing thoroughfare between the fur markets of Montreal and the French administrations of Louisiana.

For a good part of the eighteenth century, Terre Haute—"high earth"—was the dividing line between the French administration of Quebec and the colonial authority of New Orleans. Terre Haute prospered following its designation as the Vigo County seat in 1818. The current French Neo-baroque-style limestone courthouse was built in 1888.

The Memorial Hall, 219 Ohio Street across from the courthouse, is Terre Haute's oldest building, built in 1834–36 as a branch of the Second State Bank. The impressive Greek Revival structure was later used as the local Grand Army of the Republic Memorial Hall. It is currently an attorney's office.

A confluence of transportation modes helped continue Terre Haute's development. The *Florence,* the first steamboat on the Wabash, churned to the banks in 1823. As the town was the northernmost navigable spot on the river, it became the entrepôt of the middle Wabash Valley. The National Road from Washington, D.C. (today's U.S. Highway 40) arrived in 1838. The Wabash and Erie Canal, America's longest artificial waterway, eventually stretching from Lake Erie at Toledo to the Ohio River at Evansville, reached Terre Haute in 1849, offering an outlet for the Wabash Valley products. The railroads arrived soon after, in 1852.

Initially, the agricultural bounty of the valley was the primary industry. Salted pork, hominy, and whiskey were the main exports of the region.

The pre–Civil War rise of iron works, foundries, and rolling mills fueled by abundant Wabash Valley coal precipitated the town's almost congenital labor management strife. By 1881, Terre Haute hosted a midwestern labor conference that eventually created the American Federation of Labor from several craft unions.

Terre Haute's rough-and-tumble union scene spawned Eugene Debs, one of the luminaries of the American labor movement as well as the Socialist Party's perennial presidential candidate. His house is located at 451 N. Eigth Street, an unpretentious two-story house as befits the champion of the working class. The structure is also the home of the Eugene V. Debs Foundation, a labor organization dedicated to Deb's ideals, as well as a library with his papers.

Drive 18: Economic Meditation
Terre Haute to Williamsport

The Temple of Labor at 201 S. Fifth Street is the headquarters of the Central Labor Union, which was established in 1890. Debs lay in state in the temple following his death in 1926. The temple houses memorabilia for both Debs and Samuel Gompers, the founder of the American Federation of Labor.

"The District" in Terre Haute ran north on Second and Third Streets and spread into the sidestreets, including Cherry Street, famous for its wide-open gambling parlors and elaborate bordellos. Born at the edge of the district in the mid-nineteenth century, Hoosier icons Theodore Dreiser and Paul Dresser watched the promenade from their windows and front porch, marking both of them for life. Theodore Dreiser's classics, *Sister Carrie* and *Jennie Gerhardt,* tell the stories of daughters of people forced into prostitution by economic necessity. His masterpiece, *An American Tragedy,* continued his theme of capitalism overwhelming the modest dreams of common men.

Life along the Wabash affected his brother Paul Dresser in another way. Dresser wrote "On the Banks of the Wabash, Far Away," by far the song most associated with Indiana. Dresser was sent at the age of 15 to the St. Meinrad Catholic seminary to be trained as a priest. Evidently it didn't take, as he ran away and changed his name. He favored the high life and was a devotee of fancy bordellos and gambling casinos while penning dozens of hit songs. Dresser was considered to be the nation's most popular composer in his turn-of-the-century heyday.

The Paul Dresser home, a small two-story brick home, can be seen in Fairbanks Park along the Wabash. It was moved from the original location at 318 S. Second Street. Take Fairbanks off of US 41 to the park.

The Historical Museum of the Wabash Valley at 1411 S. Sixth Street has one of Dresser's pianos, as well as a collection of other historical memorabilia. The museum is in the heart of the Farrington's Grove Historic district, a haven of 800 homes and commercial structures dating from the mid-nineteenth century. The tree-lined streets are lined with fine examples of Greek Revival, Queen Anne, Romanesque, and Italian Renaissance homes. It is listed on the National Register of Historic Places.

The Indiana Theatre at Seventh and Ohio Streets is another example of Terre Haute's early twentieth-century florescence. The grandiose 1,660-seat cinema is an Andalusian fantasy, with Moorish ceilings, mosaic floors, and elaborate ceramic ornamentation. The theater boasts the state's largest indoor screen.

A block away at Eigth and Ohio Streets, the Scottish Rite Cathedral also serves as a theater, and an extravagant one at that. It was built in 1915 and 1916 as the Hippodrome Theatre in a German-Renaissance style with lions heads balefully gazing from the gables.

The Sheldon Swope Art Museum at 25 S. Seventh Street features exceptional examples of 1930s and '40s-era regionalist painters such as

Edward Hopper, Grant Wood, and Thomas Hart Benton. It is located in a 1901 Renaissance-revival building with an Art Deco interior.

Should the kids be restive, Inland Aquatics at 10 Ohio Street is a land-locked depiction of the ocean, with the largest living coral reef display in the country, and a saltwater fish hatchery.

At 820 Wabash Street, the Terminal Arcade Building was built in a bombastically neo-classic Roman style as a terminal for the local interurban trolley company as well as housing offices and retail shops. The Hulman and Company Building at Nineth and Wabash Streets is a touch more sober: a red-brick Romanesque Revival building that houses the Hulman wholesale grocery business and their renowned Clabber Girl baking powder factory, as it has for more than a century. The Hulmans are best known for their long-time stewardship of the Indianapolis 500 racetrack.

Another Hoosier made his fame in Terre Haute. Basketball star Larry Bird became the highest-paid rookie in NBA history when he joined the Boston Celtics for a stellar career. Larry Bird's Home Court Hotel on US 41 has four of his NBA Most Valuable Player trophies in the lobby. You can view his Olympic gold medal, mementos and photographs of his illustrious career, and then shoot baskets from the parquet floor of his Boston Garden Restaurant.

There is another trophy of a big-footed man out in a modest southside neighborhood. At 1105 S. 12th Street, Big Shoe's Barbecue serves some of the best ribs on the planet. Willie Jackson's father-in-law started the place back in 1947, serving folks from his backyard. "Size 13 was pretty big back then," Jackson said, so the name stuck.

Proceed west on US 40 across the Wabash 1.8 miles to West Terre Haute. Originally a French town, West Terre Haute retained French speakers into the 1930s. At one time it was a prosperous coal mining town, but is now a modest suburb of Terre Haute.

Turn north on Indiana Highway 150 and drive 4.8 miles to St. Mary's-of-the-Woods College. It is the mother house of the Sisters of Providence, founded in 1840 to serve the German and French Catholic communities of the southern Indiana region. Although the number of women entering the convent has declined, St. Mary's is still the home of 350 sisters. The Mother Theresa Theodore Guerin Historical Museum features artifacts of early Catholic ministry in the region and a history of the Sisters of Providence.

Beginning late in the nineteenth century, St. Mary's began offering degree programs for women and has pioneered new career paths for women, particularly non-traditional students. There are more than 20 specialized academic areas.

The college boasts some handsome turn-of-the-century buildings in Italian Renaissance style and a particularly charming Baroque Revival church.

The Church of the Immaculate Conception was completed in 1886 and is lit by Bavarian stained glass windows.

Return to Terre Haute and proceed north 11.9 miles on IN 63 to Clinton. The road is running through the Wabash bottoms, swooping over humpy hills as the river flows down a partially filled pre-glacial valley through a rich fertile land.

The gray-green stripper pits that dot the roadsides speak of the coal deposits that underlay the valley. Nearly 40 million tons of Indiana coal are extracted annually. While deep mining predominated in earlier production, most mining today is surface strip mining, done with monstrous draglines that munch the earth like fantastic creatures. The region is pocked with small mining communities that have fallen on hard times as the industry has consolidated and labor-efficient mining techniques have supplanted the older backbreaking ways.

Roadside signs for Vopi's Italian salami and restaurants like Zamberletti's herald Clinton, a northern Italian coal mining town on the Wabash. During the coal boom between the 1870s and 1920s, the town attracted more than 25 nationalities, including many Italians. The mines declined after the 1920s, but the Army ordnance plant north of Clinton stabilized employment beginning in World War II.

Clinton remains an Italian enclave, albeit distinctly of the Hoosier variety. There are several Italian restaurants in town, serving something that vaguely recalls the cuisine of the old country. The annual Labor Day Weekend Little Italy Festival is a town-wide celebration of Italian-ness. There are grape stomps and bocci games, polka dances, gondola rides on the Wabash, and more Italian street food than you can imagine. The local lovelies dress in traditional Italian costumes and the grape-arbored Museo del Vino opens for wine tastings under the vines.

The Immigrant Park at Ninth and Clinton Streets is a small, wrought iron–fenced park with a fine statue of a young immigrant carrying a suitcase, waving goodbye with a confident look on his face. The statue (which stands on a pile of faux coal) and bull's head fountain were cast in Torino, Italy. A riverside classical "Four Seasons" fountain, surrounded by grape vines, terraces, and a promenade at Elm and Water, also reflects Clinton's Italian pride.

Return to IN 63 and proceed north through a panorama of broad, open fields. Turn west on US 36 and drive 4.8 miles to Dana.

It's a vast prairie vista, under a blue dome of sky. Iconic silos and enormous feed mills mirror the fertility of the soil. Trains thunder across the landscape like slender messages. They rumble through Dana's red-brick downtown, past a modest white clapboard house with lace curtains and a few touches of classical trim, the home where journalist Ernie Pyle was born before going off to find his fame as a World War II correspondent.

When World War II swept millions of Americans into its maelstrom, Pyle trotted along with them, from the European theater to the war in the Pacific, chronicling the war as the dog soldier saw it. Pyle was shot and killed by a Japanese machine gunner on Ie Shima near Okinawa in April 1945.

The state of Indiana moved Pyle's birthplace from its original rural setting to the railroad side at Maple and Briarwood Streets in Dana and made it a state historic site. There are two Quonset huts that house the visitor center with its multi-media World War II stories and scenes.

Two miles north of Dana on IN 71, there is a seven-story turn-of-the-century round barn. Originally it was built as a labor-saving scientific chicken coop. Chicks went in the top floor and emerged from the bottom as fryers.

Return via US 36 to IN 63 North. The earth alternately swells and then relaxes again into prairie. Newport is 6.9 miles north, county seat of Vermillion County, called the "shoestring county" because it is 37 miles long, but averages only seven miles in width. The Beaux Arts limestone Vermillion County courthouse was built in 1925.

Vermillion County, while one of the smallest in the state, produces almost twice the corn and beans per acre as its neighbors. It also has one of Indiana's largest coal mines.

Newport was the site of a 1909 automobile hill climb. The 140-foot-high, 1,300-foot-long climb at the edge of town was a daunting challenge for the early cars, and the event drew big crowds until its demise in 1915. The hill climb for vintage cars was revived in 1963 and it remains a popular October event.

The courthouse square is pure Americana with Gidget's Deli Market and a military mural on the side of the local American Legion. Across the way, a small frame building houses the Newport Chemical Stockpile Outreach Office, a chilling reminder of America's Cold War history.

The Newport Chemical Stockpile just west of town was established in 1941 by the Department of Defense for warfare chemical production on 22,000 acres of land. The plant produced the explosives TNT and RDX as well as heavy water production for the Manhattan Project that culminated in the atomic bomb. The plant also produced the lethal chemical nerve agent VX which can kill a human in fifteen minutes with less than a pinpoint drop. In 1968, VX production was halted, though the facility continued to store the entire U.S. VX stockpile. While there has never been a fatality associated with production of the nerve agent, the region around the plant has long lived with the potential of a chemical disaster. The Newport Chemical Stockpile Outreach Office provides tours of the facility every second and fourth Wednesdays of the month.

Continue north on IN 63. The Cayuga Power Plant is a 1,006-megawatt generating facility. As the road crosses Little Vermillion River, it is near the site of Harrison's Crossing, where William Henry Harrison and his army forded the river en route to his battle with the Indian confederacy at the 1811 Battle of Tippecanoe.

At the Warren county line 6 miles past Newport, the rich fields and plump white barns of the prairie give way to abrupt hills. Waterman, 2.8 miles to the east on IN 234, was known as Lodi during the heyday of the Wabash and Erie Canal. Lodi was a major port with locks and dam.

Forty feet wide and 4 feet deep, the canal snaked along the Wabash and Maumee Rivers back to Lake Erie. Packets and freight boats coursed across the prairie and through the forest to the sounds of boatmen's horns and cries of "ste-a-dy ste-a-dy." Passengers traveled in relative luxury in the packets, with stylishly dressed canalmen in slouch hats and top boots as their squires. The line boats hauling freight presented a more raffish scene—the boats like floating packing crates and the boatmen renowned for their "brigandish guise."

In the peak years the canal bustled with commerce: 7 million pounds of bacon, 2 million bushels of corn, 1 million of wheat, thousands of perches of peaches and stone, hooppoles (staves used to bind barrels), glass, ale, tobacco, and clocks floated down the stream.

But within a quarter century, the big ditch became a bog of silted channels, leaking banks, and weary locks. The canal had its greatest impact on the Wabash Valley in northern Indiana, where the dependable transportation link back to the Great Lakes transformed communities like Huntington, Logansport, and Wabash. The upper valley's population increased 500 percent from 1830 to the canal's decline.

U.S. Highway 136 is 13.9 miles north on IN 63. Turn east 3.3 to Covington.

Covington, another canal town, is the seat of Fountain County. The courthouse dates to 1937, and murals inside depict the history of the county. Major General Lew Wallace, hero of the Mexican War and author of *Ben Hur,* grew up in Covington and started his law practice there.

The Hetfield Home at 417 Liberty is one of the region's oldest houses, dating back to the 1830s. The Federal-style brick house was the home of a county official who also owned interests in flour and woolen mills. The building is now a law office.

Return west on US 136 to IN 263 and drive north 10.1 miles to West Lebanon which dates to 1869 when the Wabash Railroad passed through town. Proceed 5.2 miles east on IN 28 to Williamsport.

Williamsport is an early town on the Wabash, site of a horse ferry across the river. The settlers were from Maryland, Ohio, and Pennsylvania and with the aggregate of historic architecture, the town retains an air of the eastern seaboard.

The Warren County Historical Society Museum is on Monroe Street by the railroad tracks in an antique building, featuring the history of the county. Farther down Monroe, the Gothic Presbyterian Church is a picturesque example of the style. The Tower House at 303 Lincoln is a Tuscan-style 1854 mansion built by a local merchant. The High House at 404 East Monroe is an 1850s sandstone tavern built in the Federal style.

The highest waterfall in Indiana, Williamsport Falls, drops 67 feet in the middle of the small town—a thin silver torrent falling into a fern-strewn and lichened grotto. The Fall Branch that forms the falls is a scenic walking stream above the falls.

Drive 19: Parke County
Covered Bridge Capital

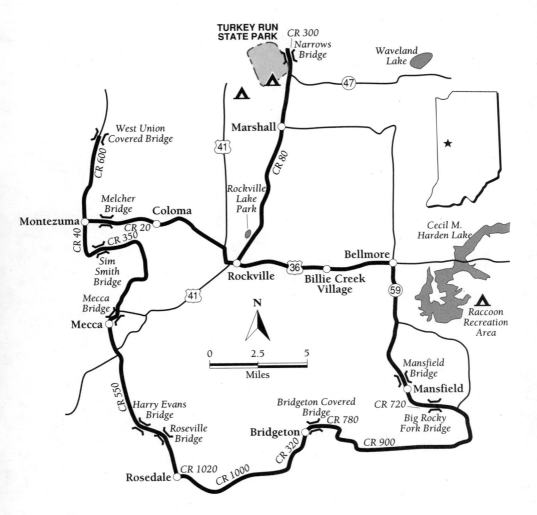

TURKEY RUN STATE PARK

CR 300

Narrows Bridge

Waveland Lake

47

West Union Covered Bridge

CR 600

Marshall

41

CR 80

Rockville Lake Park

Melcher Bridge

Coloma

Montezuma

CR 20

CR 40

CR 350

Cecil M. Harden Lake

Sim Smith Bridge

Rockville

36

Bellmore

Billie Creek Village

Mecca Bridge

41

59

Mecca

N

Raccoon Recreation Area

0   2.5   5

Miles

Mansfield Bridge

Mansfield

CR 550

Harry Evans Bridge

Bridgeton Covered Bridge

CR 720

CR 780

Roseville Bridge

Bridgeton

Big Rocky Fork Bridge

CR 900

CR 320

Rosedale

CR 1020

CR 1000

Previous Page: *Dogwood livens up a picnic spot in Lincoln State Park.* (Drive 3)

Left: *Louisville, Kentucky's skyline as seen from historic Clarksville.* (Drive 1)

Below: *Amish Acres in Nappanee, the heartland of Indiana's Amish.* (Drive 26)

Facing Page: *Tippecanoe County Courthouse in Lafayette.* (Drive 19)

Facing Page: *An Indiana family farm.* (Drive 25)

Above: *A summer sunset at a Michigan City pier.* (Drive 28)

Left: *Sunflowers stretch for rays along a hilltop.* (Drive 13)

Facing Page: *Maples and a handslpit rail fence add beauty to Indiana's fall foliage. (Drive 11)*

Above: *Autumn harvest and Halloween fun in western Indiana. (Drive 21)*

Right: *The Lincoln Living Historical Farm at the Lincoln Boyhood National Monument. (Drive 3)*

Following Page: *A covered bridge near Cataract Falls State Park. (Drive 9)*

19

Parke County
Covered Bridge Capital

General description: The 50-mile drive loops through the rural beauty of Parke County, home of the largest collection of covered bridges in the nation. Located on the edge of the last great glacier advance, the county is a rumpled quilt of diverse topography.

Special attractions: In Rockville: Billie Creek Village, historic downtown square, and national historic district, and historical museum; Terre Vin Winery. In Mansfield: Rolling Mill and covered bridge. In Bridgeton: Mill and covered bridge. In Montezuma: Reeder Park canal boat turning basin and canal route; Turkey Run and Shades State Park; Raccoon Recreation Area. En route: 32 covered bridges.

Location: Western Indiana.

Drive route numbers and names: U.S. Highways 41 and 36; Indiana Highway 59; and County Roads 210 West, 600 West, 40 West, 100 South, 420 West, 1020 South, 1000 South, 320 North, 780 South, 900 South, 720 South, 80 East, and 300 East.

Travel season: The drive is over roads of various types, from U.S. highways to gravel roads. All are in good condition, but inclement weather may make back roads tedious. Heavy snow can make some of the roads difficult. The county's roads become more crowded during its annual festivals, though it remains an attractive destination.

Camping: There are several campgrounds in the county, including Raccoon State Recreation Area, Turkey Run State Park, and Cherokee Village and Campground, Marshall. The first two are state-operated and the last is commercial.

Services: There are services in Rockville: hotels, restaurants, shopping, movies, etc. Gas and food are available in Montezuma and Rosedale. Smaller villages such as Mecca and Mansfield have food, particularly during festivals.

Nearby attractions: The Ernie Pyle Memorial at Dana is west on US 36; the Italian community of Clinton is 25 miles south on US 41.

 **The drive**

Approaching Rockville, the ornate Parke County anchors a vintage Victorian square with brick-faced Italianate commercial buildings housing a variety of establishments. The G&M Variety Store, craft stores, and antique shops share the square with lawyers' offices and abstract companies. The Soda Shop sits resolutely on the corner with its Art Deco signage. The marquee of the 1920s Ritz Theater is still lit up, offering almost up-to-date Hollywood fare to the smalltown crowd. The town remains the county seat of yore, the bustling center of an agricultural county.

While Parke County may be a rural place, it is an internationally famous one. Millions travel annually to Parke County to visit the unique collection of covered bridges—many more than a century old—that span the countless streams and creeks winding through the scenic countryside. Of the 52 1/2 covered bridges the county once owned (they shared one bridge with neighboring Vermillion County), 32 still stand tidy and resplendent.

The 1883 Rockville Train Depot east of the courthouse on Ohio Street (Route 36) is the local tourist information center, with precise maps of this up-and-down county. Should the route laid out in this chapter whet your appetite for more, the local driving map shows five color-coded driving routes.

The covered bridge route begins on Howard Avenue, northeast of the courthouse square off Market Street. Proceed north on County Road 210 West through corn and bean field vistas 2 miles to CR 20 North. The shambling town of Coloma is an old Quaker community.

The 1896 Melcher Bridge is 2.2 miles farther west, built by J. J. Daniels to span Leatherwood Creek. Covered bridges were designed to shield the floor timbers from the elements as well as preventing horses from shying as they crossed the running water. Note the entrance to the bridges resemble a barn opening, increasing the horses' sense of order. J. J. Daniels favored a square-cut top opening, while his bridge-building rival J. A. Britton used an arched opening. There are some bridges in the county where one end is arched and the other squared-off, the result of one builder getting the original contract and the other the repair contract, each marking his work with his signature style.

As you wind through the rural countryside redolent of the nineteenth century, there are stark white reminders hanging high on utility poles that the horrors of the modern era are nearby. The bulbous white plastic objects are VX nerve gas sirens erected by the Parke and Vermillion County Emergency Operations. (See Drive 18.) One is just past the wooden hump-back bridge.

Past the Melcher Bridge 1 mile, turn north on CR 600 West. The West Union Bridge, built by J. J. Daniels in 1876, is the longest bridge in Parke County at 315 feet long. The bridge crosses Sugar Creek on hand-cut sandstone piers. The sign warning to cross the bridge at a walk is a remnant of horse and buggy days when the canter of a horse could set up damaging vibrations. Marching Civil War troops also had to fall out of cadence to avoid damaging the structure.

The West Union Bridge and all but one Parke County bridge are supported by Burr arches, the internal frame that carries the structure's weight. The Burr arch was patented in the 1820s by Theodore Burr, a cousin of Aaron Burr. The arch and the internal framing member were made of poplar because of its resistance to moisture and insects the builders used steam to bend the timbers into the required arch shape and white oak for the flooring because of its strength.

In the days when all the work was done by hand, it took six months to a year to build a bridge. All the beams were hand-hewn with a broad ax and adze and fastened with wooden pegs. The only metal in the bridges were nuts and bolts connecting the largest timbers.

Just to the right of the bridge, there was a Wabash and Erie Canal feeder ditch and turning basin, where the canal boats could anchor or turn around. The first canal boats reached Parke County in 1839, though financial problems and the rise of railroads sent the canal into a sharp decline within a few decades. The hamlet of West Union was one of the early settlements on the canal.

Montezuma, located 4.5 miles south on CR 600 West, was a major canal town. Remnants of the canal can be seen as thickety trails along the road into the town. Founded in 1821 on the site of an Indian village, Montezuma boomed during the canal days. Reeder Park on Water Street is the site of Benson's Basin, an enormous anchorage whose shape can still be seen. The traces of the canal can be seen along Canal and Pond Streets.

Until just recently, the old wooden Brady Boarding House frequented by the Irish workers stood on Water Street. Mrs. Brady charged 25 cents for a night's lodging but was said never to turn away a penniless sojourner, saying, "He might come back and pay me sometime."

Railroads made it to Parke County not long after the canal. By 1860 locomotives were chuffing across the landscape, changing the human culture in its wake. Montezuma was one of the towns that precipitously declined when the trains arrived. Later railroad towns like Bloomingdale withered when the railroads pulled up their tracks and left grassy mounds running off to the empty horizon.

Proceed south on CR 40 North 1.3 miles to the 1883 Sim Smith Bridge. It was built over Leatherwood Creek by J. A. Britton. The bridge is reputed to be haunted—the sound of a cantering ghost horse being heard for many years.

Maintenance of the covered bridges is done with a variety of resources. The Indiana State Covered Bridge Repair Fund appropriates $2,500 a year per bridge. While the intent is good, the money doesn't go far. Luckily, many private individuals pitch in to help the county, providing money and time to the upkeep of the structures. The Parke County Adopt-A-Bridge organization raised almost $14,000 from 1995 to 1997 and helped put a new cedar roof on the Thorpe Ford Bridge near Rosedale.

Continue east onto CR 350 West which turns south. Proceed 1.4 miles to CR 100 South and turn west. The Arabia cemetery on the west side of the road is a picturesque one with some fine headstones, including one for Civil War soldier Joseph Crew with a carved militiaman standing at rest with his rifle.

County Road 100 South segues into CR 420 West going south to Mecca. Mecca was a booming railroad town at one time. The fine seams of clay were Mecca's key to success, providing the raw material for three clay plants at one time. The Mecca Bridge is the site of the annual Covered Bridge Festival Dance, and the Mecca Schoolhouse next to it is an oft-used meeting spot.

The Mecca Tavern in the center of town is not really in Mecca. The town lines conveniently careen around it, as taverns are not allowed in the town limits.

Follow CR 550 West going south out of town. The Harry Evans Bridge is 4.8 miles south and the 1910 Roseville Bridge is just south of it. It is a double span of 263 feet over Big Raccoon Creek, one of the area's best canoeing streams. The bridge crosses over to Chauncy Rose's (of Rose Hulman fame) sand mines. The distinctive green color of the original Coca-Cola bottle made in Terre Haute is due the characteristics of Parke County sand.

South 1 mile, the Longhorn Tavern Restaurant was built by long-time movie cowboy Tex Terry. He was the black-hatted bad guy of a hundred Hollywood westerns of the Tom Mix and Gene Autry era before retiring back to his home county. For decades the region's schoolchildren thrilled to his arrival for convocations in his vast car decorated with steer horns and six shooters. Today, the restaurant serves everything from sandwiches to full dinners. Their catfish fiddlers are local favorites.

Rosedale, 1 mile farther south, is an old coal mining town, part of Chauncy Rose's empire. The heyday of the mines was the first half of the twentieth century when more than 13 million tons were wrested from the ground. It was a dawn-to-dusk mining existence, for $1.50 a day. At its peak, the town had a population of almost 1,500. John Dillinger bestowed his agile bank-robbing skills on Rosedale and then escaped to the wilds of southeast Parke County, where he hid after many of his Indiana exploits.

Proceed east from Rosedale on CR 1020 South which becomes CR 1000 South. The broad fields along the road are high-quality potato fields. Turn north at CR 320 North into Bridgeton. It is 8 miles from Rosedale to Bridgeton.

Bridgeton was founded in 1818 on the banks of the Big Raccoon Creek. The village was the site of the first timber bridge in the county in 1849 which collapsed in 1857, and another which fell into the creek a decade later. The current one, built by J. J. Daniels, has lasted a touch longer—since 1868.

Daniels constructed the double-arch, 247-foot-long bridge with the hand techniques of the day. As in many covered bridges, the flooring is cambered to give with the weight of traffic and spring back to shape. Original advertising still graces some of the interior wood.

Built in 1870, the Bridgeton Mill is the fourth on the site. It was converted from water to electric power in 1957. Today the mill is the last family-owned operating grist mill in the county, grinding out corn meal and flour for the festival-day hordes that descend on the otherwise soporific hamlet. The village hosts a Maple Festival, a Mountain Man Festival, Coon Tail Run (antique car, truck, and tractor show), the Covered Bridge Festival, and Covered Bridge Christmas. —

The Masonic Lodge beside the mill is one of the oldest in the state. It is a moon lodge, which meets the first Saturday after the full moon. During the summer, sounds from the swimming hole across the creek from the mill are reminiscent of a James Whitcomb Riley poem.

Proceed east on CR 780 South which becomes CR 900 South. It will turn north in 7 miles. In 1.5 miles turn west on CR 720 South to Mansfield. The Big Rocky Fork Bridge crosses Big Rocky Ford Creek in 0.5 mile. Built in 1900 by the ever-busy J. J. Daniels, it is 72 feet in length. The bridges were known locally as "kissing bridges" as swains took advantage of the momentary privacy to steal a kiss. The bridges still exert a romantic pull as proposals are made and weddings held under their roofs.

Mansfield hosts the annual Covered Bridge Festival and swamps the town with thousands of vendors and vast throngs of fair-goers.

The Mansfield Roller Mill State Historic Site is a pristine example of an 1880s flour mill, when mills shifted from stone gristmill to roller grinding. The mill's roots reach back to 1819, when James Kelsey and Francis Dickson laid out a sandstone foundation out beside Raccoon Creek. The current mill was built by Jacob Rohm in 1880 and modernized in 1893 to the new-fangled roller process, producing mass-marketed flour and meal. Because of the efficiencies gained by the roller process, the mill could be run with only three men.

By 1929, the mill couldn't compete with industrial flour mills and it was converted into a local feed mill. From 1933 to 1967, the mill was maintained with the machinery intact. It passed through a number of hands who added some ersatz touches such as the non-functioning water wheel (the mill was run by two water turbines located under the mill). In 1990, the mill was listed on the National Register of Historic Places and in 1995 given to the state government as a historic site.

Proceed 5 miles north on Indiana Highway 59 to U.S. Highway 36 West. Billie Creek Village is 4.4 miles west. Billie Creek Village is a re-created turn-of-the-century village with vintage buildings and three covered bridges. The village dates back to the mid-1960s when local movers and shakers decided to develop the county as a year-round tourist destination. Several antique buildings from Rockville and the surrounding county were moved to the site to initiate a "living museum," with old-time craftspeople and products. Festivals and special events began, and today the village is at the center of the Parke County phenomenon.

The Billie Creek General Store was originally built between 1850 and 1860 in the Quaker town of Annapolis in northern Parke County. When the B&O railroad chose to go through the town of Bloomingdale 0.5 mile south, the store followed, and it rested there until 1968 when it again migrated. Since then it has anchored Billie Creek Village and boasts the crafts of 84 Wabash Valley crafters as well as pioneer toys and geegaws for all ages. It also has the bridge-building tools of master builder J. A. Britton.

The village has a demonstration maple sugar camp, tapping 300 trees in the early spring. In the summer, their herb garden is a riot of more than 50 pioneer herb plants. A 1913 schoolhouse portrays the educational ways of rural Indiana. A burr mill spins corn into meal as it did at its original home near Alamo, Indiana, before a tornado flung it into a hundred pieces, necessitating a particularly tedious restoration.

Two churches grace the village, a charming 1886 clapboard Catholic church with a "living heart"–entwined friezeboard and the 1859 Union Baptist Church. A governor's house, livery stable, print shop, common's gazebo, sundry craftsmen's building, all add to the verisimilitude.

Festivals and special events happen virtually every month. During the Covered Bridge Festival, the village is awash with people enjoying the fun. Their Civil War Days is Indiana's largest re-enactment.

Proceed west to Rockville, and turn north on Erie Street across from the Depot tourism information office. Erie Street will become CR 80 East. Six miles north, the small town of Marshall sits primly on the plain. In the middle of town, a lighted World War I victory arch still leaps over the main street, one of only two victory arches left in the state.

The Poplar Grove Cemetery at the north edge of town is a well-cared-for place. The lawns are immaculate and the lanes are plowed on any day with a hint of snow. The cemetery board is recompensed, certainly an unusual occurrence for a small town graveyard. All because the place had the good fortune to have a widow's million dollars bequeathed to maintain it in perpetuity.

Three miles north, the road enters the grounds of Turkey Run State Park, the state's second oldest after Brown County State Park. The road becomes CR 300 East. Half a mile later the road approaches the scenic Narrows of Sugar Creek, a limestone pinch point that the 1882 Narrows Bridge leaps across. The Narrows Bridge is the only one maintained by the state as it is located in Turkey Run State Park.

The Narrows is part of Salmon Lusk's 1,000-acre government military grant and the site of his mill, which he built to the north of the bridge. His brick 1841 house with a louvered cupola sits on the bluff overlooking the bridge site. It is said Lusk situated the bridge so he could watch the travelers crossing from his house.

His son John inherited the house and the 1,000-acre tract, living the balance of his life in a melodramatic isolation. A man with strong tastes and a dislike of his fellow man, he harbored a particular distaste for members of the Masonic order, believing they wanted to poison him. Local legend says Lusk liked to climb on the roof of the covered bridge and rail at crowds of passers-by, inflaming himself to particular ire if he thought the group might include a few Masons. At the height of his fulmination, Lusk would leap from the bridge, ostensibly to cleanse himself from the imagined Freemason contamination.

Ironically, Lusk's need for isolation, and his love of the forest, saved the woods for generations of Hoosiers. In 1919, five years after John Lusk's death, the state of Indiana bought the property from the estate and it became Turkey Run State Park.

20

Sugar Creek

From Thorntown through Shades and Turkey Run State Parks

General description: The 38-mile tour runs from Thorntown along Indiana Highway 47 to IN 234 en route to Shades and then down to Turkey Run on IN 47, paralleling Sugar Creek.

Special attractions: Crawfordsville, Shades and Turkey Run State Parks.

Location: Western Indiana.

Drive route numbers and names: Indiana Highways 47 and 234; County Roads 600 West and 400 South.

Travel season: All roads are paved and in good condition, but heavy snow may make some of the roads difficult.

Camping: There are campgrounds at Shades and Turkey Run State Parks, and Country Park Campground 7 miles northeast of Crawfordsville at Darlington.

Services: There are full services at Crawfordsville and gas and groceries in the vicinity of the parks.

Nearby attractions: Parke County (See Drive 19).

 **The drive**

The drive begins in Thorntown on Indiana Highway 47 where the confluence of Sugar and Prairie Creeks provided exceptional hunting grounds for the Miami Indians. An Indian village here dates back to at least 1719, known as Ka-wi-a-ke-un-gi—"place of thorns." Local lore has it the name comes from an Indian maiden who, distraught over the deaths of two competing suitors, pierced her heart with the thorns that grew there.

In the eighteenth century, French Jesuits established a mission at the village and made a European religious center for the territory to proselytize the Indians. Following the nineteenth-century Indian wars and the spurious treaties that uprooted tribes from their traditional homes, Thorntown became one of the principal Indian reservations west of Pittsburgh. In 1818 the federal government granted a 64,000-acre reserve to the Eel River Miami, centered on Thorntown.

Ten years later, the Miami acceded to pressure from the American

Drive 20: Sugar Creek
From Thorntown through Shades and Turkey Run State Parks

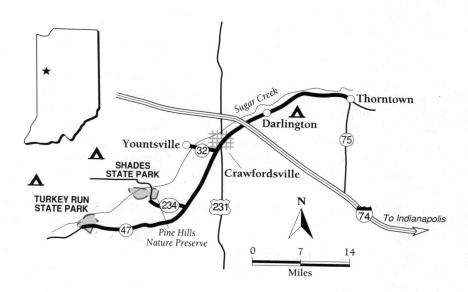

government and encroaching settlers and granted the land back to the government. The Miami retreated to another reservation near Logansport following the treaty signing. North of Thorntown on IN 47, a historical marker on the north side of the road indicates the burial place of Chief Chapadosia and Chief Dixon who fought to the death over the Thorntown treaty. They were buried in full ceremonial dress in a square grave, sitting facing one another.

Cornelius Westfall bought the land for $4 an acre the next year and the first settlers lived in the abandoned Miami houses. The Thorntown Heritage Museum is located in a Gothic structure at Main and Vine Streets and has a history of the Thorntown area as well as Native American artifacts.

Proceed west on IN 47. The Montgomery county line is 4.9 miles down the road. The county was formed in 1822 in the western part of land taken from the Indians in the New Purchase treaty that opened the central part of Indiana to European settlement. The flat prairie of the northern part of the county gives way to the heavily forested sections in the south. The route parallels Sugar Creek, a wild and scenic stream in its lower sections.

Sugar Creek bisects the western edge of the flat, glaciated Tipton Till Plain that extends far to the north. The creek begins many miles to the east near Tipton, Indiana, and rapidly becomes a broad, open stream, cutting a deeper streambed through sandstone and siltstone as it drains west toward the Wabash, forming the high bluffs and picturesque canyons of Shades and Turkey Run State Parks. It is considered the best canoeing river in the state and is certainly the most popular. Canoe rentals are available in Crawfordsville and in and near the state parks.

Darlington is 5 miles west, an early toll road town. The Darlington Toll Gate House on Main Street is a tiny 1880s gatehouse for the corduroy toll road made of felled timbers laid horizontal to one another, which made for a bone-bruising transit across the landscape. The Darlington Covered Bridge is 1.2 miles ahead on Coutny Road 600 East. Built in 1867, the 166-foot bridge is still paved with wooden blocks. At one time, this peaceful scene was in the midst of four factories and mills operating on Sugar Creek.

The Art Deco National Guard Armory at Franklin and Main Streets is from another era entirely. Built at the height of the streamline craze in 1936, the building looks ready for a movie set.

Crawfordsville is 7.3 miles west on IN 47. The town was platted in 1823. Since the mid-nineteenth century, the town has been a prosperous manufacturing center, making coffins, nails and wires, gloves, barrels, foundry items, and bricks. The Midstates Wire dates back to 1900 and is still a major employer. R. R. Donnelley, world-renowned printer, is another long-time company in Crawfordsville, beginning in 1923. The company's Indian-head logo carved in limestone on a tall brick tower overlooks the vast plant on the western edge of town. (See Drive 18 for more information on the cultural and educational side of Crawfordsville.)

Yount's Mill, near Yountsville, was an early industry on Sugar Creek. The mill site is 4 miles west of town on IN 32, where a historical marker is located. The last surviving building is still standing. During the Civil War, the textile mill was a major supplier of woolen Union uniforms, employing 300 workers. It closed in 1905.

The grave of the last surviving Revolutionary War veteran, George Fruits, who died at the age of 114 years, is located farther east. Drive 2.4 miles to CR 600 West and turn left. Proceed 3 miles to CR 400 South and turn right 0.3 mile to Stonebraker Cemetery. The Stonebraker House, 0.3 mile farther down the lane, dates to the 1820s, made of brick fired on the place.

Return to Crawfordsville and turn south on IN 47. Drive 7.9 miles to IN 234 and turn west to Shades State Park. Established more than half a century ago, the founders envisioned the 3,000-acre park as a primitive retreat from the pressures of modern urban life. The shadows of the deep forests gave the area its name.

Compared to nearby Turkey Run, it is relatively undeveloped, intended for the use of nature lovers who like to take their environments straight.

Crawfordsville's General Lew Wallace, author of Ben Hur, built a fantastical library with his royalties. Photo courtesy of Montgomery County CVB.

There are 8 miles of hiking trails with exotic names like Devil's Punch Bowl and Maidenhair Falls. Sugar Creek has carved elaborate sandstone bluffs providing spectacular vistas from the tops of places like Prospect Point, 210 feet over the stream, and the obligatory Lover's Leap.

The area's use as a recreational area dates to the 1860s when a mineral springs near Devil's Punch Bowl attracted health-seekers. A wooden inn was built in 1887. Today all of the structures have long disappeared and the only substantial development is the turfed Roscoe Turner Flight Strip for light airplanes.

The Pine Hills Nature Preserve 0.8 mile north on IN 234 is a remarkable landscape of deep gorges and jagged hills. Rare ferns and fragile wildflowers prosper in the moist environs. Four slender stone ridges called "backbones" rise from the valley floor in hump-backed formation, Clifty Creek on one side of the sidewalk-width ridges, Indian Creek on the other. The two streams join at Honeycomb Rock and flow into Sugar Creek. Stands of massive white pines are the largest in the state.

While proposals to turn Pine Hills into a state park began in 1927, it took another three decades for it to transpire. The preserve was the first conservation project of The Nature Conservancy, purchased in 1960 and turned over to the state in 1961. The 470-acre plot is notable for its unique geological and biological features as well as the historical impact of humans. The Mill Cut Backbone was notched in the 1860s with a 20-foot cut for a mill flume. Giant-sized line drawings of passenger pigeons, last seen in Indiana in 1902, are atop Devil's Backbone along with a devil's face carved in 1910. The intent of the Corps of Army Engineers to impound Sugar Creek and form a reservoir that would cover the white pines with 30 feet of water was squelched with citizen opposition. The preserve was named as a national Natural Landmark in 1970.

Deer's Mill Covered Bridge is 0.6 mile north on IN 234, built by Parke County master builder J. J. Daniels in 1876. A canoe launch is adjacent to the bridge.

Return to IN 47 and turn south. The Parke County line is 6.6 miles. (See Drive 19 for Parke County information.) Turkey Run Country Club lies on the north and manmade Waveland Lake is to the south just before the line. Turkey Run State Park is 6 miles west.

Turkey Run is the second oldest in the state park system, established in 1916. When the state acquired adjoining land from recluse John Salmon, it acquired the intently stewarded land-grant virgin forests that he had saved from timber interests for several decades. The park's 2,382 acres hold the state's largest stands of virgin forest.

It is by far the most developed of the string of Sugar Creek parks, with tennis, swimming, canoeing, horseback riding, bicycling, and picnic areas. There are 13 miles of hiking trails. A founding-era suspension bridge leads over Sugar Creek to the dappled wonders of the Rocky Hollow–Falls Canyon Nature Preserve, an alluvial forest with waterfalls and stands of old-growth hardwoods: towering black walnuts, hickory, sycamore, and stands of hemlock and other evergreens. A rustic state inn, cabins, and campgrounds offer a full range of accommodation.

A monument to the "Father of the State Parks," Richard Lieber, and journalist Juliet Strauss stands near the inn. Both were instrumental in saving the forests for the park. Strauss wrote a column for the Rockville paper as well as national publications about the area. Lieber was the founder and director of the state park system after a successful business career. He died while visiting McCormick's Creek, the first state park, in 1944. His remains are buried in an old-growth forest near the pioneer log church. Another log cabin in the park overlooking Sugar Creek has an exhibit on his life.

21

Boilermakers to Indiana Beach

A drive along the Wabash and then to a resort region

General description: The 35-mile drive covers the route of history that encompasses Indian battles and early commercial centers as well as vintage resort areas.

Special attractions: In Lafayette and Tippecanoe County: Purdue University, Clegges Botanical Gardens, Tippecanoe Battlefield, Prophetstown, Wolf Park.

Location: Western Indiana.

Drive route numbers and names: Indiana Highways 25 and 43, and U.S. Highway 421.

Travel season: Except when heavy snow can drift into huge banks covering the highway, the roads are fine year-round. Indiana Beach booms during the summer season.

Camping: Monticello has Indiana Beach Camp Resort and Yogi Bear's Jellystone Park.

Services: There are full services in Lafayette and Monticello: hotels, restaurants, shopping, movies, etc. Gas and food are available in Battle Ground, Delphi, and Americus.

Nearby attractions: Jasper County, with its Jasper-Pulaski State Fish and Wildlife Sanctuary, is just north of Monticello.

 # The drive

The drive begins in West Lafayette, home of the Purdue Boilermakers. (The university and town are covered in Drive 18.) By far, the most locally momentous event happened in the early morning of November 7, 1811, when 600 Indian warriors crept through the mists to attack invading Territorial Governor William Henry Harrison's army of 900 soldiers.

Led by the Shawnee prophet, Tenskwatawa, the brother of Tecumseh, warriors of seven allied Midwestern tribes sought to drive the Europeans from Native American land and protect nearby Prophetstown, the capital of the Indian Confederacy. While relatively untested in battle, Harrison's men repelled the attack that lasted several hours. Though most commentators assess the battle as less than a clear-cut victory for the American army, it broke Tenskwatawa's power in the alliance.

The state purchased the battle site in 1836 and erected a 92-foot obelisk in 1908. It is now a National Historic Landmark that encompasses about 100 acres.

Drive north on Indiana Highway 43 (River Road) from State Street in West Lafayette. The Indiana State Soldiers' Home Historic District, 3.6 miles from State Street, is a state property used for community gatherings. The grandiose Greek-Revival Indiana State Soldiers' Home dates to 1895 when Indiana established a home for destitute veterans and widows of veterans.

Proceed 1.6 miles on IN 43 to Burnett Road and turn right, then turn left 0.5 mile later onto Ninth Street and drive 1.5 miles to Prophet Street and turn left. A marker 0.7 mile ahead indicates the Prophet's Rock on a bluff over Burnett's Creek, where Tenskwatawa urged his forces to battle, exhorting them with promises of immunity from the soldiers' bullets with a magic potion he had made. After the battle when the dead and wounded were being carried into the camps, Tenskwatawa blamed the failure of his magic potion on a woman who inadvertently touched the kettle in which it was brewed.

Trails connect Prophet's Rock with the Tippecanoe Battlefield. Return to Ninth Street and proceed 0.1 mile to the battlefield. The obelisk memorializes the army's casualties—188 dead and wounded. The Native Americans suffered at least 35 dead, though historians conjecture the number was much higher.

The location of Prophetstown is 1.1 miles southeast of the nearby town of Battle Ground on IN 225. Tecumseh and Tenskwatawa established the town, which was laid out in a right-angled grid at the junction of the Wabash and Tippecanoe Rivers in 1808 as a confederacy center and training ground for up to 1,000 warriors. It was an orderly place with crops grown yearly and intoxicants banned.

It was built on the site of an earlier Wea settlement that the Americans burned in 1791. The recently established Prophetstown State Park is currently planted with 110 acres of prairie grasses and forbs. A Council House is the center of a Prophetstown Living History Village. Plans for a museum and education center are nearing completion and groundbreaking was scheduled for July 1999.

Wolf Park, begun by a Purdue professor, is located on Jefferson Street just north of the IN 225 intersection. For decades, the park's wolf pack has gathered to howl at the moon, most often in accompaniment with a gathered throng of homo sapiens. Visitors learn about pack behavior and social strata and have the opportunity to watch their interactions. The park's small herd of bison also allows visitors to watch the pack at work, testing the buffalo for weakness.

The Wabash Heritage Trail runs for 13 miles along the river starting at the battlefield. It passes through Lafayette and West Lafayette, through a number of parks and natural areas offering great hiking, birdwatching, and history lessons.

Return to Lafayette and proceed northeast 1.2 miles from the intersection of IN 25 and U.S. Highway 52 (Sagamore Parkway) to County Road 200 North. Drive 1.5 miles to CR 400 East and turn right. The Jerry E. Clegg Memorial Botanical Garden is just beyond. The 14-acre garden located on the banks of Wildcat Creek is dedicated to plants native to Indiana.

Drive 21: Boilermakers to Indiana Beach
A drive along the Wabash and then to a resort region

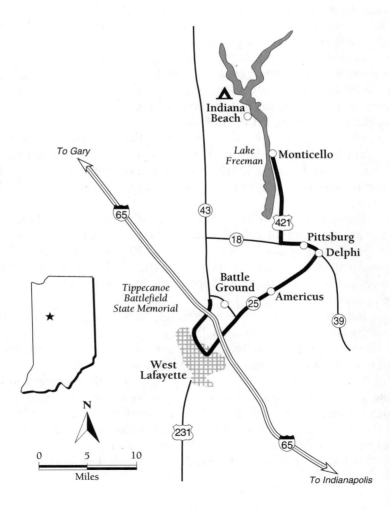

On the ravined wooded site, springtime bluebells and shooting stars counterpoint the flowering dogwood and redbud. When the heat of summer threatens to wilt you, the shady groves provide a respite.

The 1847 Ely Homestead, a two-story Federal-style structure, is located on CR 200 North, just to the right after the intersection. The upright home reflects the esthetics of the Ohio Western Reserve where builder Henry Ely migrated from in 1825.

Return to IN 25 and drive northeast. In 5.5 miles, the mouth of the Tippecanoe River can be seen emptying into the Wabash that is paralleling the highway.

The Tippecanoe is the largest tributary of the Wabash, stretching 166 miles up into Indiana's lake country and passing through two of the biggest natural ones, Webster and Tippecanoe. In the upper stretches, it drains 88 natural lakes and acts as a regulator for the whole watershed. It is described as the clearest stream in the state, where unique aquatic grasses and a profusion of waterfowl and fish prosper.

At Monticello, not far upstream, the construction of two mammoth dams stockaded the river, creating Lake Freeman and Lake Shafer, the terminus of the drive. Below the second dam, the river flows unimpeded between craggy bluffs until its junction here with the Wabash, the clear Tippecanoe marrying with the muddy Wabash.

The nearby town of Americus hardly reflects the grandeur of its founding. Laid out in 1832, it was envisioned as the western terminus of the Wabash and Erie Canal. But the diversion of the canal to Lafayette left the dream high and dry, and it has survived since as a trading center for the area farmers.

The Carroll county line is 5.5 miles north of the mouth of the Tippecanoe, named for the Maryland Revolutionary War leader, Charles Carroll. The county was originally settled in the 1820s with a French trading post located just north of Rockfield near the Wabash. The dense forests and good canoeing rivers—the Wabash, Tippecanoe, and Wildcat Creek—made good fur trading.

Today the county is overwhelmingly agricultural, with more than 95 percent of the land in cultivation. In spite of that, picturesque Wildcat Creek as it flows through Carroll and Tippecanoe Counties has been recognized by the state for designation as a natural and scenic river.

Turn north on US 421 which is 1.8 miles further. Proceed to Delphi. Note the marker 1 mile north noting the New Purchase treaty boundary that wrested most of central Indiana from Native American control.

Delphi is a Wabash and Erie Canal boomtown. Established in 1828 as the county seat, the town's fortunes flared when the canal reached it in 1840. Until the last canalboat passed through in the 1870s, Delphi was an important port. As is the case in much of canal-era Indiana, the railroad came through in the 1850s, severely impacting canal commerce.

There are several imposing examples of fine period architecture, reflecting the town's former prosperity. The Barnett-Seawright House at 203 East Monroe is a Greek Revival structure built in 1857, with Italianate elements added later. The courthouse on Main Street was built in 1916. A courthouse bell used from 1841 sits under the stained-glass rotunda. A county museum is housed in the basement of the courthouse.

From the courthouse, turn left on Washington Street and drive 0.5 mile to the stone arch bridge over the Wabash and Erie Canal. Canal Park stretches on both sides of the old waterway. The county has 19 bridges deemed historically significant, including two covered bridges and four older stone arch bridges to vintage steel Warren Pony and Pratt Thru Truss bridges. Maps to the historic bridges are available at the county museum, as well as maps to the 11 Delphi Historic Trails that crisscross the town.

Deer Creek at the southern edge of town is another of Hoosier poet James Whitcomb Riley's fishing holes. It was here on the banks of the bluffed and sun-dappled stream that Riley got his inspiration for "On the Banks o' Deer Crick." Riley Park memorializes the peripatetic poet.

Return to US 421 and turn north. Pittsburg is another canal town, platted in 1836. The brick commercial structures of Main Street hark back to halcyon days when the town thronged the dock at the sound of the boatman's trumpet.

Lake Freeman is 4 miles north on US 421. It was formed when the Insull Corporation—a.k.a. Indiana Hydroelectric Power Company, which later became NIPSCO—dammed the Tippecanoe River with the 0.3-mile-long Oakdale Dam. The result was a 2,800-acre lake that quickly became a local fishing and boating favorite. Since the lake is privately owned, the shoreline is crowded with summer and weekend homes and cottages.

The lake stretches 7 miles along the highway north to Monticello, best known as a resort town. Monticello was platted in 1834 on a bluff overlooking the Tippecanoe River and named for President Thomas Jefferson's Virginia home. The town dozed for many decades; the major events seeming to be the tornadoes that swept down periodically. The 1872 Italianate-style James Culbertson Reynolds House at 417 N. Main Street obviously missed the tornado damage. James Reynolds was a successful farmer, merchant, and politician.

But the town's torpor lifted in the 1920s when plans were announced to build the two massive dams that created Lake Freeman and Lake Shafer north of Monticello.

The Insull Corporation erected the 1,200-foot-long Norway Dam north of the city in 1923. The resulting 1,291-acre Lake Schafer, ringed by 50 miles of shoreline and dotted with summer homes, stretches 4 miles up the former river. Proceed down Sixth Street to the west shore of the lake.

Indiana Beach, the premier lake playground, was opened under the name Ideal Beach in 1926 as "The Hoosier Riviera" by entrepreneur E. W. Spackman. The Riviera consisted of a bathhouse and sand beach where he rented ten small boats. Spackman erected the Ideal Beach Ballroom in 1930 to cash in on the Big Band craze. Groups such as Duke Ellington, Louis Armstrong, Glenn Miller, Tommy and Jimmy Dorsey, and Benny Goodman played there.

As musical tastes changed, so did the acts. Bill Haley, the Beach Boys, Chicago, Alice Cooper, and Sonny and Cher replaced the Big Band era in the venue, now called the Roof Garden Lounge. When Jefferson Airplane played in 1967, the admission was $3.25. Amusement rides along the beach arrived in 1947: merry-go-round, Ferris Wheel, and Rolo Plane. In 1951, Ideal Beach became Indiana Beach, and the growth hasn't stopped.

Now there are three roller coasters and giant waterslides among dozen of rides that are jammed into a manmade peninsula boardwalk that extends into the lake. Hundreds of hotel rooms and campsites are clustered around the amusement facility. The *Shafer Queen*, Indiana Beach's paddlewheeler, hauls nostalgic passengers around the lake daily in season.

22

Rensselaer and the Kankakee River
Dance of the Cranes

General description: The 68-mile route crosses the drained bed of the Great Kankakee Swamp through some of the nation's most productive farmland. State Fish and Wildlife Areas strung along the Kankakee River like beads on a string are remnants of the historic wetland environment.
Special attractions: In Brook: Hazelden, Willow Slough and LaSalle State Fish and Wildlife Areas, and birdlife at Jasper-Pulaski State Fish and Wildlife Area.
Location: Northern Indiana
Drive route numbers and names: U.S. Highways 231 and 41 and Indiana Highways 16 and 10.
Travel season: The fall and spring bird migrations are good times to explore this area. Winter can bring snowfall that will drift across roads, though snowplows are ubiquitous.
Camping: There is camping at Willow Slough and Jasper-Pulaski State Fish and Wildlife Areas.
Services: There are full services in Rensselaer. Gas and food are available at the numerous gas stations/convenience stores that sprout at the area's highway intersections.
Nearby attractions: Lake Shafer with its many recreational facilities is south at Monticello.

 ## The drive

The drive begins in Rensselaer, founded at the Falls of the Iroquois River, which never amounted to much in this case, given the unending flat landscape. The falls were a small rock ledge the river tumbled over. The first white settler made his way here in 1836, but within a few years sold out to enterprising Dutchman James Van Rensselaer from the upper Hudson Valley, who constructed a grist mill.

Van Rensselaer laid out the town as the county seat, and the Jasper County courthouse on Van Rensselaer Street is evidence that the town kept the honor. The Romanesque-late Gothic-style structure was built in 1896 to 1898. Turn left onto Indiana Highway 114 (Cullen Street) and proceed 1.9

miles. The Historical Log Cabin Museum is located in the Jasper County Fairgrounds. The 1872 cabin has a collection of vintage county materials.

Collegeville, home of St. Joseph's College, is 0.3 mile south of Rensselaer on U.S. Highway 231. Founded in 1889, the college is now a four-year liberal arts school, though it served as a seminary for priests at one time. The Chicago Bears used the campus for preseason training from 1944 until 1974 at the height of Coach George Hallas' reign. Hallas Hall is named after the coach who was a heavy contributor to the school.

The three-story brick structure on the east side of the highway is Drexel Hall, the former St. Joseph's Indian Normal School. Young Native American students were brought from Michigan, Wisconsin, Minnesota, and the Dakotas to be taught "industrial" skills, such as farming, tailoring and carpentry on the school's 420 acres. The Philadelphia heiress Katharine Drexel funded the school with a $50,000 gift in 1888, but by 1896 the school was closed. The distance from their families caused few students to want to stay with the program. Only six out of the first class of 50 remained to graduate.

Proceed 4 miles south and turn west on IN 16. Drive west 11.2 miles to Brook. Hazelden, home of author George Ade, is on the south side of the road beside the Iroquois River. Ade was a prolific humorist, writer, columnist, and playwright. He and Neil Simon share the honor of having three Broadway plays running simultaneously.

The sprawling Tudor-style mansion Ade built in 1904 sat on 417 acres alongside the Iroquois River. Ten acres of manicured lawns surrounded the house and formal garden. A baseball diamond, golf course, and swimming pool awaited his stellar guest list, ranging from Will Rogers and boxer Gene Tunney to General Douglas MacArthur and presidential candidate William Howard Taft.

Proceed west 3.7 miles on IN 16 to US 41 and turn north. Drive 9.7 miles across the low sand hills that separate the Iroquois' watershed from the Kankakee River to County Road 100 North to Willow Slough Fish and Wildlife Area. Opened in 1953, the 9,670-acre reserve is a haven for game and waterfowl thriving in the area's sand ridges and marshes. Willow Slough is the vestige of shallow Beaver Lake, part of the immense Kankakee swamp that stretched for over 0.5 million acres—5,300 square-miles—in the northwestern corner of the state along the Kankakee River from today's South Bend to Momence, Illinois.

Beaver Lake stretched for 28,500 acres. Before developers drained the swamp in 1853, this corner of Newton County was covered by water 3.5 feet deep. The lake bed is dry now, and strong southwest winds can lift enough ancient silt from the bed to cause instant brown-outs on nearby Interstate 65.

Drive 10.5 miles north through fields of dark mucky soil along US 41

North to LaSalle State Fish and Wildlife Area. The LaSalle Fish and Wildlife Area contains remnants of the Great Kankakee swamp in its 3,640 acres.

Prior to the nineteenth century, the Kankakee region was a vast complex of swamp, marsh, slough, bayou, and slurry, the largest freshwater marsh in the country. Through it the Kankakee River crossed 90 miles of ground, writhing through 2,000 bends in 250 miles of stream. Six months of the year, half of Indiana north of the Wabash was flooded. In high water, freight canoes could be paddled over the portages from one watershed to another.

The Kankakee Swamp was a spectacular wildlife refuge where millions of fur-bearing animals lived in the wetland, joined by clouds of waterfowl: ducks, Canada geese, blue herons, and sandhill cranes. The fur-crazed French traders were the first to mine the swamp, and the Americans, including the tycoon John Jacob Astor, were right behind. By 1855 the Kankakee was overtrapped, and the stage was set for the next chapter.

Drive 22: Rensselaer and the Kankakee River

Dance of the Cranes

The Indiana legislature passed the first motions to straighten the river and drain the swamp in 1848, and in 1858 developers formed the Kankakee Valley Draining Association. Oxen began pulling enormous plows through the muck, digging V-shaped ditches 2- and 3-feet deep. By 1882, there were 30,000 miles of tile drain in the state, most in this near-aquatic corner.

But it took the arrival of the first steam dredge boat in 1884 to get the swamp drained. The Indiana State Legislature authorized $60,000 in 1893 to blast the limestone barrier at Momence. When laborers finished their job, the ancient swamp began to give way to relatively dry land.

By the turn of the century, the straightening of the channel left 85 bends where 250 had been. The sluggish five-inch drop became a brisk 15-inch fall down a 90-mile ditch from the headwaters to the junction with the Illinois. Speculators created a land boom in the waterland. Investors became wealthy raising muck crops like onions and potatoes, and grain crops in the sandy soils that slowly rose to the sunshine.

To add to the bounty, drillers found oil pooled a mere hundred feet beneath the onions at the turn of the century. The hamlet of Asphaltum remains as a memory of the short-lived boom.

Into the 1920s, the region remained a premier sporting destination for the country's hunters and fishermen, as it had since the 1870s. Up and down the stream, posh hunting clubs served a coterie of wealthy sportsmen from New York, Washington, Philadelphia, and Boston, as well as across the Midwest, drawn by the promise of up to a hundred birds a day. At Thayer (1.1 miles north on IN 55), hunting lodges stood along the winding banks—the Diana and the Ahlgrim's Park among them.

By the 1920s, bridges stood high and dry where the river once ran, and the legislature was busy redrawing county lines that used to follow the curlicues of the river.

The fields, striated with the endless rows of crops following the neat grids of the government surveyors, stretched unchecked to the treelines of the tamed and tidy river.

Crossing the quiet stream, its banks run straight as a die on a diagonal across the checkerboarded landscape. Kankakee River Ditch is the name given to it on the state maps.

Proceed 13.8 miles west on IN 10 to US 231 North. Drive 3 miles north to IN 10 East and drive 12.6 miles to Jasper-Pulaski State Fish and Wildlife Area. The area—7,995 acres—is one of Indiana's largest remaining wetlands. It also is a primary state pheasant hatchery as well as having display cages of game birds and large native mammals. The facility provides an essential breeding and nesting ground for migrating waterfowl, including the spectacular sandhill cranes. More than 30,000 cranes arrive each fall in their migration to Florida and Georgia. Flocks of birdwatchers also arrive yearly to climb the observation towers and watch the curious dance of the cranes.

23

The Wild Life: Indians and Circuses

A drive along the Upper Wabash

General description: The 50-mile drive explores the Upper Wabash River, the spiritual home of the Miami Indian tribe.

Special attractions: In Huntington: Historic Forks of the Wabash and Dan Quayle Center and Museum. In Marion: Mississinawa Battlefield. Seven Pillars of the Mississinawa. In Peru: Circus Hall of Fame. Wabash and Erie Canal towns. In Logansport: Little Turtle Waterway Park and the Cass County Carousel.

Location: Northern Indiana.

Drive route numbers and names: U.S. Highway 24; Indiana Highway 124; and County Roads 500 East, 300 East, 200 South, 650 West; Division Road, and Frances Slocum Trail.

Travel season: Peru Circus Days in the summer bring large crowds to the area. The roads are all in good condition, though winter can bring drifting snows.

Camping: There are state campgrounds at Mississinawa Reservoir and Salamonie Lake, and private campgrounds at Peru's Honeybear Hollow Family Campground and Logansport's France Park.

Services: There are full services at Huntington, Wabash, Peru, and Logansport. Gas and food are available at numerous places en route.

Nearby attractions: James Dean's birthplace and grave are located in Fairmont, south of Marion. Frances Slocum State Recreation Area.

 ## The drive

The drive begins on the west side of Huntington at the junction of U.S. Highway 24 and Indiana Highway 9 at the Forks of the Wabash Park. It is where the Little River joins the Wabash at the southern end of the Long Portage, the historic link between the Atlantic and the Gulf of Mexico. Up-river at Fort Wayne, Indians and French voyageurs portaged from the junction of the Maumee over to the Little River, and in the process traversing from the great watershed of the St. Lawrence to that of the Mississippi. In high water, the portage was a short distance, but for much of the year it was a long haul through wetlands from one river system to the other.

When the first French traders arrived, the Wabash was considered the home of the Miami Indians and their Algonquian kinsmen—the Delaware, Kickapoo, Potawatomi, and Shawnee. The relatively tolerant French coexisted with the Miami, also inveterate traders, for nearly a century, often using the forks as a convenient locale for commerce.

In the post–Revolutionary War period, white incursions seeking land for settlement precipitated several battles, with Miami Chief Little Turtle's Indian forces emerging victorious. But Little Turtle's defeat by General Mad Anthony Wayne in 1796 spelled the end of Miami hegemony in the Wabash Valley. A series of treaties ceded increasing tribal land to the settlers. Miami chiefs and government negotiators signed the last treaty in 1840 here at the Forks of the Wabash. In 1846, the Miami, the last Indian tribe in Indiana, moved west of the Mississippi to Kansas.

The centerpiece of the park is the Chiefs' house, home of Jean Baptiste Richardville, the Civil Chief of the Miami tribe from 1816 to 1841. A skilled negotiator, Chief Richardville received large tracts of land and a substantial sum of money from the 1818 Treaty of St. Mary's, as well as sizable considerations from treaties signed at the Forks in 1834, 1838, and 1840. Richardville operated a trading post at Fort Wayne and his son-in-law, Lafontaine, controlled the porters that hauled the freight over the Long Portage.

The park re-creates the days of conflict and amelioration with festivals, interpretation, living history, and a visitor center with many exhibits. The park includes a reconstructed German settler house circa 1850s that displays the accouterments of the day.

Huntington was once a Miami village called Wepecheange—"place of flints." Located on the Little River, it was platted as the county seat in 1834 and grew sporadically until the arrival of the Wabash and Erie Canal accelerated the town's development. Huntington was long known as a center of limestone production, though the quarries were exhausted by 1900. It has been a small agricultural and manufacturing town since.

The best known Huntingtonian is J. Danforth Quayle, vice president under George Bush. Quayle grew up in the river town, practiced law here, and helped publish the local paper. He continues to use the town as his legal address and announced his latest campaign for president from a local restaurant, as he has all of his campaigns.

The Dan Quayle Center and Museum at 815 Warren Street is the only vice-presidential museum in the country. It offers exhibits and programs relating to the office of the vice president, since five vice presidents have come from Indiana.

The downtown is a redoubt of vintage brick and limestone commercial buildings, anchored by a neo-classical limestone Huntington County Courthouse with an Italian mosaic tile rotunda floor. A county museum is on the fourth floor.

Drive 23: The Wild Life: Indians and Circuses
A drive along the Upper Wabash

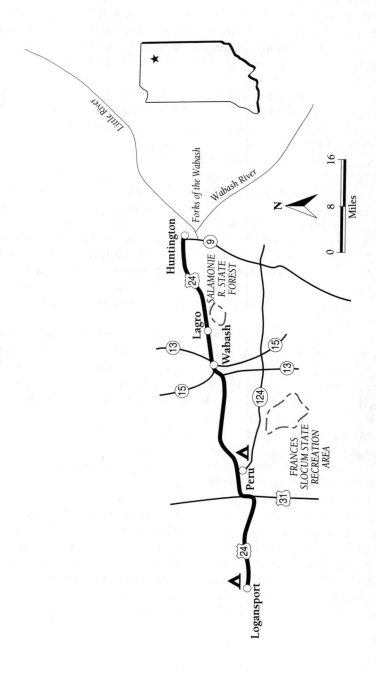

The Federal-style 1844–45 Moore Building at the northwest corner of Jefferson and Market Streets is a vestige of Huntington's canal days. It was the first brick building in the town.

Proceed west 12.5 miles on US 24 past limestone ledges and along the route of the Wabash and Erie Canal to Lagro. It was founded in 1829 and named after a Miami chief. Lagro was a major port on the canal, and the red-brick St. Patrick's Catholic Church at Main and Harrison is a remnant of the Irish canal workers who arrived to dig the ditch in 1834. The present church was dedicated in the 1870s.

The downtown is a down-at-the-heels memory of Lagro's brief heyday. Turn south on IN 524 to Washington Street and turn left. The small park three blocks away contains a cabin and the Kerr Locks, built in 1834–38. Though now high and dry, the finely dressed stone lock walls remain, curved to ease the canal boats into the lock.

Lagro is best known for the Irish War when warring Irishmen rioted in 1835 and state troops were called out to quell the battle, arresting more than 200 canal workers. The ringleaders were tried and jailed in Indianapolis, but the rest were sent back to their shovels and barrows.

Salamonie Reservoir and State Forest is located at the south edge of town. Hanging Rock is 2.1 miles south on Division Road, an 84-foot-high hunk of Silurian reef that towers above the countryside, providing a promontory for vistas. The small 610-acre forest has camping and trails for hikers, horses, and cross-country skiers. The reservoir is a 2,855-acre pool that stretches 17 miles.

Proceed west 4 miles on US 24 to County Road 500 East, turn north, and drive 1.9 miles to CR 300 North. Hopewell Church is nature-writer Gene Stratton Porter's childhood church. Her brother Leander, model for Laddie in her 1913 novel of the same name, is buried in the cemetery. Gene Stratton Porter was born on a 240-acre farm 0.5 mile north of the church.

Return to US 24 West. Wabash, 1.5 miles west on US 24, is another canal town that hung on as a small industrial city and county seat. Some of the vintage structures still have doors on the canal side to facilitate loading onto the boats. Look behind the buildings at Canal and Wabash Streets to get a sense of Venice-style Wabash.

The 15-acre Paradise Springs park at the corner of Allen and Market Streets re-creates the momentous treaty grounds, where the American government in 1826 once again required the Miami and Potawatomi to cede more land. With the signing of the treaty, the tribes gave up a wide swath of their northern Indiana and southern Michigan land and acquiesced to the Wabash and Erie Canal to pass through their remaining reserve.

The current courthouse is a pastiche of Greek Revival, Italianate, and Romanesque styles, erected in 1878–79. Just west of the courthouse, the

Wabash County Historical Museum houses artifacts of local resonance, including Native American materials, canal memorabilia, and a collection of war-related items including statues of a Union soldier and sailor who stand guard at the entrance.

The canal in the upper valley did far better than farther south, in part because it operated in that halcyon canal period before railroads came down the tracks. Railroads reached Wabash in 1856, nearly two decades after the Wabash and Erie arrived. It is railroad history, however, that immortalized the town in song. "The Wabash Cannon Ball" celebrates the Norfolk and Western train that barreled through town and down the riverside track, running between Detroit and St. Louis.

In 1880, Wabash became the first electric-lit city in the nation. Today Wabash is best known for its connection to the Honeywell Corporation, which began as a local heating concern in 1900. The heat control/thermostat corporation, Honeywell, Inc., is now one of the nation's 100 largest companies. Downtown at Hill and Carroll Streets, the Honeywell Memorial Center is an architecturally significant civic center that boasts a fine collection of Hoosier School paintings, including work by T. C. Steele, Marie Goth, and C. Curry Bohm. The original exterior has some charming bas-reliefs of recreation-related objects like roller skates.

The requisite mansion of the local nabob, the Honeywell House, is located at 720 N. Walnut Street. The home, built 1959–1964, is furnished with fine Louis XIV and Louis XV pieces. Following a 1974 fire and the death of Mrs. Honeywell, the house was bequeathed to the Indiana University Foundation, which opens the building for special events.

Continue 10.7 miles west on US 24 to Peru, "Circus Capital of the World." Platted in 1829, the city became the winter home of several major circuses such as Wallace-Hagenbeck, Sells-Floto, and the American Circus Corporation. In the golden age of the circus in the 1870s, 12 large circuses crisscrossed the continent, a traveling aggregate of wild animal acts, performers, clowns, grifters, and con men, leaving a path of delighted locals and disgruntled city fathers in their wake. They moved down the silver tracks, and Peru stood at a handy intersection with trains leaving in all directions.

Each winter, as many as seven troupes returned to roost in the small Indiana town, with many famous performers such as Emmett Kelly and Clyde Beatty using Peru as their permanent address. As their performing careers ended, many of the veterans of the big top returned to Peru to retire.

The Depression hit the circus world hard, and by the 1940s Peru's days as the winter home were over. The memories almost faded until 1956 when the National Convention of the Circus History Society met in Peru. Circus City Festival, Inc., a nonprofit organization celebrating Peru's circus past, was formed in 1960 and the annual circus festival began. The yearly circus parade is now an eagerly awaited event. The Circus City Center where it all happens is located in a renovated brick lumberyard at 154 N. Broadway. The building also houses a fine exhibit of Peru circus history.

East 2.5 miles on IN 124 at the confluence of the Wabash and Mississinawa Rivers, the International Circus Hall of Fame is the site of the largest winter circus quarters in the world. In its heyday, the 3,000-acre farm had more than 40 buildings and barns sheltering the animals and wagons of several circuses, including the American Circus Corporation and Buffalo Bill's Wild West Show. One pasture held the herd of 100 zebras, another held 1,000 giant circus horses. Sixty elephants walked the grounds. Lions roared from the Hoosier barns. Today, an old sign that reads "Elephants-Big Cats" still hangs over the entrance to a looming yellow barn.

Behind it, another gargantuan structure, originally the circus wagon building, houses the Hall of Fame Collection, honoring the luminaries of the Big Top from the eighteenth-century beginnings to the 1920s Golden Days to modern performers like Gunther Gabel-Williams. The museum has more than 40 wagons and calliopes, artifacts, props, costumes, posters, hand-bills, and lithographs from circuses around the world.

The winter quarters began in 1891 when Ben Wallace bought the farm of Miami Chief Francis Godfroy, who received the land as a government grant in 1826. The Greek Revival house was built in the 1870s. The Godfroy Cemetery where he and other Miami and their white spouses are buried is 5 miles east of Peru on IN 124 on the north side of the road.

The International Circus Hall of Fame hosts daily circus performances under the Big Top throughout the summer. The steam calliope burbles and whistles and the local animal trainer gives "tiger talks." The facility is a National Historical Landmark.

Return west toward Peru on IN 124, cross the Mississinawa and turn south on Frances Slocum Trail. Cole Porter's parents' Southern Colonial house, Westleigh, is in the first scene of "Night and Day" which told the life story of the Peru native. Just down the road, the bucolic white frame "Old Fashioned Garden" farm is Porter's grandmother's house, and the inspiration for his first popular song, "Old Fashioned Garden."

Cole Porter was a master of American popular song, famous for such Broadway hits as "Anything Goes," Kiss Me Kate," and "Can-Can." He captured America with songs like "Night and Day," "In the Still of the Night," "You're the Top," and "Don't Fence Me In."

Return to IN 124 and proceed west to CR 300 East and turn south. The site of the Osage Village, one of the largest Miami villages, is nearby, memorialized by a large boulder with a bronze plaque on the right side of the road. Tecumseh assembled the braves of a dozen tribes here in 1812, attempting to persuade them to join his confederacy in the War of 1812.

Colonel J. Campbell burned the village in 1813. The brick house to the south is yet another of Jean Baptiste Richardville's homes.

Drive south 1.2 miles to CR 200 South and turn left. The Seven Pillars of the Mississinewa, a sacred site of the Miami Indians, is across the stream. The pillars symbolize "the Great Father," and figures prominently in tribal ritual and lore. Much of the area's land was part of the Miami Reserve until 1840 when the last treaty forced the tribe west of the Mississippi. The 6,000-member Miami Nation of Indiana, which is reasserting itself in the local area, recently bought the land across the river from the Pillars for tribal rites and festivals.

Return to IN 124 and proceed east to CR 650 West and turn south. Drive 2.8 miles to Frances Slocum Cemetery. Slocum, "the White Rose of the Miami," was a Miami Indian woman, Maconaquah, who was kidnapped as a young girl from her Pennsylvania Quaker family by three Delaware braves. Raised by a childless couple, she became wholly integrated into tribal ways, later marrying a Miami chief. At an elderly age, she was reunited with her Pennsylvania family, but chose to remain with her Miami family. She died at the age of 74 and was buried in an upright position in the Miami cemetery. The flooding of the area for the Mississinewa Reservoir necessitated the relocation of the graves to this spot.

Return to Peru. At the Wabash River bridge at Broadway, the old Toll House stands on the northeast corner. The 1840 structure is the oldest in town. In canal days, boats unloaded at the south end. The Wabash County Courthouse is a neo-classical structure built in 1911. Cole Porter's birthplace is located at 102 E. Third Street.

Drive west 14.1 miles on US 24 to Logansport. The road twists and turns a bit as it winds through a forested section. Named for a Shawnee chief who died fighting for the American forces near Fort Wayne in the War of 1812, Logansport is situated at the confluence of the Eel and Wabash Rivers. The canal made the town flourish, and the railroad's coming in 1855 transformed it into a rail center. By 1860, it was one of the Midwest's main hubs and repair depots. The Iron Horse Museum on South Fourth Street is located in the former Pennsylvania Railway Station, filled with railroad kitsch and memorabilia. The Cass County Historical Society Museum at 1004 S. Main Street is located in an 1853 Italianate home, and has a large collection of Cass County pioneer and Native American artifacts.

Cass County is second only to Miami County in Native American population. They have celebrated the heritage with the well-designed Little Turtle Waterway park along the Wabash. The monument features granite insets honoring the Miami and Potawatomi tribes and a granite map of the Wabash watershed showing the locations of 1812 Miami villages. A statue of Little Turtle is planned.

Another Logansport park is located on the Eel River on Tenth Street. The 1895 Riverside Park boasts a magnificent National Historic Landmark, the Cass County Carousel, a perfectly preserved Dentzel merry-go-round, carved by Gustav Dentzel and his artisans more than 100 years ago. It has delighted four generations of Cass County kids with its whirling charms one of only three intact Dentzel carousels left.

24

Indiana Lakeland
Warsaw to North Webster

General description: The drive proceeds from Warsaw past Tippecanoe Lake and winds around Lake Wawasee.

Special attractions: Tippecanoe Lake, Lake Wawasee, and Lake Webster.

Location: North central Indiana.

Drive route numbers and names: Indiana Highways 15 and 13; U.S. Highway 6; County Roads 775 East, 1300 North, 900 East, 850 East, 1000 North, and 500 North and East; and North Shore Drives.

Travel season: This is a long-time summer playground, so accordingly, the place hops from Memorial Day to Labor Day. Winter can bring deep snows that make travel on the back roads precarious until the snow plows come through.

Camping: Warsaw has camping at Hoffman Lake Camp and Pic-A-Spot Campground.

Services: There are full services in Warsaw, Syracuse, and North Webster, and gas and food at numerous places en route.

Nearby attractions: The Amish areas of Lagrange and Elkhart Counties are 20 miles north.

 The drive

The drive begins in Warsaw, the county seat of Kosciusko County. Following the Indian treaties that opened the land for settlement, the county was organized in 1835 and 1836. The county was named after the Polish Revolutionary War hero, Thaddeus Kosciusko, and the city after the capital of his homeland. More than 90 lakes dot the county, including Indiana's largest natural lake, Wawasee.

Settlers named Warsaw as the county seat in 1837. The courthouse is an 1880s French Second-Empire structure with a mansard roof, topped with an octagonal clock tower. The third-floor courthouse still retains the original fireplaces, though the heavy legal lifting is now done across the street at the modernist justice building that opened in 1982.

The two-block courthouse area was designated a historic district in 1982, and the Saeman Building at Buffalo and Center Streets is the centerpiece. The Italianate structure has retained its original cherry and walnut woodwork and stained glass transoms. The old county jail at Indiana and Main Streets, two blocks west of the square, is also in the district. It houses the Warsaw Museum which has a large genealogical library and county mementos, with a particular focus on the Civil War.

The town has a diversified industrial base, but is a center of surgical prosthetics and artificial joints, a specialty that dates back to 1895. The county is also known as the "Egg Capital of the Midwest" with millions of eggs laid yearly. Mentone, on the county's western edge, celebrates their status with a 3,000-pound concrete egg on the main drag that they light up at night.

Another vintage business is the Warsaw Cut Glass Factory which has operated since 1911. Proceed 3 blocks east on Center Street to Detroit Street, then go south 4 blocks. The first floor has an exhibit of antique glass and a showroom of new material.

Winona Lake, southeast of Warsaw, was the western outpost of the Chautaqua movement. It is a summer resort and religious revival center. Each summer thousands from Chicago, New York, and the Midwest traveled via the Pittsburgh, Fort Wayne, and Chicago Railroad to the lakeside town for elucidation and exhortations. An early twentieth-century evangelist in the area was Billy Sunday. His house, a small wooden bungalow, can be seen at 1111 Sunday Lane.

The Winona Christian Assembly dates back to 1895, the result of the collusion of influential men like food-processor H. J. Heinz, auto manufacturer John Studebaker, and Dr. J. Wilbur Chapman, a famous evangelist. Following Sunday's death in 1935, the Free Methodist Church World Headquarters was established here, and the Grace Brethren Church followed, which also operates the nearby Grace College and Seminary. Tens of thousands still arrive annually for the services held in the Billy Sunday Tabernacle.

Return through Warsaw to Indiana Highway 15 and drive north. The road crosses Tippecanoe River below Tippecanoe Lake, where it receives the waters of the seven-lake Barbee chain. It winds between tree-lined banks, with bluffs and grassy islands decorating the stream.

In 5.5 miles, turn east at Leesburg to 707-acre Tippecanoe Lake. It is the state's deepest and one of the hundreds of kettle lakes left in northeastern Indiana when the glaciers retreated. The lake is secluded in a picturesque valley, an ideal place for a stroll, picnic, or boat excursion.

Oswego at its southern end is a small resort village that was an early settlement on the site of Chief Musquabuck's Indian village and tribal reservation. Pound's Store located at Armstrong Road and Second Street is the oldest business in the county, beginning in 1838. It is now maintained by the county historical society as a museum and contains many original fixtures and furnishings.

Return to IN 15 North. Drive north 5.6 miles to Milford, the first town settled in the county by pioneers drawn to the rich prairie. Later the Cincinnati, Wabash, and Michigan Railroad boosted the town's prospects with its arrival in 1870.

Continue north 3 miles to the junction of U.S. Highway 6 East. Proceed 5 miles east to IN 13 and turn south. Drive 2 miles to Syracuse. Founded in the 1830s, the town was destined to be a resort town. The first hotel was called the Rough and Ready, and two distilleries and a barrel-making factory were among its first businesses. Today Syracuse is primarily a resort town with four lakeside parks that dozes through the winter. It sits at the end of Syracuse Lake, a 564-acre bay of adjoining Lake Wawasee.

Take IN 13 to Washington Street, follow it to North Shore Drive and

Drive 24: Indiana Lakeland
Warsaw to North Webster

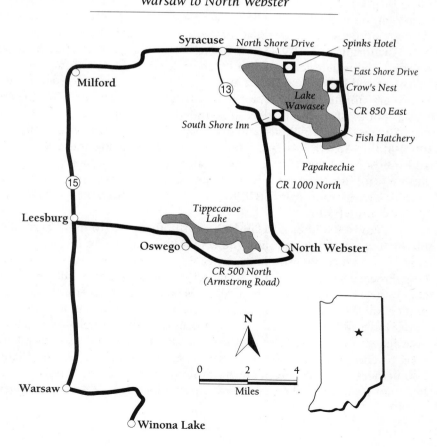

turn right. Follow this to East Shore Drive and go 0.7 mile across the railroad tracks, turn left and continue 0.6 mile to Lake Wawasee. Named for Miami Chief Wau-was-aus-see, the 2,618-acre lake is the largest natural lake in Indiana. A dam built at Syracuse in 1834 raised the water to its present level.

A marker noting the boundary line of Chief Papakeechie's former reservations is on the right, Indian land that extended into Noble County. The sprawling former 130-room Spink Hotel and gambling casino is 0.4 mile farther. In its heyday it was a pink stucco destination for the moneyed classes. Built in 1925, it operated as a Catholic seminary and prep school from 1948 until the 1970s. It is now condominium apartments.

The Wawasee Golf Club is left on County Road 775 East. It was founded by Eli Lilly in 1891. The section of lakeshore became a refuge for Indianapolis industrialists. The two-story brick home across the street was built by J. K. Lilly, Eli's son. Just west of the house, a Greek Revival home was built by Indianapolis Speedway founder James Allison.

Turn right on CR 1300 North in 0.5 mile, drive 1.3 miles, and then turn right on CR 900 East. The Crow's Nest Yacht Club is 3 miles south. It was one of the seven hotels that thrived on the lake in the 1930s.

Turn right on CR 950 East 0.4 mile past the yacht club, which will proceed a non-defunct state fish hatchery located on an isthmus between Wawasee and Lake Papakeechie, a 300-acre lake that is restricted to property owners around the lake. Prior to construction of a dam in 1910, the area was a sponge of six small lakes surrounded by wetlands.

Proceed to CR 850 East and drive 1.2 miles. The Tri-County State Fish and Wildlife Area, a 3,487-acre reserve, has 39 manmade and natural lakes and ponds, used for wildlife viewing and mushroom gathering as well as hunting and fishing. A 10-acre nature preserve that was part of Chief Papakeechie's reservation from 1828 to 1834 is within the refuge. It has a self-guided nature trail.

Follow CR 850 East to CR 1000 North, then west to IN 13 and follow the highway northwest around the lake. The South Shore Inn was located along here, a local favorite in its day.

Proceed south on IN 13. A marker noting the Continental Divide between the Great Lakes and the Gulf of Mexico is half 0.5 south—less dramatic than the one on top of the Rockies, but momentous nonetheless.

North Webster is 5 miles south. It is another summer playground town, cutesied into a faux Camelot for the most part. Webster Lake is a deep kettle lake, reaching a depth of 45 feet, with a surface of 585 acres. The *Dixie*, a double-decker sternwheeler, churns around the lake as she has since 1929. It is another devout lake drained by Tippecanoe River. Weimer Park was a popular camp meeting site on the lake dating to 1915, and the Indiana Conference of the Methodist Church has church grounds at Epsworth Forest Park on a road of the same name. The park was organized in 1924 named after the birthplace of John Wesley, founder of Methodism.

Oswego at the south end of Lake Tippecanoe can be reached via CR 500 North, which is 0.7 miles south of North Webster on IN 13. County Road 500 North, which becomes Armstrong Road, leads to Oswego in 5.8 miles.

25

Wintertime Cheer to the Austere Life

A loop from Angola to the homeland of the Indiana Amish

General description: The tour starts in Angola where the heaviest snowfalls in Indiana from the lake-effect of Lake Michigan engenders the winter recreation of Pokagon State Park. The drive continues through Auburn, famous for the Auburn-Cord-Duesenberg Museum to Amish country at Shipshewana and home of one of the country's most famous flea markets.

Special attractions: In Angola: Pokagon State Park and Lake James. In Auburn: Auburn-Cord-Duesenberg Museum. In Rome: Gene Stratton–Porter State Historic Site. In Shipshewana: Menno-Hof Mennonite-Amish Visitor Center and Shipshewana Flea Market and Auction.

Location: Northeastern Indiana.

Drive route numbers and names: Indiana Highways 827, 120, 8, 35, 6, 127, 727, and 9; U.S. Highways 20 and 6; and Interstate 69.

Travel season: Wintertime is a special season here for winter sports opportunities. The region falls in the lake-effect snow belt, so be prepared for some storms.

Camping: There are campgrounds in Angola: Pokagon State Park, Camp Sack-In, and Circle B Park. The Pigeon River State Fish and Wildlife Area at Mongo has Class B sites. Shipshewana has Riverside Campground and Shipshewana Campground.

Services: There are full services in Angola, Auburn, Lagrange, and Shipshewana. Gas and food are available at numerous places en route.

Nearby attractions: Elkhart County, with its large Amish population is just west, and the lake country around Wawasee and North Webster is southwest.

 The drive

The drive begins in Angola, the Steuben County seat. The New England–flavored courthouse reflects the Yankee origin of many of the town's earliest settlers, who migrated from New England, New York, and the Western Reserve areas of Ohio that were the home of New Englanders after the Revolutionary War. The courthouse with its elaborate belfry and Italianate brackets

Drive 25: Wintertime Cheer to the Austere Life

*A loop from Angola to the homeland
of the Indiana Amish*

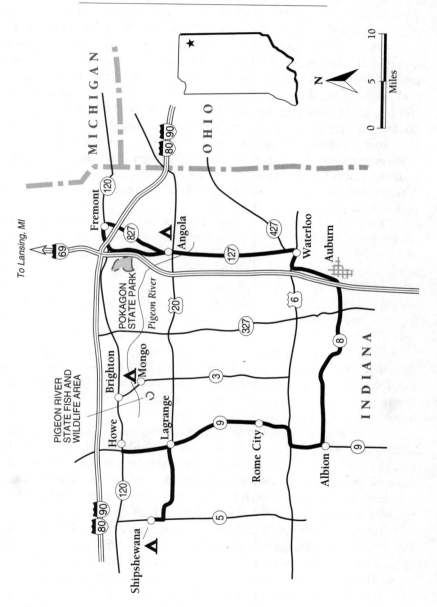

was built in 1867 and 1868 of native timbers. The jail just behind was finished about a decade later, also with local materials. Local laborers dredged the marl and blue clay from nearby Lake James to make the bricks.

The county historical society maintains the Hartman House at 901 West Maumee Street. The 1890s house has a collection of historical items including a tapestry that hung in the Territorial Capitol in Vincennes.

Tri-State University is west on Maumee Street 4 blocks, and then south 2 blocks on Darling Street. Founded in 1884, the four-year college boasts a museum dedicated to an alumni who sparked a thousand protests. The General Lewis B. Hershey Museum honors the long-time director of the Selective Service System. Hershey ran the draft from 1941 to 1970. The museum contains his papers, furniture, and military memorabilia.

Just southwest of the campus, Fox Lake has been a playground for Midwestern black families since the 1920s when strict segregation plagued Indiana. From the Roaring 20s until the 1960s, it was primarily used by African–Americans, and today most of the lakefront property is still owned by black families.

There are 101 lakes in Steuben County and three navigable rivers. Five nature preserves are open to nature enthusiasts on a daily basis. The lake-effect of Lake Michigan and prevailing westerlies bury the region in a blanket of snow that lasts most of the winter. Accordingly, locals and visitors take advantage of the natural assets of the region to turn it into a four-season playground. Fishing, boating, swimming, and hiking enliven the warm months, and cross-country skiing, tobogganing, snowmobiling, ice-fishing, and traipsing through the winterland trails spice up the cold ones.

Take Indiana Highway 127 North 0.6 mile to IN 827 East (Mechanic Street). Drive 6.9 miles to Fremont at IN 120. Fremont is on the Vistula Road that traversed from Lake Erie at Toledo to Lake Michigan at Chicago, the route for French Jesuits toting Christianity to the Indians, and Mormons trailing Brigham Young to the West.

Drive west 3.5 miles to IN 127 and turn south. The entrance to Pokagon State Park at IN 727 is 1.8 miles south. Established in 1925, the 1,195-acre park is located on Lake James, one of the largest lakes in Indiana. The park offers a variety of recreational facilities including a unique toboggan run down a 1,780-foot iced slide. The vintage Potawatomi Inn has 142 guest rooms and has been ranked as one of the top 25 resorts in the Midwest.

Proceed south on IN 127 through Angola and drive 16 miles south to U.S. Hgihway 6, then go east 1.4 miles to Interstate 69 South. Auburn is 5.4 miles south. Each Labor Day Weekend more than 200 Auburns, Cords, and Duesenbergs—luxury roadsters synonymous with the Roaring '20s high life—return to their birthplace in Auburn, along with 200,000 people celebrating the Golden Age of Motoring with a festival and a classic car auction.

The Auburn-Cord-Duesenberg Museum at 1600 S. Wayne Street is housed in the Auburn Automobile Company's art deco administration building and showroom, built at the height of the streamline era. The chandeliers, elaborate terrazzo floors, and grand staircase are all original, as are the hundred classic automobiles housed there.

Proceed west 16.8 miles on IN 8 through a land of rolling glacial moraines to Albion. While one of the smaller towns in the county, Albion's central location gave it the county seat honors. The Richardsonian Romanesque courthouse was built in 1888–89. The Old Jail Museum next door is housed in an 1875 jail. Turn north on IN 9 and proceed 4 miles to US 6. Turn east 1.4 miles to IN 9. Rome City and the Gene Stratton Porter State Historic Site is 3 miles north.

The town is situated on Sylvan Lake, an 1830s reservoir for a canal to connect Lake Michigan with the Wabash and Erie Canal, another of the projects that went bust in the canal days. French and Irish workers each took a side of the canal-in-progress as their home.

The Gene Stratton Porter State Historic Site honors the naturalist and author who wrote *Freckles* and *Girl of the Limberlost* among many others. Porter lived here from 1914 to 1919 and adjacent Wildflower Woods were the inspiration for many of her stories.

Proceed north on IN 9 through lake and northern moraine country. Lagrange County is home to a large Amish community which relocated here from Lancaster County, Pennsylvania, in the 1840s. More than 20 percent of the county's population is Amish. Be alert for slow-moving buggies and wagons. Also please refrain from photographing the Amish.

The town of Lagrange is the county seat, 12.3 miles north of Rome City. The brick and sandstone courthouse was built in 1879 in a Renaissance-Revival style with a 125-foot-high bell tower. Along the west side, Amish tie their patient horses to the hitching posts. On the two-story square, Foltz Bakery serves traditional sweet things to the local townspeople.

Proceed north on IN 9 to Howe. It's a quintessential small Indiana town, with scrupulously mowed lawns and well-maintained older homes nestled in shady yards. The Kingsbury House on the square on Third Street is a finely wrought yellow brick hotel built in 1863, replacing another hotel that dated back to 1835, but burned.

The Howe Military School at the north edge of town on IN 9 was founded in 1895. From 1884 to 1895 it operated as a grammar school. The Norman-style St. James Chapel is modeled on the Magdalen College Chapel at Oxford, England, an appropriate motif for this Episcopal Church–affiliated school. The chapel was built in 1902–1914. The interior has stone floors, hand-carved walnut pews, and an Italian triptych. The remains of several Episcopal bishops reside in the chapel crypt. On Sundays at noon in the spring and fall, the uniform-clad cadets wheel and turn in military review and parade.

Turn east on IN 120. The land begins to open up; tile drains and pumps appear. Turn south on IN 3 and drive 3.3 miles south to Mongo. Flapping laundry drying in the sun and houses without electric wires running to them tell of an Amish area. The broad tan fields are known as English Prairie.

A red bank barn (called a bank barn because of the slope or bank that runs to the second floor, a vestige of Pennsylvania Dutch architectural design) is on the right with the name "Aldrich" proudly painted on the front.

Mongo has garnered regional fame for succulent honeydew, muskmelon, and cantaloupe melons that thrive in the sandy soil. Originally named Mongoquinong, Potawatomi for "Big Squaw," the town straddles the Pigeon River at the mill pond that is the river's origin. The river sweeps out of sight around a willow-lined bend on its way to a confluence with the St. Joseph's River 36 miles away. It is considered one of Indiana's best canoeing and float streams, and rental places abound.

The Potawatomi were the original inhabitants of the pond, and French and American fur traders joined them in the 1830s. An 1832 Greek Revival house stands at West and Second Streets, with the sign for a defunct interior design firm out front. A 1915 Mongo Bank Building with Prairie-style stained glass and fine detailing is now a bar. To the east, the now empty Olde Mongo Hotel stands resolute with an ornate Victorian cupola on top.

The Lagrange Phalanx, part of the Fourierist communal movement, was founded near Mongo in 1844. Forty families—120 people—lived in a 210-foot-long building with shared dining, supervised by councils of industry, commerce, and education. They raised produce and livestock on 1,500 acres of fine farmland. Though communal in all aspects, they issued stock and paid dividends. The commune failed in two years after dissensions tore the community apart, as did a similar community at Brighton 3.5 miles north.

East of Mongo on CR 300 North, the Pigeon River State Fish and Wildlife Area is an 11,500-acre facility. A nature preserve in the area has the largest tamarack bog forest preserve in Indiana. Shallow Lake is a waterfowl production area that has helped nurse Canada Geese back to healthy levels after near extinction.

Proceed south on IN 3 to US 20 and turn west. Proceed 18.3 miles through Lagrange to IN 5 North and drive 1.5 miles to Shipshewana. Giant grain elevators announce the town. The town was founded in 1889, named after a local Potawatomi chief. The town is best known for the sprawling Shipshewana Flea Market and Auction, where more than 1,000 vendors offer their treasures every Tuesday and Wednesday. Work horse and livestock auctions happen throughout the season.

Winter-weather enthusiasts enjoy Pokagon State Park's toboggan run.
Photo courtesy of Steuben County Tourism Bureau.

An antique auction is every Wednesday with as many as 12 auction-eers simultaneously hollering out their cadences to rings of intent bidders. Goods range from 50s junk to high-end country antiques that make their way to the big city antique shops and dealers. In the auction-barn restaurant, diners share communal tables as Amish girls in prayer caps and shin-length dresses, whisk plates of farm food to the patrons. Antique dealers and tony mavens pass the salt to bearded farmers with Red Man Tobacco belt buckles, and chats about original paint and resale get mixed in with gimlet-eyed discussions of feeder calves and work horses.

Down IN 5 North, the Wana Cup restaurant is another place offering Amish and Mennonite food. In the evening it becomes a happening place, the hitching posts filled as the young courting couples gather for soft-serve ice cream and a little post-chores chat.

The Menno-Hof Mennonite-Amish Visitor Center across the road from the flea market is one of the nation's most respected interpretive centers. Within the barnlike museum, visitors can learn about the history, customs, and lifestyles of the Amish and Old Order Mennonites that make the region their home.

The Amish trace their origins to the early 1500s when a priest named Menno Simons preached against the non-scriptured teaching of the Dutch church. He taught that only willing adults should be baptized, and there should be a strict delineation between church and state. A movement known as the Anabaptists rose from his beliefs.

In 1693, a conservative Swiss, Jacob Amman, preached an even more austere brand of anabaptism, urging beards for married men, plain dress for both sexes, and shunning from the community for those not adhering to the rules. Amman's preaching split the Anabaptist community, and those that followed him became known as Amish.

Eventually both the Mennonites and Amish were driven from Europe for their beliefs, particularly their resistance to military service, as both sects are pacifistic. Many moved to the early Pennsylvania colony, invited by Quaker William Penn.

The Amish and Old Order Mennonites share many beliefs including pacifism, adult baptism, and plain lifestyles. The Amish, remembering their days of persecution, have no central religious authority, electing their local deacons, ministers, and bishops from the congregation. There are no Amish churches, as they continue to meet in homes every other Sunday.

A south German dialect called "Pennsylvania Dutch" is used in the home and church, though it has evolved into its own parlance, enlivened with colloquialisms and English words. Northern Indiana Amish can no longer converse in German with their southern Indiana brethren, being forced to use English instead. The families are large and divorce is almost non-existent. Farming is still the preferred vocation, though many men now work in the area factories (particularly woodworking and the RV industry) and on construction crews.

The Amish educate their children in small Amish schoolhouses scattered through the region, with an Amish woman most often serving as teacher. Children are educated up to the Eighth grade when they leave to pursue their traditional occupations. Until school consolidations in the 1960s, the Amish children were educated in public schools, but the Amish opposed their children being bussed to faraway institutions and instead choose to set up their own facilities within a buggy ride of home.

26

Indiana Amish Heartland
Nappanee to Goshen

General description: This 55-mile drive explores the northern Indiana heartland of the Old Order Amish, beginning in Nappanee and running through Amish farmland to Bonneyville Mill.

Special attractions: Amish Farms, Amish Acres, Old Bag Factory, and Bonneyville Mills.

Location: Northern Indiana.

Drive route numbers and names: Indiana Highways 119, 4, and 5; and County Roads 16, 34, 37, and 250 West.

Travel season: Amish country is year-round, though heavy snows slow things down. There are many Amish buggies on the roads, so caution is vital.

Camping: Eby's Pines Campground at Bristol in the northern part of the county and Elkhart Campground in Elkhart.

Services: There are full services in Napannee, Goshen, and Middlebury. Gas and food are available at Bristol.

Nearby attractions: Shipshewana's Menno-Hof Amish-Mennonite Museum and famous flea market and auction are just east.

 **The drive**

The drive begins in Nappanee, a railroad town founded in 1874. The town has capitalized on the allure of the plain Amish, and there is an abundance of black buggy art painted on local signs. Area strip malls all seem to have Amish and country themes and crafts, and it's hard to ignore the fact that this is Amish country.

Amish Acres, an 80-acre re-creation of a working Amish farm has given the town its lodestone. The farm began in 1874 when Christian and Moses Stahly bought it. The farm includes the original house with appropriate furnishings, the smaller Gross Dawdy Haus where the grandparents lived, and several vintage farm, buildings including the grand Schweitzer barn. It operated as a working farm among the Stahly, Nissley, and Kuhns family until 1969 when the current owners purchased it on the auction block to prevent it from being turned into an industrial site.

More than 250,000 people a year visit the farm, experiencing the

Drive 26: Indiana Amish Heartland

Nappanee to Goshen

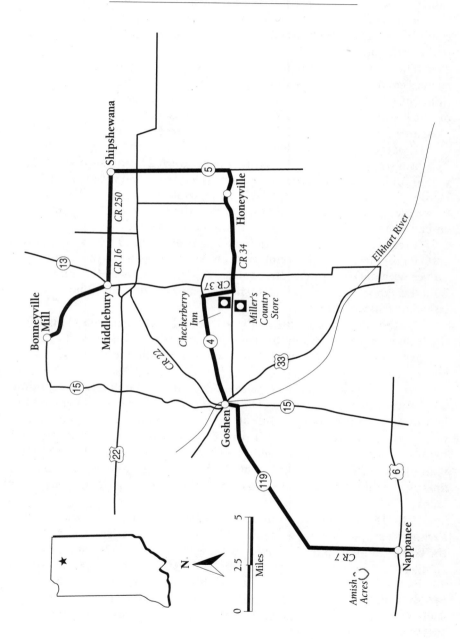

rustic life of the Amish of yesterday (and today, for that matter, since things don't change much on an Amish farm). The place still exhales the air of a calm yesterday, even with a 400-seat barn restaurant serving Threshers' Dinners, a musical theater operating in a restored 1911 round barn, and relocated log houses serving as shops for crafts, soda, meat and cheeses, and homemade fudge.

The farm acts as a living museum. Women carry out everyday tasks such as candle making, quilting, and outdoor baking, while the men engage in maple sugaring, cider making, and animal husbandry. The farm is listed on the National Register of Historic Places and served as a heritage tourism pilot area for the National Trust for Historic Preservation.

Proceed to the east edge of town and turn north on County Road 7. The road passes several Amish farms where bearded farmers work the fields with draft horses, and teams of as many as a dozen used in spring plowing. Herds of cows lay in leisure beside great white barns. Tall silos hold the provender of the year to satisfy the herds in the winter. Austere farmhouses sit beneath towering windmills spinning in the breeze.

Proceed north 5 miles to Indiana Highway 119 and turn to the northeast. Black buggies with bonneted women trip down the road, pulled by horses with dark shining coats, some crossing the highway like moving silhouettes. Young Amishmen with snappy fedoras ride behind horse-drawn cultivators like charioteers.

To the southwest, rolling hills are dotted with small woodlots. Tree-lined streams wind through the fields. The air is tinted with the smell of hay and manure—livestock's "useful byproduct" according to the local tourism brochures.

A hummocky golf course with a requisite gated golf course "community" announces the outskirts of affluent Goshen. City fathers platted Goshen in 1831, but it took a while to boost its fortunes enough to warrant incorporation in 1854. It is still primarily an insular agricultural trading town, in character if not in revenues. The growth of the locally owned recreational vehicle industry has created a burgeoning class of parvenus who are responsible for the bloated lakeside homes that ring the region's many lakes.

The 1870 Elkhart County Courthouse at the center of town reflects the town's suspicions. An octagonal limestone booth with a carved frieze at the corner of Main and Lincoln Streets was built by the WPA in the Depression at the behest of the town fathers. Banks stood at the adjacent corners and bank robber John Dillinger roamed the land. Police manned the bulletproof booth from 1939 to 1969, though it is now used by the local historical society to keep an eye on things. It is not known if they use the armored gun slits at the top of the enclosure.

Originally settled by Mennonites, the town retains a strong connection to the sect. Goshen College at Ninth and Main Streets is a four-year liberal arts college, with almost three-quarters of the students members of the denomination. With a strong tradition in peace movements, the college offers a number of courses, as well as encouraging understanding of the developing world by offering their students a 14-week sojourn in a Third World country.

The annual Michiana Mennonite Relief Sale held at the Elkhart County Fairgrounds draws thousands. Besides the three large auctions of handmade quilts, the sale features crafts from Mennonite relief villages in 33 different countries including baskets, figurines, toys, rugs, and wooden ware.

Quilts are a burgeoning cottage industry in the Amish area, often a substantial second income in Amish homes. Beginning in the 1870s the Amish women began to make bold geometric designs from blocks of solid-colored fabric, then embellished with elaborate quilting in feathered scrolls, florals, grids, and cables. They still use solid fabrics for their quilt blocks as prints are considered too worldly, though much of the piecing is done on treadle sewing machines. The quilting is still done by hand. Quilt shops advertising their wares are scattered through the area, and welcome visitors.

Of course, the quilt sale offers barrels of traditional food like head cheese and mush, apple butter, dumplings, strawberry shortcake, and whole

Amish Acres re-creates the quiet world of Amish farm families.
Photo courtesy of Amish Acres.

hog sausage. Haystacks, an Amish favorite, are a big seller. It is kind of an Amish taco salad, a layering of crackers, ground meat, rice, lettuce and tomato, peppers, olives, and corn chips, with cheese poured all over it. It is often the dish served at fund-raising Amish pitch-ins when a disaster has struck one of the insurance-shunning Amish. The haystack becomes whatever the congregation brings.

Four blocks south of the college at Westwood Avenue, turn south and drive 0.3 mile to the Elkhart River and Shoup Parsons Woods, known for record numbers of bird species. The rich natural area is used by Goshen College professors and local ornithologists.

The Old Bag Factory at Indiana and Chicago Avenues is a rehabilitated turn-of-the century industrial complex that has been reborn as a shopping destination. The structures began life in the 1890s as the Cosmo Buttermilk Soap Company followed by the Chicago-Detroit Bag Factory (later Chase Bag) which made burlap bags until 1982. "Bagology" is emblazoned on the side of the building. It was reborn as a high-end hardwood furniture workshop and showroom and artisan gallery. Unlike repetitive malls selling the same thing across the country, the Old Bag Factory features one-of-a-kind arts and crafts made by premier resident artisans and craftspeople. Goods include quilts, pottery, metal sculpture, furniture, glass windows, toys, European-style breads and pastries, hand-carved cameos, and gourmet chocolates.

Take IN 4 east from Goshen through rolling farmland. Grazing ponies and well-cared-for horses are alongside the road. Buggies clop down the road. Spotted cows graze and lay chewing their cud in farmlots. Because of the high proportion of Amish farmers, Elkhart County ranks first in the number of cows and the amount of milk produced in the state. The farms are smaller than average—133 acres versus the state average of 242. Almost half of the county's farms are less than 50 acres.

From Goshen, 5.9 miles, turn south on CR 37. The Checkerberry Inn 1 mile south is a touch of rustic luxury amidst the hilly farmland. The 100-acre retreat features a gourmet dining room and 14 guest rooms. Their slogan, "There's something to be said for tranquillity," could be the theme for the whole Amish region.

Continue south to CR 34 and turn right. Proceed 0.5 mile to Miller's Country Store, a traditional Amish establishment. A windmill sits beside the barn, black buggy, and well-kept kitchen garden. A small white phone booth sits in the parking lot, attached to a rancorous bell. (While the Amish aren't allowed phones in the *house,* it doesn't mean they can't have them nearby). Miller's offers a variety of bulk foods and Amish essentials. While there is a hitching post outside, there are no gas pumps.

An old Amish school bus awaits its horse and students. Photo courtesy of Amish Acres.

Change is coming to the Amish world. Half of the men now work in non-farming occupations. Where the plainest of porch rail spindles used to be, turned and adorned spindles now stand. The bike shop just down the road tells of a conservative bishop's change of heart, allowing a vehicle that previously was forbidden. Roller bladers skate down the country lanes between farms. Previously the vast majority of shopping was done at country stores like Miller's. Now there is a hitching rack at the Walmart in Goshen, and there is a small local industry of van drivers who do nothing but provide taxi service for Amish shopping trips and medical visits.

A charming rural tableaux lays below, an impressionist's landscape of farm and barn and stark, unadorned houses. Farther east on CR 34, towering electric pylons march across the landscape, passing archly past houses distinctly not hooked up to the grid.

Proceed 4.5 miles to Honeyville past more buggies than cars. A road sign reads "Speed Limit 3.5" at the outskirts of the hamlet as imperious draft horses munch in the pasture. The Honeyville General Store is at the heart of the community, an old 1850s country store that experienced a second chance. It closed in the 1960s but a Michigan quilt and antique dealer found it and reopened it as a place of commerce for local Amish families and passers-by. It has a variety of Amish necessities and favorites like stove pipe, hats, Indian Corn Soap, kazoos, harmonicas, and flutes. Amish baked goods are available for refreshment. Across the road, the current proprietor also purveys fine French and English antiques at White Swan Antiques and Gifts.

Proceed east on CR 34 through a popcorn-growing region (a popular and profitable crop in the area) to IN 5 North. Go north 7.6 miles to Shipshewana. (See Drive 26 for information on Shipshewana.) Drive west on Middlebury Street which becomes CR 250 West. At the west edge of town an octagonal barn was built by Manuel Yoder and his sons in 1907 and 1908. Yoder determined that the shape would give additional strength as well as usable space.

Small signs along the road advertise honey, eggs, cheese, maple syrup, and popcorn for sale, but not on Sunday. As involved and active as the Amish are in agriculture and commerce, they resonate to a divine spiritual reality. They see their duty to keep "un-spotted from the world" and separate from the desires, intents, and goals of the worldly people. An Amish cemetery, a *graabhof,* is beside the road, as plain and simple as their lives.

Middlebury, 6.5 miles west of Shipshewana, is another center of Amish culture and related kitsch. County Road 250 turns into CR 16 on the way to Middlebury. Main Street offers an old-time hardware store. Like many towns in the northeastern part of the state, Middlebury was founded by Yankees. It was named after Middlebury, Vermont, by Vermonters who arrived in 1830.

Das Dutchman Essenhaus, considered Indiana's largest family restaurant with over a thousand seats, is west of town at IN 20 and Wayne Avenue. It is more hearty farm fare—noodles, biscuits, dressing, potatoes, roast beef, fried chicken, ham, and pies—of course, pies. It is the Land of Happy Calories. "Would you like noodles on those potatoes?" as the local joke goes.

Take CR 8 northwest out of town along the Little Elkhart River. The road curls over the rocky glacial moraines left from the last great ice age 15,000 years ago, and twists through forests past small streams before re-entering open ground. Most of northern Indiana was part of the Michigan Territory, but was ceded to Indiana to give the state a port on the Great Lakes. This area, as most of the state, was wrested from the indigenous Indian tribes in a series of treaties in the first 40 years of the nineteenth century.

Bonneyville Mills is 4.5 miles northwest of Middlebury. Established in the 1830s, Bonneyville Mills was envisioned by Edward Bonney as the beginning of a great Midwestern metropolis centered around his grist and sawmill. The mill was near the Toledo to Chicago Trail and canals were sure to follow the Little Elkhart. But the railroad passing the mill by deflated any of those dreams. Bonney sold the mill, ran a tavern, and later fled as fugitive from a counterfeiting charge.

The mill was never modernized into a roller mill, remaining an old-style stone grist mill. In the Depression, the mill owners added hydroelectric generation to their offerings, providing 45 customers with electric current. it hung on until the 1960s, producing livestock feed and "Famous Buckwheat Pancake Flour." In 1968, a county group bought the mill and continued the tradition of very slow mill grinding. The rustic mill remains as Indiana's oldest continuously operating grist mill, now surrounded by a 222-acre park, offering trails through meadow, marsh, hillside, and valley, and dozens of picnic sites.

27

Lake Maxinhuckee Loop

Plymouth to beautiful Lake Maxinhuckee

General description: The 35-mile drive loops from Plymouth around Lake Maxinhuckee and back to Plymouth.

Special attractions: Twin Lakes, Chief Menimonee Monument, Lake Maxinhuckee, Culver Military Academy, Potawatomi Wildlike Park.

Location: North central Indiana.

Drive route numbers and names: U.S. Highway 30, and Indiana Highways 17, 117, 10, and 331.

Travel season: This is a summer playland from Memorial Day to Labor Day. Graduation weekends at Culver Military Academy can fill the area up. Winter can bring deep drifting snows until the snow plows come through.

Camping: The Plymouth Jellystone Camp Resort has 1,500 campsites.

Services: There are full services in Plymouth and Culver. Gas and food are available at several convenience stores en route.

Nearby attractions: South Bend, with Notre Dame and the Studebaker Museum, is 20 miles north.

 **The drive**

Deep natural lakes dapple Marshall County, and the Yellow and Tippecanoe Rivers cut across the county. Marshall County sits at the eastern edge of the wetlands that stretched for 5,300 square miles southward from South Bend in the pre-settler days. Much of Marshall County's agricultural land is drained soil, and the primary produce are muckland crops: onions, potatoes, hay, corn, oats, and mint. All across the mucklands of northern Indiana, mint was a major crop. Cut like hay, it was stomped in a Hoosier version of a grape crush, and then distilled in specially made outbuildings. The glacial moraine highlands around Culver, Pretty Lake, and Twin Lakes are the home of many orchards that thrive in the well-drained soils.

Tourism and resort life are a major part of the lakeland economy. Many of the state's most attractive lakes are tucked into the county—Lake of the Woods, Twin Lakes, and Lake Maxinhuckee to name a few.

The loop begins in Plymouth, the Marshall County seat. Settlers organized the county in the 1830s on land that the Menominee tribe previously owned. The nearby swampland caused endemic outbreaks of malaria, and periodic fires retarded the town's growth. But as the wetlands were drained and the city sorted out its fire department, the small town stabilized. It incorporated in 1851 and reached city status in 1873. Besides producing automotive and plastics parts, the area is known as a top pickle producer, the county being among the top 3 percent in cucumber production in the nation.

The courthouse is a Georgian-revival structure with Corinthian columns and an impressive clock tower, completed in 1872. Somewhat incongruously, the square is ringed with residences rather than businesses. One residence that doubles as an essential business is located at Madison and Walnut Streets. The Simons House is now the Van Gilder Funeral Home.

The Marshall County Historical Museum is in the historic Lauer Building also located in downtown Plymouth at North Michigan and Garro Streets. It houses exhibits on local history, gristmill wheels, farm implements, a schoolhouse bell, Potawatomi artifacts, and decorative arts. Period rooms

Drive 27: Lake Maxinhuckee Loop

Plymouth to beautiful Lake Maxinhuckee

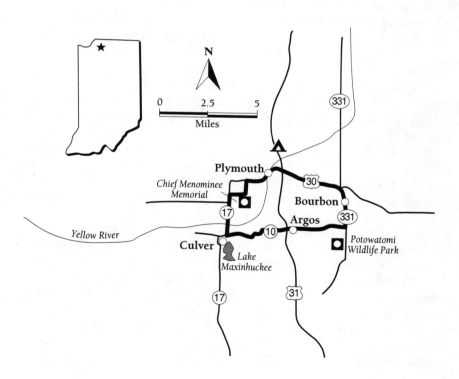

depict life between 1870 and 1910, including a child's room, a kitchen, and a vintage parlor.

Drive along the east side of the courthouse square south for 2 blocks to Center and Washington Streets and the Plymouth Fire Engine House that serves as the local visitor center. Built in 1875, the station has a red-brick watch tower.

East of downtown three blocks on La Porte Street, the cantilevered Iron Footbridge lightly leaps over the Yellow River. Erected in 1898 to help develop the area across the river, the "footpath of iron" is only 6 feet wide. There was an adjacent iron vehicle bridge, but it was replaced in the 1920s.

Centennial Park, the flagship of the municipal park system, is north on Michigan Street, just south of U.S. Highway 30. Depression-era WPA workers built the rustic entrance gate to the park. Rich in labor but short on money for materials, the workers used stones scavenged out of riverbeds and farmers' fields to construct the arch.

By far the town's biggest yearly event is the Blueberry Festival. Over 600,000 people throng the streets for the three-day event held over Labor Day weekend each year. The parade lasts two hours, and the fireworks display is one of the Midwest's largest.

Proceed west 1.7 miles on Indiana Highway 17 to South Olive Trail. Turn south and proceed 3.1 miles to West 13th Road, turn west and drive 1.2 miles to South Peach Road. The Chief Menominee Monument is 0.4 mile north. The Indiana State legislature appropriated $2,500 in 1909 for the life-sized granite statue that was erected here. It is said to be the first monument erected by a state to a Native American.

In 1832, Potawatomi Chief Menominee signed a treaty that guaranteed "forever" 14,000 acres to the Potawatomi for their many villages along the region's lakes and streams. There were more than 100 wigwams at Twin Lakes alone.

In the spring of 1838, the government lured a number of chiefs to a treaty parlay, and convinced them, with the help of threats and whiskey, to sign over their land and migrate west of the Mississippi. With the Treaty of Yellow River, the government bought the 14,000 acres the Potawatomi had in perpetuity for $1 an acre. Menominee protested that he had not signed the document and the young chiefs were drunk when they signed.

Because of the resistance of the Potawatomi, the governor sent General John Tipton to remove the Indians from the land. Tricking the tribe into meeting for a counsel at the Catholic mission, troops were able to then place the Indians under arrest. The tribe was eventually forced on a 61-day march to Kansas, with very little water and detestable food. Along the way, 60 escaped and made their way home. But 42 died from the horrible conditions, including Chief Menominee. The march was known as the Trail of Death.

Culver Academy's Black Horse Troop is the largest remaining cavalry in the U.S.
Photo courtesy of Marshall County CVB.

Proceed 0.8 mile past the lakefront to West 12th Street and turn left. Drive west 2.7 miles to IN 17. Drive south across the Yellow River through Burr Oak to IN 10 and Culver.

Yellow River is another sluggish meandering northern wetland river that has been drained, straightened, and pacified, particularly in the reaches to the west where it contributed to the great Kankakee Swamp. East of Knox and into Marshall County, the river is allowed to roam free in its original banks as it cuts through the massive Maxinhuckee Moraine, a high bank of land left by the retreating glaciers 15,000 years ago. The river winds through a green, scenic valley with calming hills and glittering lakes.

Culver, just off IN 10, has been a resort town since the nineteenth century, and its wide streets and comfortable homes reflect the presence of old money. A fine new park stretches along the lakefront. Culver sits on the shores of 1,850-acre Lake Maxinhuckee, the state's second largest natural lake.

Follow Lakeshore Drive to Academy Road. Turn left and the road leads into the 1,800-acre campus of the Culver Military Academy. The campus buildings are designed to lend an air of medieval Europe, with Tudor-Gothic, Italian Renaissance, French, and Belgian esthetics worked into structures.

When Henry Culver founded the academy in 1895, his goal was to form men out of boys through the rigors of the military system. Accordingly the school is renowned for the pageantry and pomp of its military ritual and ceremony. Alumni include playwright Joshua Logan, Senators Evan Bayh and Lowell Weicker, George Steinbrenner, Hal Holbrooke, Gene Siskel, Jonathan Winters, and Roger Penske.

The academy is best known for the Black Horse Troop, the largest remaining cavalry in the United States. Public appearances of the troop began in 1898, and it participated in President Woodrow Wilson's inauguration parade in 1913. Since then, the troop has performed in ten other inauguration parades as well as hundreds of other events. The troop has drills almost every summer Sunday.

The Vaughn Equestrian Center on campus is the largest indoor riding hall in the nation, 300 x 90 feet, with grandstands for 800 people. The east portion of the center has stall space for 134 horses and tack rooms with equipment custom-tailored for each animal. The Armory north of the Equestrian Center houses blacksmith and leathersmith shops and private boarding stalls for the students' horses from home.

Proceed 10.1 miles east on IN 10 to Argos. The leafy town was a stagecoach stop on the old Michigan Road (US 31 today), named by vice president Schuler Colfax in the Grant administration. It is a traditional dairy farming area.

Proceed 7.2 miles to IN 331. The Potawatomi Wildlife Park, located 2.5 miles south of IN 10, is a 200-acre facility that has wetlands, fields, ponds, and forests bordered by the Tippecanoe River. There are 5 miles of trails and excellent birding and wildlife viewing.

Potawatomi villages extended along the Tippecanoe, including the largest, Aubbeenaubbee, which was near the southern county line. The 166-mile-long Tippecanoe River, known as Kethippecamunk to the Potawatomi, was an important early waterway. It flows through two of the state's largest lakes—Tippecanoe and Webster—and helps regulate the levels of the 88 lakes it drains.

Proceed north on IN 331 through Old Tip Town and Tippecanoe to Bourbon. Founded in 1836 by a native of Bourbon County, Kentucky, the town was a lumber and woodworking center after the railroad arrived in 1853. The small town continued the woodcrafting tradition with butter tub, boat oar, and furniture manufacturing for many decades, before switching to artificial—joint manufacturing—a medical technology company.

At Center and Main Streets, the Old Town Pump is a 1929 re-creation of a town landmark. The colored rock monument with the carved pump on top memorializes the community gathering spot. U.S. Highway 30 is 1 mile north on IN 331. Turn west and proceed 9.3 miles to Plymouth.

28

Dunes and the Big Lake
Indiana's Lake Michigan shoreline

General description: The 25-mile drive covers the lakeshore from Gary to Michigan City.

Special attractions: Steel industrial complexes, Indiana Dunes National Lakeshore, Paul H. Douglas Center for Environmental Education, Bailly Homestead, Chellberg Farm, West Beach, Homes of Tomorrow, Kemil Beach, and Mount Baldy.

Location: Northwestern Indiana.

Drive route numbers and names: U.S. Highway 12, and County Roads 500 East and 1400 North.

Travel season: Each season seems to offer a different delight for the Dunes area, from the holiday bustle of summer to the quietude of winter. Wintertime snowstorms can disrupt traffic a bit, but snow plows arrive fairly quickly.

Camping: There are campgrounds at both the Indiana Dunes National Lakeshore and the Indiana Dunes State Park, as well as Yogi Bear's Jellystone Park Camp in Porter.

Services: There are full services in Miller and Michigan City. Gas and food are available at numerous places en route.

Nearby attractions: The urban excitement of the Calumet cities and Chicago are just to the west. Michigan City with its lighthouse and outlet malls is just east.

 The drive

The Indiana Dunes National Lakeshore Park enchants people. The wind piles the sand into wandering mountains, carving it into arabesques and curlicues and calligraphic etchings of air. The light dances endlessly on the lake, a bowl of gray-green glass moving kinetically to the blue horizon as the beach grass bows to the lake breeze, a tableaux of mustard, pewter, and pale green.

But the Dunes sit in an odd juxtaposition to one of the world's great industrial complexes, the great steel-making factories of the Calumet Region. Look down the beach from the dunes and a vast assemblage of black and rust-colored elevators and mill buildings and spuming and flaring smokestacks hulks on the lakeside. Beyond them, the tall towers of Chicago levitate in the haze. It is certainly a unique national park.

Thanks to many decades of dedicated conservation work, there are more than 15,000 acres of state and national parks and natural areas that stretch 18 miles along the Indiana lakeshore, with the most diverse flora and fauna in the entire Midwest. Among all of the National Parks, the Indiana Dunes National Lakeshore is the fourth highest in plant and animal diversity. The prairie meets the eastern deciduous and northern conifer forests at the southern end of Lake Michigan and the topographic relief of the Dunes offers a variety of altitudes and habitats for plants to thrive in lusty diversity.

The state and national parks offer an array of educational facilities and activities, including 15 nature trails to quaking bogs, moving dunes, ponds, savannas, prairies, and beaches.

The Dunes tour begins at U.S. Highway 12 in Gary. Take the exit marked Dunes Highway off of Interstate 90, just west of the interchange with Interstate 65. U.S. Highway 12 follows the route of the Calumet Beach Trail, a major Indian route between the Great Lakes and the Mississippi. Later the U.S. military used the road between Chicago and Detroit, and in the 1830s a stageline ran along the lake. The Dunes Highway opened in 1923.

Take US 12 to Lake Street in Miller, an affluent section of Gary, and proceed north through the cozy downtown. The Miller Bakery Cafe at 555

The Indiana Dunes National Seashore offers a touch of big water.
Photo courtesy of Porter County.

Drive 28: Dunes and the Big Lake

Indiana's Lake Michigan shoreline

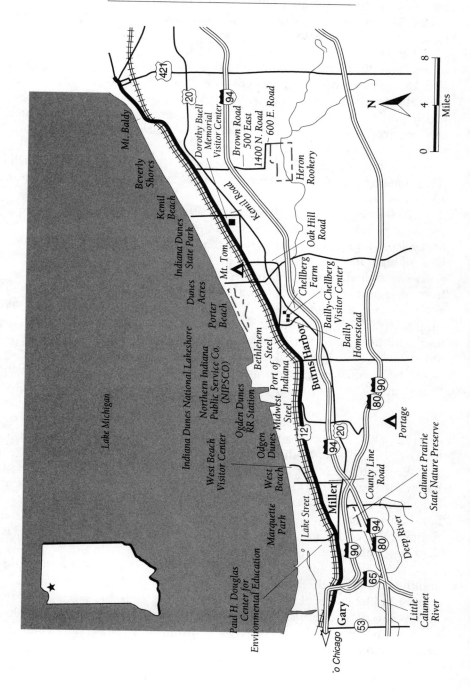

Lake Street is a well-respected area restaurant. The National Lakeshore begins at the northern edge of town. Marquette Park Beach on the lakeshore bustles with basking crowds in the summer and is a quiet escape in the winter. The dark silhouttes of the steel mills hug the curve of the lake to the west.

Return to US 12 and drive east. The Paul H. Douglas Center for Environmental Education at the National Lakeshore is just north of the highway. It is the park's largest nature center, with interactive exhibits and an animal room with many of the area's representative species. Behind the Center, the Miller Woods Trail leads past cattailed ponds to the very rare black oak savanna, a great place to see woodland wildflowers in the spring, and prairie flowers in the fall.

County Line Road, 2.2 miles east of Lake Street, leads to West Beach. It is a winding road through a varied terrain of towering dunes, low marshes, and scrub forests.

West Beach, with its visitor center, bath house, and lifeguards is one of the most popular beaches. Dune Succession Trail offers a glimpse into the life cycles of dunes. Long Lake is the largest of the interdunal ponds, reached by a hiking trail.

The Indiana dunes are the result of wind-blown sand that was left from ice-age lakes that predate Lake Michigan. Until the glaciers melted enough to open up the Straits of Mackinac, the lakes drained down the Illinois River. When the straits opened up, the lakes found their present level and the wind blew the remaining sand into the piles that abound yet today.

The National Lakeshore proceeds east and surrounds the town of Ogden Dunes, an upscale bedroom community of the Calumet and Chicago region.

A South Shore Line Station is on US 12 at Hillcrest Road. The electric commuter line extends from South Bend to the Randolph Street Station in the Loop of Chicago, hauling millions of commuters annually.

Proceeding east on US 12, the Midwest Steel complex at the Port of Indiana is just east of Odgen Dunes, which adjoins Bethlehem Steel and a large Northern Indiana Public Service Company power plant at Burns Harbor. Midwest and Bethlehem are two of the largest steel producers in the Calumet Region. Inland Steel is the largest in terms of land, and US Steel is the biggest producer.

The Calumet Region sits at the intersection of the coal of Appalachia and the iron ore of the Lake Superior Mesabi Range. The lakeside location and the availability of cheap wild land drew developers and capitalists early in the century. The development of the Calumet Region began in the 1890s when industrialists sought cheap land near Chicago for what can politely be called nuisance industries.

An Indiana Dune National Seashore naturalist untangles the web of nature for visitors.
Photo courtesy of Porter County.

Hammond got its start as an enormous slaughterhouse town. Whiting became the home of the gargantuan refinery that rolled its first tanker of kerosene out in 1890. The refinery still looms over the town. In 1901, Inland Steel began at Inland Harbor in East Chicago, and in 1905, US Steel began in Gary.

Today, the mills are highly automated, and buffeted by competition from abroad and domestic mini-mills. The armies of steelworkers that used to march into the mills are sharply diminished, and the steel output is far below the peak years. The industrial cities of Gary and East Chicago are sad remnants, full of Edward Hopper scenes and constellations of solitary street people.

But the flames still flare from the steel furnace stacks, and the 285-ton ladles of liquid steel still pour golden flows. And the thousands of red-hot steel slabs still race down the lines at 45 miles-an-hour on their way to the rolling mills where immense pressure squeezes them into coils 1/16th of an inch thick and 4,000 feet long.

The historic isolation and intense industrial development combined with the eastern and southern European, Southern African-American, and Mexican settlement gives the Calumet Region a distinct flavor that is closer in affinity to the big-shouldered bravado of Chicago than the agricultural ethos of the rest of Indiana.

Just past the Midwest Steel Complex, the National Lakeshore park headquarters and the Bailly-Chellberg Visitor Center is on the south side of the road. A 2-mile trail adjacent to the Bailly-Chellberg Visitor Contact Center connects the 1835 Bailly Homestead of French-Canadian pioneer Joseph Bailly, and the turn-of-the-century Chellberg Farm, farmed until 1972 by the Swedish Chellberg family.

Bailly settled in the area in 1822 on the Little Calumet River where the Sauk and Potawatomi Trails joined, the first white man to settle in north-west Indiana. For a decade it was one of only two trading posts between Detroit and Chicago. The Bailly family occupied the 42-acre homestead until 1918 when it became a Catholic Retreat. In 1971 it became part of the National Park.

The adjacent Chellberg Farm is a restoration of a turn-of-the-century Swedish homestead. The area had a Swedish settlement when Anders Chellberg arrived in 1863. His descendants continued to operate the farm until 1972. It includes the 1885 farmhouse, a Swedish-style post-and-beam barn, chicken house, corncrib, and sugarhouse.

Returning toward US 12, turn left on Oak Hill Road and drive 0.7 mile to Augsburg Swensk Skola, a tiny Swedish chapel and school. It was originally built as a large tool shed, but was given in 1889 to the local Lutheran congregation for use as a school. In 1930, it was dedicated as a church, now considered Indiana's smallest.

Across US 12 from the visitor center, the 2.5-mile long Cowles Bog Trail winds through a wetland to a secluded beach. The bog is a registered natural landmark where botanist Henry Chandler Cowles' intensive study of plant succession in the tamarack swamp became a landmark ecological work.

Adjacent to the bog, Dune Acres is an exclusive residential area that has some of the highest dunes on the shoreline. The entrance to Indiana Dunes State Park is a mile past Dunes Acres off of US 12. The 2,182-acre

The big ones lurk off shore for Lake Michigan charter-boat fisherman.
Photo courtesy of Porter County.

park contains a long sand beach and nature center. Mount Tom is the highest point along the Indiana shore at 192 feet. Mount Holden and Mount Jackson are nearby, only a few feet smaller. The park has a number of "blowouts" where wind currents from the lake have eroded the land and created desert depressions devoid of vegetation.

The Indiana Dunes State Park Nature Center is particularly strong in children's programming. Trail 9 leads through forested sand dunes, past the rim of the Beach House Blowout, and then along the ridge of the first dune inland from the beach. There are some wonderful views of the lake though the last virgin pines in the region.

When industrialists wanted to mine Mount Tom for its sand in 1916, the uproar created the "Save the Dunes" movement. The Indiana legislature voted to purchase lakefront land in 1923, and the park was established in 1925.

Proceed east on US 12 through a forested section of road and marsh below the road. The Dunes Park Railroad Station is on the north side of the road. Just east of Kemil Road, the Dorothy Buell Memorial Visitor Center is the starting point for the Ly-Co-Ki-We Trail System, a series of loops through diverse habitats.

Above popular Kemil Beach, the five remarkable Century of Progress Homes look oddly out of place, an architectural compendium of art deco, sci-fi, and Florida. Built for the 1933 Chicago World's Fair as examples of innovative materials and construction techniques, they were floated and trucked to Beverly Shores after the Fair.

The town of Beverly Shores dates to 1947, though two Colonial-style structures, the Old North Church on West Beverly Drive and the Wayside Inn on Jameson Avenue, look much older. They too were built for the World's Fair as part of the Colonial exhibit and barged over to Beverly Shores after the show. Today, Beverly Shores is an enclave of Lithuanians, who have recreated a bit of the Baltic in this little lakeside town.

The Heron Rookery, a 368-retreat for Great blue herons and other birdlife, is located 3.1 miles south of US 12 at Beverly Shores. Take Brown Road (CR 500 East) to CR 1400 North and turn east. Proceed to CR 600 East and the rookery. The Heron Rookery Trail runs through the center of it. Return to US 12 and proceed east 3 miles.

On the lakeshore at Beverly Shores, Mount Baldy, 140 feet high, offers the combination of a scenic beach and a giant wandering dune. Pushed by wind and waves, Mount Baldy migrates southward about four feet a year. When the winds are right, the moving dunes make a sound like a deep bass viola—what locals call the singing sands.

Appendix: Sources of More Information

For more information on lands and events, please contact the following agencies and organizations.

Drive 1: River to River

Vincennes/Knox County
Convention and Visitors
Bureau
27 North 3rd Street
Vincennes, IN 47591
800-886-0400

Daviess County Visitors
Bureau
1 Train Depot Station Street
Washington, IN 47501
800-449-5262

Paoli Chamber of
Commerce
210 West Court Street
Paoli, IN 47454
812-723-4769

Clark/Floyd Convention
and Visitors Bureau
305 Southern Indiana
Avenue
Jeffersonville, IN 47130
800-552-3842

Drive 2: Greek Revival Indiana

Ohio River Scenic Route,
Inc.
University of Southern
Indiana
8600 University Boulevard
Evansville, IN 47712
800-489-4474

Switzerland County
Convention and Visitors
Bureau
209 Ferry Street
Vevay, IN 47043
800-HELLO VV

Rising Sun/Ohio County
Convention and Visitors
Bureau
218 South Walnut Street
Rising Sun, IN 47040
88-RSNG-SUN

Madison Area Convention
and Visitors Bureau
301 East Main Street
Madison, IN 47250
800-559-2956

Drive 3: The Haunts of Young Abe Lincoln

Perry County Convention
and Visitors Bureau
645 Main Street
Tell City, IN 47586
888-343-6262

Spencer County Visitors
Bureau
P.O. Box 202
Santa Claus, IN 47579
888-444-9252

Drive 4: Land of the Indiana Germans

Perry County Convention
and Visitors Bureau
645 Main Street
Tell City, IN 47586
888-343-6262

Dubois County Convention
and Visitors Bureau
610 Main Street
Jasper, IN 47547
800-968-4578

Drive 5: Hoosier Forest Loop

Crawford County Tourism
Board of Directors
6225 East Industrial Lane
Leavenworth, IN 47137
888-846-5397

Perry County Convention
and Visitors Bureau
645 Main Street
Tell City, IN 47586
888-343-6262

Drive 6: The Road to Utopia

Evansville Convention
and Visitors Bureau
401 Southeast Riverside
Drive
Evansville, IN 47713
800-433-3025

Historic New Harmony
P.O. Box 579
New Harmony, IN 47631
800-231-2168

Drive 7: Southern Indiana Amish

Daviess County Visitors
Bureau
1 Train Depot Station Street
Washington, IN 47501
800-449-5262

Paoli Chamber of
Commerce
210 West Court Street
Paoli, IN 47454
812-723-4769

Washington County
Chamber of Commerce
210 North Main Street
Salem, IN 47167
812-883-4303

Drive 8: Brown County Loop

Nashville/Brown County
Convention and Visitors
Bureau
P.O. Box 840
Nashville, IN 47448
800-753-3255

Drive 9: Sweet Owen

Spencer/Owen County
Chamber of Commerce
46 East Market Street
Spencer, IN 47460
812-829-3245

Drive 10: Culture to Culture

Monroe County
Convention and Visitors
Bureau
2855 North Walnut Street
Bloomington, IN 47404
800-800-0037

Nashville/Brown County
Convention and visitors
Bureau
P.O. Box 840
Nashville, IN 47448
800-753-3255

Columbus Area Visitors
Center
5th and Franklin Streets
Columbus, IN 47202
800-468-6564

Drive 11: Autumn Loop 1

Lawrence County Tourism
Commission
1116 16th Street
Bedford, IN 47421
812-275-7637

Drive 12: Autumn Loop II

Bloomfield Chamber of
Commerce
P.O. Box 144
Bloomfield, IN 47441
812-384-8995

Drive 13: Early Indiana: The Whitewater Valley

Brookville/Franklin County
Chamber of Commerce
P.O. Box 211
Brookville, IN 47012
765-647-4150

Drive 14: The Old National Road

The Indiana National Road
Historic Landmarks
Foundation of Indiana
P.O. Box 284
Cambridge City, IN 47327
765-478-3172

Richmond/Wayne County
Convention and Visitors
Bureau
701 National Road East
Richmond, IN 47374
800-828-8414

Henry County Convention
and Visitors Bureau
3900 South Memorial
Drive
New Castle, IN 47362
800-676-4302

Greater Greenfield
Chamber of Commerce
One Courthouse Plaza
Greenfield, IN 46140
317-462-4188

Drive 15: Underground Railroad

Richmond/Wayne County
Convention and Visitors
Bureau
701 National Road East
Richmond, IN 47374
800-828-8414

Drive 16: Mansions to Barns

Hamilton County
Convention and Visitors
Bureau
11601 Municipal Drive
Fishers, IN 46038
800-776-8687

Drive 17: The Big Empty

Putnam County
Convention and Visitors
Bureau
2 South Jackson Street
Greencastle, IN 46135
800-82W-INDY

Montgomery County
Convention and Visitors
Bureau
412 East Main Street
Crawfordsville, IN 47933
800-866-3973

Drive 18: Economic Meditation

Terre Haute Convention
and Visitors Bureau
643 Wabash Avenue
Terre Haute, IN 47807
800-366-3043

Clinton Chamber of
Commerce
292 North 9th Street
Clinton, IN 47842
765-832-3844

Parke County Convention
and Visitors Bureau
401 East Ohio Street
Rockville, IN 47872
765-569-5226

Drive 19: Parke County

Parke County Convention
and Visitors Bureau
401 East Ohio Street
Rockville, IN 47872
765-569-5226

Drive 20: Sugar Creek

Montgomery County
Convention and Visitors
Bureau
412 East Main Street
Crawfordsville, IN 47933
800-866-3973

Parke County Convention
and Visitors Bureau
401 East Ohio Street
Rockville, IN 47872
765-569-5226

Drive 21: Boilermakers to Indiana Beach

Greater Lafayette
Convention and Visitors
Bureau
301 Frontage Road
Lafayette, IN 47905
800-872-6648

Greater Monticello
Chamber of Commerce
and Visitors Center
116 North Main Street
Monticello, IN 47960
219-583-7220

Drive 22: Rensselaer and the Kankakee River

Fowler Chamber of
Commerce
P.O. Box 293
Fowler, IN 47944
765-884-0570

Jasper-Pulaski Fish and
Wildlife Area
R.R. 1 Box 216
Medaryville, IN
219-843-4841

Drive 23: The Wild Life: Indians and Circuses

Huntington County
Convention and Visitors
Bureau
305 Warren Street
Huntington, IN 46750
800-848-4282

Wabash County
Convention and Visitors
Bureau
11 South Wabash Street
Wabash, IN 46992
219-563-1168

Peru/Miami County
Chamber of Commerce
2 North Broadway
Peru, IN 46970
765-472-1923

Logansport/Cass County
Chamber of Commerce
300 East Broadway
Logansport, IN 46947
219-753-6388

Drive 24: Indiana Lakeland

Koscuiski County
Convention and Visitors
Bureau
313 South Buffalo
Warsaw, IN 46580
800-800-6090

Drive 25: Wintertime Cheer to the Austere Life

Steuben County Tourism
Bureau
207 South Wayne Street
Angola, IN 46703
800-LAKE-101

Auburn Chamber of
Commerce
136 West 7th Street
Auburn, IN 46706
219-925-2100

Lagrange County
Convention and Visitors
Bureau
502 North Detroit
Lagrange, IN 46761
800-254-8090

Drive 26: Indiana Amish Heartland

Amish Country/Elkhart
County Convention and
Visitors Bureau
219 Caravan Drive
Elkhart, IN 46514
800-377-3579

Drive 27: Lake Maxinhuckee Loop

Marshall County
Convention and Visitors
Bureau
220 North Center Street
Plymouth, IN 46563
800-626-5353

Drive 28: Dunes and the Big Lake

Lake County Convention
and Visitors Bureau
5800 Broadway
Merrillville, IN 46410
800-ALL-LAKE

Porter County Convention,
Recreation, and Visitor
Commission
800 Indian Boundary Road
Chesterton, IN 46304
800-283-8687

Index

Page numbers in **bold** refer to maps.

Page numbers in *italics* refer to photos.

About the Author

Douglas Wissing is a writer and world traveler who lives in Bloomington, Indiana. He writes for publications such as the *New York Times, Washington Post, Chicago Tribune, National Geographic Traveler, Travel Holiday, Travel and Leisure, Details, ARTnews,* and *Saveur.* Wissing's *Traveling the Ohio River Scenic Route* explored the national scenic byway running along the Ohio River. His next project is a biography of renowned Tibetan explorer, Dr. Albert Shelton. A descendant of eighteenth-century French fur traders in Vincennes, Wissing is as Hoosier as you get.